ideals Christmas and Holiday COOKBOOK

This special volume features three of our best-selling cookbooks guaranteed to inspire exceptional Christmas fare and unique menus for holidays and celebrations throughout the year.

You'll also discover international Christmas cuisine as well as old family favorites in these keepsake cookbooks from IDEALS:

Book I
Christmas Cookbook

Book II
All Holidays Cookbook

Book III
Christmas Around the World
Cookbook

Ideals Publishing Corp.
Milwaukee, Wisconsin

Introduction

Chestnuts roasting by the fireside, cookies baking in the oven, lavish desserts being decorated with loving care—these are some of the special sights, smells, and sounds that make the Christmas season an exciting time for the preparation and enjoyment of food.

You'll find satisfaction in combining favorite traditional foods with new dishes that may become future treasured family recipes. This cookbook contains our select kitchen-tested recipes to give you fresh ideas for preparing appetizers, beverages, main dishes, and desserts as well as serving special menus for your Christmas dinner and New Year's Eve buffet. There are also great recipes for cookies, breads, and candies to provide you with unique gift ideas for family and friends.

This beautiful Ideals Christmas Cookbook will be a special keepsake for you or a memorable gift to share with others during the Christmas season and throughout the year.

ISBN 0-8249-0005-7

Book I

Christmas
COOKBOOK

Contents

Appetizers

Sandwich Wreath

20 party rye slices
20 party pumpernickel slices
  Butter or margarine, softened

Spread bread with butter. Spread 10 slices of rye bread with Deviled Ham Spread; the remaining 10 slices with Chicken Salad Spread. Top sandwiches with the pumpernickel slices. To form wreath, arrange sandwiches around rim of a round plate. Decorate with a velvet or satin bow.

Deviled Ham Spread

1 4½-ounce can deviled ham
¼ cup chopped celery
½ teaspoon Worcestershire sauce

Combine all ingredients.

Chicken Salad Spread

1 4¾-ounce can chicken spread
¼ cup chopped apples
1 tablespoon sour cream

Combine all ingredients.

Glazed Meatballs

Makes 5 dozen meatballs.

1 pound lean ground beef
½ cup dry bread crumbs
⅓ cup minced onion
¼ cup milk
1 egg
1 tablespoon snipped parsley
1 teaspoon salt
⅛ teaspoon black pepper
½ teaspoon Worcestershire sauce
¼ cup shortening
1 12-ounce bottle chili sauce
1 10-ounce jar grape jelly

Mix beef, crumbs, onion, milk, egg, and next 4 seasonings. Gently shape into 1-inch balls. Melt shortening in a large skillet; brown meatballs. Remove meatballs from skillet; drain off fat. Heat chili sauce and jelly in skillet until jelly is melted, stirring constantly. Add meatballs and stir until coated. Simmer 30 minutes. Serve hot in a chafing dish.

Note: Put toothpicks in a few of the meatballs and place a dish of toothpicks beside chafing dish.

Creamy Cheese Ball

1 8-ounce package cream cheese, softened
2 cups (8 ounces) crumbled blue cheese
⅓ cup flaked coconut
1 teaspoon finely grated onion
1 teaspoon Worcestershire sauce
¼ cup flaked coconut
¼ cup chopped pecans
¼ cup minced parsley

Combine cheeses; cream well. Blend in the ⅓ cup coconut, onion, and Worcestershire sauce. Cover and chill at least 6 hours. Before serving time, combine remaining ingredients on piece of waxed paper. Form cheese mixture into a ball and roll in the coconut, pecan, parsley mixture until completely covered. Place on a platter. Serve with crackers.

Basic Fondue

½ pound American cheese, cubed
½ pound Colby cheese, cubed
1 cup milk (or ¾ cup milk and ¼ cup white wine)

Combine all ingredients and simmer, stirring often. Add milk or wine mixture to thin as necessary. For dipping, use cubed French bread, ham cubes, small meatballs, mushrooms, tiny onions, cauliflowerets, large shell macaroni, and wiener puffs.

Note: To make wiener puffs, cut wieners into ¾-inch pieces. Bring to a boil in a little water. This will cause them to puff up.

Party Wieners

Makes ¾ cup sauce.

    Frankfurters, Vienna sausages or cocktail wieners
⅓ cup prepared mustard
½ cup currant jelly

Cut meat into bite-size pieces. Mix mustard and jelly in a 1-quart saucepan. Add meat. Cover and simmer for 10 minutes. Serve on toothpicks with crackers.

Cheese Buds

Makes 60 cheese buds.

2 cups flour
½ pound butter or margarine, softened
½ pound grated cheese, room temperature
    Salt and ground red pepper to taste
    Pecan halves

Blend flour, butter, cheese, and seasonings. Pinch off small bits the size of a half dollar and place on a cookie sheet. Top with a pecan half. Bake at 400° for 15 minutes or until brown. Cool.

Chicken Livers in Sherry

½ cup butter
2 pounds chicken livers, halved
1½ teaspoons salt, divided
¼ cup minced onion
¼ cup sherry or white wine
½ teaspoon Tabasco sauce

Heat butter in a large skillet. Add half of the liver; sprinkle with ¾ teaspoon salt. Brown quickly on both sides. Place in a chafing dish. Add remaining liver to skillet and sprinkle with remaining ¾ teaspoon salt. Brown and place in chafing dish. Add onion to skillet; cook until tender but not brown. Stir in sherry and Tabasco sauce; heat, stirring occasionally, until all drippings are loosened from the pan. Pour into chafing dish. Heat, stirring frequently, 10 minutes or until livers are done. Serve with cocktail picks.

Appetizer Cheese Tray

A simple cheese tray is one of the easiest of appetizers to create. Begin with a centerpiece of club cheese in its attractive brown crock. Surround with slices of tangy blue or smoky provolone. Add cubes of brick, Monterey Jack or Muenster cheese. Slices or wedges of Cheddar and Colby cheese, along with Swiss, add to an interesting selection. Garnish with crisp vegetables such as radishes, cucumber slices, celery, and carrot sticks and olives. Crackers and sesame sticks add contrast. For special occasions, make balls of Edam and serve in the cheese's own bright red shell.

Tomato Teaser

1 pint cherry tomatoes
½ pound bacon, cooked and crumbled
¼ teaspoon Tabasco sauce

Cut small hole in the top of each tomato. Combine bacon and Tabasco sauce. Spoon mixture into tomatoes. Serve on toothpicks.

Shrimp Mold

1 10¾-ounce can tomato soup
1 8-ounce package cream cheese
2 envelopes unflavored gelatin, softened in
    ½ cup cold water
½ cup minced onion
½ cup chopped celery
½ cup chopped green pepper
1 cup mayonnaise
3 cans small shrimp

Combine soup and cream cheese in top of double boiler; heat until blended. Add remaining ingredients; mix well. Pour into a greased mold. Chill 24 hours. Unmold and serve with crackers or rye bread rounds.

Beverages

Hot Apricot Grog

Makes 7½ cups.

    1 46-ounce can apricot nectar
    2 tablespoons lemon juice
 1½ cups brandy
      Lemon slices
      Whole cloves

Pour apricot nectar, lemon juice, and brandy into a large saucepan. Bring to a simmer. Ladle into mugs or punch cups. Garnish each serving with a lemon slice studded with a clove.

Cranberry Punch

Makes 30 servings.

    4 cups cranberry juice
 1½ cups sugar
    4 cups pineapple juice
    1 tablespoon almond extract
    2 quarts ginger ale

Combine first 4 ingredients. Stir until sugar is dissolved; chill. Add ginger ale just before serving.

Christmas Cider

Makes 16 servings.

    2 quarts apple cider
    1 cup brown sugar
    3 3-inch sticks cinnamon
    1 teaspoon whole cloves
    1 teaspoon salt

Heat cider to boiling. Lower heat; add remaining ingredients. Simmer 15 minutes. Strain and serve.

Festive Punch

    1 package fruit-flavored Kool-Aid
 1½ cups sugar
    1 6-ounce can unsweetened frozen orange juice
    1 6-ounce can frozen pink lemonade

Add all ingredients, one at a time, to a gallon jar; add water to make 1 gallon. Stir until dissolved.

Traditional Eggnog

Makes 25 to 30 servings.

  12 eggs, separated
    1 cup sugar
    1 quart milk
    2 cups bourbon
    1 cup Jamaica rum
    1 quart whipping cream, whipped
      Nutmeg

Beat egg yolks slightly. Gradually add sugar; beat until smooth. Pour in milk, bourbon, and rum; stir until well mixed. Beat egg whites until they form stiff peaks; fold egg whites and whipped cream into yolk mixture, gently but thoroughly. Serve cold with freshly grated nutmeg on top.

Punch Cubes

      Juice of 2 lemons
      Juice of 2 oranges
    2 bananas, mashed
    1 cup canned crushed pineapple and juice
  ¾ cup sugar
    1 cup water

Combine all ingredients; blend well. Pour into ice cube trays and freeze. To serve, place 3 or 4 cubes in a glass and pour chilled ginger ale over cubes. Garnish with a maraschino cherry or mint leaves, if desired.

Wassail

Makes 1 quart.

 1½ cups sugar
    4 cups boiling water
    3 whole allspice
    6 whole cloves
    1 tablespoon ground ginger
    1 1-inch stick cinnamon
 1⅓ cups orange juice
  ⅔ cup lemon juice

Combine sugar and 2 cups of the boiling water; boil 5 minutes. Add spices, cover and let stand 1 hour. Add remaining water and fruit juices; mix well. Strain. Heat to boiling. Serve immediately.

Soups

Cream of Potato Soup

5 large potatoes, pared and sliced
½ cup sliced carrots
6 slices bacon, cooked and crumbled, drain reserving 2 tablespoons fat
1 cup chopped onion
1 cup sliced celery
1½ teaspoons salt
¼ teaspoon white pepper
2 cups milk
2 cups light cream or evaporated milk
Cheddar cheese, shredded
Parsley

Cook potatoes and carrots in boiling water until tender. Drain. Sauté onion and celery in the 2 tablespoons bacon fat. Combine all ingredients except cheese and parsley. Simmer 30 minutes. Garnish each serving with Cheddar cheese and parsley.

Pimiento Bisque

2½ tablespoons butter or margarine
2½ tablespoons flour
5 cups milk
½ teaspoon grated onion
¾ cup chopped pimiento
Salt and pepper to taste

Melt butter in a saucepan; add flour and mix well. Add milk. Cook until thick, stirring constantly. Add onion, pimiento, salt and pepper. Heat, stirring occasionally. Do not boil.

Ham Bone Soup

1 trimmed ham bone
6 quarts water
1 medium can tomatoes
1 teaspoon dried parsley
2 ribs celery, sliced
3 peppercorns
2 tablespoons barley
3 carrots, sliced
Salt
½ head cabbage, cut up
2 large potatoes, diced

Place ham bone in a two-gallon kettle; add water, tomatoes, parsley, celery, peppercorns, barley, carrots, and salt to taste. Boil for 2 hours. Add cabbage and potatoes; cook 30 minutes.

Note: More carrots, cabbage, and a little catsup can be used to improve the flavor. The ham bone does not need to be trimmed too much, as all parts of ham add to the flavor.

Beef Tingler

Makes 5½ cups.

2 10¾-ounce cans condensed beef broth
2 10¾-ounce soup cans water
¼ cup brandy
¼ cup whipping cream
⅛ teaspoon vanilla extract
Dash nutmeg
⅛ teaspoon grated orange rind

Combine soup, water, and brandy in a saucepan. Heat, stirring occasionally. In a separate bowl, combine cream, vanilla, and nutmeg; beat until cream just mounds. Fold in orange rind. Serve on soup.

Oyster Bisque

1 dozen large raw oysters, shucked, diced, drained, reserve 1 cup liquor
3 cups milk
1 cup heavy cream
1 slice onion
2 ribs celery
1 sprig parsley
1 bay leaf
⅓ cup butter or margarine, melted
⅓ cup flour
1¾ teaspoons salt
½ teaspoon Tabasco sauce
Chopped chives

Place oysters and liquor in a saucepan. Bring to a boil over low heat. Pour into a bowl and set aside. In the saucepan scald milk and cream with onion, celery, parsley, and bay leaf. Strain. Blend butter, flour, salt, and Tabasco sauce. Slowly stir in scalded milk. Stir over low heat until thick. Add oysters and liquor. Heat and serve with chopped chives.

Tossed Mushroom Salad

Makes 12 servings.

- 1 head romaine lettuce
- ¼ pound mushrooms, sliced
- ¼ cup lemon juice
- 1 quart chicory, cut into bite-size pieces
- 1 quart escarole, cut into bite-size pieces
- 2 to 3 heads endive, cut into bite-size pieces

Arrange romaine leaves with ends up around the sides of a large salad bowl; set aside. Place mushrooms in a separate bowl; sprinkle with lemon juice. Drain. Combine chicory, escarole, and endive with mushrooms. Shake Dressing and pour over salad greens and mushrooms; toss. Place in salad bowl.

Dressing

- ⅔ cup salad oil
- ½ cup tarragon vinegar
- 2 tablespoons sugar
- 2 teaspoons garlic salt
- 1 teaspoon seasoned salt
- ¼ teaspoon pepper

Combine all ingredients in a covered jar; shake to mix. Refrigerate 30 minutes before using.

Yuletide Salad

- 2½ cups crushed pineapple, drained, reserve juice
- 1 3-ounce package lemon-flavored gelatin
- 1 3-ounce package pineapple-flavored gelatin
- ½ pound miniature marshmallows
- 1 8-ounce package cream cheese, softened
- 1 cup mayonnaise
- 1 4-ounce jar maraschino cherries, minced
- 1 cup whipping cream, whipped
- 1 3-ounce package strawberry-flavored gelatin

Add hot water to pineapple juice to make 4 cups. Stir in lemon and pineapple gelatins until dissolved. Stir in marshmallows; cool. Add cream cheese, mayonnaise, pineapple, and cherries to the whipped cream. Combine with cooled gelatin. Pour into mold; chill until set. Prepare strawberry gelatin according to package directions. Cool and spoon onto lemon-pineapple salad. Chill until firm.

Shrimp Salad Louis

Makes 4 servings.

- 1 cup mayonnaise
- ¼ cup French dressing
- ¼ cup catsup
- 1 teaspoon horseradish
- ½ teaspoon salt
- 1 teaspoon Worcestershire sauce
- ½ teaspoon Tabasco sauce
- 1 pound shrimp, cleaned and cooked
  Shredded lettuce

Combine mayonnaise, French dressing, catsup, horseradish, salt, Worcestershire sauce, and Tabasco sauce. Add shrimp; mix well. Serve on shredded lettuce.

Note: 1 7½-ounce can crabmeat may be added to shrimp in salad.

Christmas Ribbon Salad

First Layer

- 2 3-ounce packages lime-flavored gelatin
- 2½ cups hot water

Combine gelatin and hot water; stir until gelatin dissolves. Pour into a 9 x 13-inch pan. Chill until firm.

Second Layer

- ½ cup pineapple juice
- 20 large marshmallows, cut up
- 1 3-ounce package lemon-flavored gelatin
- 1½ cups hot water
- 1 8-ounce package cream cheese, softened

Combine pineapple juice and marshmallows in a saucepan. Heat until the marshmallows melt. Dissolve the gelatin in hot water. Combine the hot marshmallow mixture, gelatin, and cream cheese; mix well. Cool and pour over the first layer. Chill until firm.

Third Layer

- 1 3-ounce package cherry-flavored gelatin
- 1 3-ounce package red raspberry-flavored gelatin
- 2½ cups hot water

Combine all ingredients; mix until gelatin dissolves. Cool and pour over the second layer. Chill until firm. Cut in 2- or 3-inch squares to serve.

Gelatin Christmas Trees

- 1 3-ounce package lime-flavored gelatin
- 1 cup boiling water
- 1 envelope unflavored gelatin
- ½ cup cold water
- 1 16-ounce can fruit cocktail and juice
- 9 pointed paper cups

Dissolve lime gelatin in the boiling water. Soften unflavored gelatin in the cold water; add to first mixture and stir well. Add fruit cocktail and juice; stir. Cool at room temperature. Rinse the paper cups with water and stand in glasses, pointed side down. Pour cool gelatin mixture into cups. Chill until firm. To serve carefully unwrap the paper cup. Place gelatin tree on salad plate. Surround with cottage cheese or sour cream.

Note: Trees may be decorated with sour cream or whipped cream in a decorating tube, if desired.

Jellied Tomato Salad

Makes 6 servings.

- 1 tablespoon unflavored gelatin
- ¼ cup cold water
- 2½ cups fresh or canned tomatoes
- 1 tablespoon minced onion
- ½ small bay leaf
- ½ teaspoon sugar
- ½ teaspoon salt
  Pepper to taste
- 1 tablespoon lemon juice
- ½ cup minced cucumber
- ½ cup minced celery
  Lettuce or salad greens

Soften gelatin in cold water. Cook tomatoes, onion, and bay leaf (about 20 minutes for fresh tomatoes, 10 minutes for canned) in a saucepan. Press tomatoes through a sieve. Measure 1¾ cups, adding boiling water, if needed to fill measure. Add hot, sieved tomatoes to gelatin; stir until gelatin dissolves. Stir in sugar, salt, pepper, and lemon juice. Chill. When slightly thickened, add cucumber and celery; mix well. Pour into a mold rinsed in cold water. Chill until firm. Unmold onto a bed of lettuce.

Eggnog Holiday Salad

- 2 envelopes unflavored gelatin
- 1 16-ounce can fruit cocktail, drained, reserve juice
- 1 11-ounce can mandarin oranges, cut in half
- 1 cup flaked coconut
- 2½ cups dairy eggnog
  Dash nutmeg
  Maraschino cherries, halved, optional

Soften gelatin in fruit cocktail juice and melt over hot water. Combine with rest of ingredients. Place in a 5-cup mold; refrigerate until firm.

Creamy Fruit Salad

- 1 8-ounce package cream cheese, softened
- ½ cup mayonnaise
- 1 small can crushed pineapple, drained
- 1 4-ounce jar green cherries, drained
- 1 4-ounce jar red cherries, drained
- 2 cups miniature marshmallows
- 1 cup chopped walnuts
- 1 cup whipping cream, whipped

Blend cream cheese and mayonnaise. Add fruit, marshmallows, and nuts. Fold in whipped cream. Chill before serving.

Noel Apple Salad

- 6 apples
- ⅛ cup lemon juice
- 1½ cups chopped dates
- 1 4-ounce jar green maraschino cherries, drained and chopped
- 1 4-ounce jar red maraschino cherries, drained and chopped
- ¾ cup chopped walnuts
  Granulated sugar
- 1 cup sour cream

Partially peel apples, leaving some skin on for color; quarter and coarsely chop. Sprinkle lemon juice on apples to prevent discoloring; toss thoroughly. In another bowl combine the dates, cherries, and nuts. Sprinkle apples with sugar. Refrigerate both bowls of fruit. Just before serving, mix all together, adding as much sour cream as desired for dressing.

Poinsettia Salad

Place a slice of pineapple on a lettuce leaf. Arrange a few strips of pimiento on pineapple. Place a marshmallow in the center; top with a nut. Serve with salad dressing.

Purple Lady Salad

- 2 3-ounce packages strawberry-flavored gelatin
- 1 cup boiling water
- 1 small can crushed pineapple, undrained
- 1 can blueberries in heavy syrup, undrained
- 1 banana, chopped, optional
- 1 cup prepared whipped topping
- ½ cup chopped nuts

Dissolve gelatin in boiling water. Add pineapple and blueberries with syrup, and banana. Refrigerate until thick. Fold in whipped topping and nuts.

Christmas Wreath

- 1 3-ounce package lime-flavored gelatin
- 1 cup boiling water
- 1 20-ounce can sliced pineapple, drained, reserve syrup
    Maraschino cherries
- 1 3-ounce package red, fruit-flavored gelatin
- 1½ cups boiling water
- 1 16-ounce can whole cranberry sauce
- 1 cup whipping cream, whipped
- 1 cup salad dressing

Dissolve lime gelatin in the 1 cup boiling water; add pineapple syrup. Pour into a 6-cup ring mold. Place pineapple slices in mold, slightly overlapping; place a cherry in the center of each slice. Chill until almost set. Dissolve red gelatin in the 1½ cups boiling water and chill until partially set. Add cranberry sauce. Spoon over green layer. Chill until firm. Combine whipped cream and salad dressing. Unmold gelatin ring onto a serving platter. Place dressing in center of mold.

Cranberry Whipped Cream Salad

Makes 8 to 10 servings.

- 1 8¼-ounce can crushed pineapple, drained, reserve syrup
- 1 3-ounce package raspberry-flavored gelatin
- 1 16-ounce can whole cranberry sauce
- 1 teaspoon grated orange peel
- 1 11-ounce can mandarin orange sections, drained
- 1 cup whipping cream, whipped

Add enough water to pineapple syrup to make 1 cup. Heat syrup in a saucepan. Dissolve gelatin in hot syrup. Stir in cranberry sauce and orange peel. Chill until partially set. Fold in mandarin oranges and pineapple. Fold in whipped cream. Pour into a 6-cup mold. Chill until firm. Unmold.

Note: May be garnished with green grapes and cranberries rolled in egg white and lime- and raspberry-flavored gelatin.

Fruit Salad Dressing

- 1 can sweetened condensed milk
- 2 eggs
- ½ teaspoon dry mustard
- ½ teaspoon salt
- ¾ cup vinegar

Pour milk in a mixing bowl. Add eggs, mustard, and salt; beat slightly. Add vinegar and beat well. Store in refrigerator.

Cauliflower Salad

Makes 8 servings.

- 1 medium cauliflower, broken into flowerets
- ½ cup French dressing
- 1 small avocado, diced
- ½ cup sliced stuffed green olives
- 3 tomatoes, cut in eighths
- ½ cup crumbled Roquefort cheese
    Crisp salad greens

Cover cauliflowerets with ice water; chill 1 hour. Drain. Add dressing and let stand 2 hours. Just before serving, add avocado, olives, tomatoes, and cheese. Toss lightly. Serve on crisp greens.

Herbed Cucumbers

Makes 4 servings.

- 2 tablespoons salad oil
- 1 teaspoon salt
- 2 cucumbers, thinly sliced
- 1 small onion, sliced
- 2 tablespoons water
- ½ teaspoon Tabasco sauce
- 2 tablespoons chopped fresh thyme

Heat oil with salt in a skillet. Add cucumbers and onion. Cook over medium heat, stirring constantly, about 3 minutes. Add water, Tabasco sauce, and thyme. Cover. Cook, shaking skillet occasionally, about 2 minutes or until tender-crisp.

Minted Peas

- 1 20-ounce can peas, drained, reserve liquid
- ½ teaspoon salt
- ¼ teaspoon pepper
- 1 tablespoon margarine
- ⅓ cup mint jelly

Cook liquid from peas until ¼ cup remains. Add remaining ingredients. Simmer and serve.

Cottage Cheese-Asparagus Mousse

Makes 6 to 8 servings.

- 1 envelope unflavored gelatin
- ¼ cup water
- 1 15-ounce can cut green asparagus spears, drained, reserve liquid
- 1½ cups cottage cheese, sieved
- 2 tablespoons lemon juice
- ½ teaspoon prepared mustard
- ½ teaspoon salt
- 1 cup chopped blanched almonds

Sprinkle gelatin over water to soften. Add enough water to asparagus liquid to make 1 cup. In a 1-quart saucepan, heat liquid to boiling. Stir in softened gelatin until dissolved; cool slightly. In a bowl combine cottage cheese, lemon juice, mustard, salt, almonds, and asparagus. Add gelatin mixture. Pour into a 4-cup salad mold. Chill until firm. Unmold on salad greens.

Creamed Celery with Almonds

- 4 cups sliced celery
- 1 10¾-ounce can cream of celery soup
- ½ cup milk
- 1 teaspoon instant minced onion
- 1 tablespoon minced parsley or chives
- 1 tablespoon minced pimiento
- ½ cup toasted diced almonds

Cook celery in boiling salted water for 5 minutes. Drain. Combine next 5 ingredients; add to celery. Pour into a 1½-quart casserole. Sprinkle almonds over top. Bake at 350° for 20 minutes or until heated and lightly browned.

Delicious Potatoes

- ½ cup butter or margarine
- 1½ cups milk
- 6 medium-size potatoes, grated
- ¼ green pepper, grated
- ¼ sweet red pepper, grated (or ¼ cup chopped pimiento)
- 5 green onions with tops, chopped
- 1 teaspoon salt

Preheat oven to 250°. Heat butter and milk in a small saucepan until butter melts. Do not boil. Combine grated potatoes, peppers, onions, and salt in a 1½-quart casserole. Pour on milk. Bake 4 hours, adding more milk if necessary.

Note: Leftover portion may be pan fried for breakfast.

Candied Sweet Potatoes

- 1 cup orange juice
- 2 tablespoons butter, melted
- ½ cup white sugar
- ½ cup brown sugar
- 1 tablespoon cornstarch
- 2 1-pound cans sweet potatoes, halved or quartered

Combine all ingredients except the potatoes; mix well. Place potatoes in a greased casserole. Pour mixture over potatoes. Bake at 325° for 1 hour.

Note: To cook on top of stove prepare syrup, add potatoes and heat to serving temperature.

Glazed Carrots

- ⅓ cup sugar
- 1 tablespoon flour
- 2 teaspoons grated orange rind
- ¾ cup orange juice
- 3 cups cooked carrots

Combine sugar, flour, orange rind, and orange juice in a small saucepan. Cook and stir over low heat until thick. Pour over carrots.

Sweet Potato Balls

Makes 12 balls.

- 6 medium sweet potatoes, cooked, peeled and mashed
- ½ cup margarine
- 1 cup brown sugar
- 1 cup chopped pecans or walnuts
- 12 large marshmallows
- 2 cups crushed cornflakes

Mix sweet potatoes with margarine, sugar, and nuts. Form a ball around 1 marshmallow; roll in crushed cornflakes. Just before serving, warm balls in a 350° oven 15 minutes, or until marshmallow has softened or melted.

Note: Balls may be made ahead of time and refrigerated or frozen for later use.

Broccoli with Stuffing

- 2 eggs, beaten
- 1 onion, minced
- 1 10¾-ounce can mushroom soup
- ½ cup mayonnaise
- 2 10-ounce packages frozen broccoli, cooked and drained
- 1 cup grated Cheddar cheese
- 1 package herbed stuffing mix, prepared
- ¼ cup butter or margarine, melted

Combine eggs, onion, soup, and mayonnaise. Place a layer of broccoli in a 2-quart casserole. Add a layer of cheese. Pour a small amount of sauce over top. Repeat layers until all ingredients are used. Top with stuffing mix. Sprinkle butter over top. Bake at 350° for 30 minutes.

Squash Puffs

Makes 6 servings.

- 1 quart frozen yellow squash
- ½ cup water
- ½ teaspoon salt
- ¼ cup milk
- 3 tablespoons flour
- 1 tablespoon light brown sugar
- ½ teaspoon ground nutmeg
- ⅛ teaspoon ground black peppr
- 2 large eggs, beaten

Place squash in a saucepan with water and salt; cook until tender. Combine squash with remaining ingredients and mix well. Place into a buttered 1-quart casserole. Bake at 350° for 35 minutes.

Beets Russe

- 2 cups hot cubed beets
- ½ cup French dressing
- 1 cup sour cream, whipped
- ½ cup minced green onion

Mix beets with dressing. Place in a serving dish. Top with sour cream; sprinkle with minced onion.

Fruited Rice

Makes 6 servings.

- 1 cup sliced carrots
- 3 tablespoons vegetable oil
- 1 cup sliced green onions
- 2 cups unpeeled apple slices
- 3 cups cooked brown rice
- 1 teaspoon salt
- ½ cup seedless raisins
- 1 tablespoon sesame seed

Sauté carrots in the oil about 10 minutes. Add onions and apples. Cook 10 minutes. Stir in rice, salt, and raisins. Cook, stirring constantly, until rice is heated through. Add sesame seed and toss lightly.

Casseroles

Corn Bake

Makes 7 servings.

 3 1-pound cans whole kernel corn, drained
 1 cup milk
 2 eggs
 ½ cup ground ham
 ¼ cup grated cheese
 1 slice bread, ground
 2 tablespoons minced onion, optional
    Salt and pepper to taste
1½ cups bread cubes
 2 to 3 tablespoons butter, melted
 1 tablespoon grated Parmesan cheese

Combine first 8 ingredients; pour into a greased 10 x 6-inch baking pan. Mix bread cubes with melted butter and place over top. Sprinkle with grated Parmesan cheese. Place pan on a baking sheet and bake at 350° for 25 minutes.

Note: Chopped peppers may also be used for added color and flavor, if desired.

Sweet Potato Casserole

Makes 6 to 8 servings.

 3 medium sweet potatoes
 ½ cup margarine
 1 cup brown sugar
    Milk
 ⅛ teaspoon ground cinnamon
 ⅛ teaspoon ground nutmeg
 1 teaspoon salt
 ½ cup toasted, salted pecans

Cook potatoes until tender. Drain and mash. Add margarine, brown sugar, and enough milk to make soupy. Add cinnamon, nutmeg, and salt. Mix and place in a casserole. Pour Topping over potatoes. Sprinkle with nuts. Bake at 400° until bubbly.

Topping

 2 tablespoons margarine
 ½ cup sugar
 ⅛ cup milk
 1 teaspoon vanilla extract

Melt margarine in a small saucepan. Add sugar and milk. Cook until thick and bubbly; cool. Add vanilla and beat well.

Yuletide Scalloped Onions

Makes 8 servings.

 2 pounds small white onions
 ¼ cup butter or margarine
 ¼ cup flour
 2 cups milk
 ½ teaspoon salt
 ¼ teaspoon pepper
 1 cup grated sharp cheese
 ¼ cup chopped pimiento
 ¼ cup chopped parsley
 ½ cup bread crumbs
 1 tablespoon butter, softened

Peel onions and cook in salted water 15 minutes until just tender; drain. Place in a baking dish. Melt ¼ cup butter; add flour and blend until smooth, cooking 3 minutes. Heat milk and slowly stir into flour mixture. Bring just to a boil and cook 5 minutes, stirring constantly with wire whip. Add salt and pepper. Stir in cheese until melted; add pimiento and parsley. Pour over onions. Mix crumbs with softened butter. Sprinkle on top around edges. Bake at 375° for 15 minutes or until brown.

English Pea and Chestnut Casserole

 ½ cup butter
 1 small onion, minced
 2 tablespoons chopped green pepper
 1 cup sliced celery
 2 cans peas, drained
 1 can sliced water chestnuts, drained
 2 pimientos, diced
 1 10¾-ounce can cream of mushroom soup,
    undiluted
    Buttered cracker crumbs

Melt butter in a heavy skillet. Add onion, green pepper, and celery; sauté over medium heat, stirring often until soft. Remove from heat; add peas and chestnuts. Fold in pimientos. Arrange ½ of the vegetable mixture in the bottom of a 2-quart buttered casserole; top with ½ of the soup. Repeat layers. Sprinkle with buttered cracker crumbs. Bake at 350° for 30 minutes.

Chicken and Sweet Potato Bake

  3 chicken breasts, split or 1 fryer, cut up
 ¼ cup flour
 ¼ teaspoon salt
 ¼ teaspoon paprika
    Dash pepper
 ¼ cup oil
 ½ cup chopped celery and leaves
  1 green pepper, sliced
  1 medium clove garlic or garlic salt
 ⅛ teaspoon thyme
  1 bay leaf
    Dash rosemary
  1 10¾-ounce can mushroom soup
 ½ cup liquid (wine, broth, or water)
  1 can whole white onions, drained
  1 can sweet potatoes or 6 medium sweet potatoes, cooked

Dust chicken with flour, salt, paprika, and pepper. Sauté lightly in oil; arrange in a large casserole or pan. Add celery, green pepper, garlic, thyme, bay leaf, and rosemary to drippings. Cook 5 minutes; stir in remaining seasoned flour and gradually blend in soup and liquid. Arrange onions and sweet potatoes around chicken in casserole. Pour seasoned soup over all. Bake, covered, at 375° for 30 minutes; uncover and bake 30 minutes or until chicken is tender.

Flemish Beef Casserole

Makes 2 2-quart casseroles.

1½ pounds onion, thinly sliced
  2 cloves garlic, minced
 ¾ cup vegetable oil, divided
  4 pounds round steak, fat trimmed and cubed
 ¼ cup flour
    Salt and pepper to taste
  4 sprigs parsley, minced
 ½ teaspoon ground nutmeg
 ½ teaspoon leaf thyme
  2 bay leaves
  2 12-ounce cans beer

Sauté onion and garlic in ¼ cup oil until transparent. Remove from pan. Dredge meat in flour mixed with salt and pepper. Add remaining oil to pan and brown meat well on all sides. Line 2 2-quart casseroles with heavy-duty aluminum foil. Divide ingredients between the 2 casseroles. Place meat on bottom, spread with onion and sprinkle parsley over top. Add remaining herbs. Top with beer and an additional ½ teaspoon salt over each casserole. Cover casseroles with aluminum foil. Bake at 325° for 2 hours, or until meat is tender. Serve 1 casserole; cool and freeze the other.

Asparagus Almondine

  1 10¾-ounce can cream of chicken soup
 ¼ cup milk
  3 hard-cooked eggs, sliced
  1 cup cubed American cheese
  1 10-ounce package frozen cut asparagus, cooked and drained
  1 cup sliced almonds
 ½ cup bread crumbs
  2 tablespoons butter

Combine soup and milk. Stir in eggs, cheese, and asparagus. Spoon mixture into a buttered casserole. Sprinkle almonds and crumbs over top. Dot with butter. Bake at 350° for 30 to 40 minutes, until bubbly and slightly brown on top.

String Bean Casserole

  2 medium cans whole green beans, drained
  1 medium can Chinese vegetables, drained
  1 10¾-ounce can cream of mushroom soup
    Salt and pepper to taste
  1 medium can French fried onion rings
  1 cup grated Cheddar cheese

Combine beans, vegetables, soup, salt and pepper in a casserole. Top with onion rings. Bake at 325° for 25 minutes. Sprinkle cheese over top and bake an additional 5 minutes.

Meats

Walnut-Stuffed Beef Rolls

Makes 6 servings.

- 2 1-pound top round steaks, ½ inch thick
- ¼ cup flour
- ⅓ cup chopped onion
- ⅓ cup chopped celery
- ½ cup butter or margarine
- 2 cups bread cubes
- ⅔ cup walnuts, chopped
- ⅓ cup chopped parsley
- 1 teaspoon salt
- 1 egg
- 1⅓ cups water
- 2 10-ounce packages Brussels sprouts
- 1 10¾-ounce can beef gravy

Cut each steak crosswise into 3 uniform pieces. Sprinkle with flour; pound each side until steaks are ¼ inch thick. Sauté onion and celery in ¼ cup of the butter until tender, 4 to 5 minutes. Add bread cubes, walnuts, parsley, and salt. Cook until bread is lightly browned. Remove from heat. Stir in egg. Spread each piece of meat with walnut mixture, leaving ½ inch around edges. Roll up and secure with toothpicks. Place remaining ¼ cup butter in a large skillet. Brown beef rolls well on all sides. Add ⅔ cup water. Reduce heat to low and simmer, covered, 30 minutes, stirring occasionally. Add Brussels sprouts, beef gravy and remaining water. Heat to boiling. Cover and cook 10 minutes.

Orange-Ginger Pork Chops

- 6 lean pork chops
- ¼ cup orange juice
- ½ teaspoon salt
- 1 teaspoon ground ginger
- 6 orange slices (1 large orange)
- ¾ cup dairy sour cream

In a skillet brown chops over medium heat, 10 minutes per side. Add orange juice, cover, and simmer 30 minutes. Uncover; sprinkle chops with salt and ginger and top each with an orange slice. Cover and cook 10 to 15 minutes until chops are fork tender. Remove chops to an oven-proof platter and top each with sour cream. Place under broiler 1 minute. Serve immediately.

Pepper Steak

- 1½ pounds boneless round steak, cut cross-grain into thin strips
- 1 clove garlic, minced
- ¼ cup olive oil
- 2 large tomatoes, skinned and chopped
- 4 medium green peppers, seeded and cut into strips
- ¼ cup soy sauce
- ¼ teaspoon ground black pepper
- ½ teaspoon sugar
- 1¼ teaspoons ground ginger
- 1¼ cups beef bouillon or stock
- 2 tablespoons cornstarch

Brown the meat and garlic in olive oil. Stir in tomatoes, peppers, soy sauce, pepper, sugar, ginger, and ¾ cup of stock. Cover and cook 20 minutes or until meat is tender. Blend cornstarch with remaining stock. Stir into meat mixture, bring to boil and simmer 2 minutes, stirring constantly. Serve over rice.

Beef Rib Roast

- 1 3- to 4-rib beef roast

To make carving easier, have butcher loosen the backbone by sawing across ribs. Tie roast; place fat side up on a rack in an open roasting pan. Insert meat thermometer in the thickest part of roast. Do not add water. Roast, uncovered, at 325° to desired degree of doneness. The meat thermometer will register 140° for rare, 160° for medium and 170° for well done. For a 4- to 6-pound roast, allow 26 to 32 minutes per pound for rare, 34 to 38 minutes for medium and 40 to 42 minutes for well done. For a 6- to 8-pound roast, allow 23 to 25 minutes per pound for rare, 27 to 30 minutes for medium and 32 to 35 minutes for well done. For easier carving, allow roast to stand in a warm place 15 to 20 minutes after removing from the oven. Since roasts usually continue to cook after removal from the oven, it is best to remove them when the thermometer registers about 5° below the temperature of doneness desired. Before carving roast, remove strings. With a sharp knife, remove backbone and feather bones from roast.

Individual Ham Loaves

Makes 10 to 12 loaves.

    1 pound ground ham
    ½ pound ground lean pork
    ½ pound ground lean beef
    1 cup fine cracker crumbs
    2 tablespoons chopped onion
    2 tablespoons chopped celery
    2 tablespoons chopped green pepper
    ½ teaspoon salt
    ¼ teaspoon black pepper
    2 eggs, beaten
    1 cup milk

Combine ingredients in order listed; mix well. Shape into 10 or 12 loaves. Arrange in a baking dish; pour Sauce over loaves. Bake at 350° for 50 to 60 minutes. Baste frequently.

Sauce

    1 8-ounce can tomato sauce
    3 tablespoons vinegar
    1 teaspoon dry mustard
    1 cup firmly packed brown sugar

Combine all ingredients; mix well.

Sliced Beef in Onion Sauce

Makes 4 servings.

    1 pound chuck, shoulder or round roast, cut
      cross-grain in ¼-inch slices
    1½ teaspoons salt
      Dash pepper
    3 tablespoons vegetable oil
    1 cup water
    ½ pound large onions, cut into thick slices
    2 tablespoons flour
    1 teaspoon sugar

Season meat with salt and pepper. Heat oil in a skillet or Dutch oven; brown meat on both sides. Add ¼ cup of the water and cover tightly. Simmer gently 1 to 1½ hours, or until meat is tender. Add remaining water, ¼ cup at a time, to keep moist. Push meat to one side of pan and carefully place onions in the juice. Cover; simmer ½ hour, until onions are transparent and tender. Transfer meat and onions to hot platter; cover. Stir combined flour and sugar into juice, adding more water if needed. Heat to boiling. Pour over meat and onions.

Pork Steaks with Apple Stuffing

    6 pork steaks, ½-inch thick
    2 tablespoons vegetable oil
      Salt and pepper to taste
    3 tart red, unpeeled apples, cored and halved
      Sugar

Slowly brown pork steaks on both sides in hot oil. Season with salt and pepper. Place in shallow baking dish. Cover each steak with a layer of Apple Stuffing; top with an apple half. Sprinkle with sugar. Cover dish tightly with foil. Bake at 350° for 1 hour or until pork is well done.

Apple Stuffing

    3 cups toasted bread crumbs
    1½ cups chopped unpeeled apples
    ½ cup seedless raisins
    ½ cup chopped celery
    ½ cup chopped onion
    1 teaspoon salt
    1 teaspoon poultry seasoning
    ¼ teaspoon pepper
    ½ cup canned condensed beef broth

Combine all ingredients except beef broth. Add broth and toss lightly to moisten.

Beef Piquant in Rice Ring

Makes 6 servings.

    1½ pounds tenderized round steak, cut in 1-inch strips
    2 tablespoons chili powder
    2 teaspoons salt
    ½ teaspoon garlic powder
    4 cups hot cooked rice
    1 teaspoon onion powder
    1 cup cooked seasoned green peas
    2 tablespoons chopped parsley
    2 tablespoons vegetable oil
    1 8-ounce can tomato sauce

Season beef strips with chili powder, salt, and garlic powder. Let meat stand about 30 minutes to absorb the flavor of the spices. Combine rice, onion powder, green peas, and parsley. Toss gently. Pack into a 1½-quart ring mold. Cover and place mold in a pan of hot water until serving time. Sauté steak in hot oil about 10 minutes. Add tomato sauce. Cover and cook 10 minutes longer. Invert rice ring onto a heated platter. Fill ring with meat mixture.

Frosted Meat Loaf

1½ pounds ground beef
1 10¾-ounce can cream of mushroom soup
1 cup small bread cubes
¼ cup chopped onion
1 egg, beaten
½ teaspoon salt
  Dash pepper
2 cups mashed potato
¼ cup water
1 tablespoon drippings

Combine ground beef, ½ cup of the soup, bread cubes, onion, egg, and seasonings; mix thoroughly. Shape into a loaf. Place in a shallow baking pan. Bake at 350° for 1 hour. Frost loaf with potato. Bake 15 minutes. Blend remaining soup, water, and drippings; heat. Serve with meat.

Spicy Jelly-Glazed Pork Roast

Makes 6 to 8 servings.

1 4- to 5-pound pork loin roast
1 teaspoon salt
¼ teaspoon ground allspice
  Canned or fresh pineapple and orange slices
  Watercress, mint sprigs or parsley

Rub outside of roast with the salt and allspice. Place roast on a rack in a shallow, uncovered, baking pan. If meat thermometer is used, insert point in center of lean part of loin away from bone. Roast at 325° until done, 2¾ to 3 hours, or to an internal temperature of 170° if a meat thermometer is used. Prepare Glaze and brush on meat several times during last 30 minutes of roasting. Garnish with canned or fresh pineapple and orange slices, and watercress, mint sprigs or parsley, if desired.

Glaze

½ cup currant or apply jelly
¼ cup light corn syrup
3 tablespoons catsup
¼ teaspoon ground allspice

Combine jelly, syrup, catsup, and allspice in a saucepan. Simmer 2 minutes.

Baked Boneless Smoked Ham

1 5- to 7-pound smoked boneless ham

Place ham, lean side down, on a rack in an open roasting pan. Insert roast meat thermometer so that the bulb is centered in the thickest part. Do not add water. Roast, uncovered, in a 325° oven, allowing 15 to 18 minutes per pound. For a fully cooked ham weighing 6 pounds, this will take approximately 1¾ hours. Prepare the Orange-Raisin Sauce. During the last 30 minutes of cooking time, brush ham with ½ cup of the sauce. Serve remaining sauce hot with ham.

Orange-Raisin Sauce

¼ cup raisins
2 cups orange juice
2 tablespoons cornstarch
2 tablespoons water
½ teaspoon salt
1 tablespoon prepared mustard

Place raisins and orange juice in a saucepan. Bring to a simmer, cover and cook slowly 10 minutes. Combine cornstarch, water, salt, and mustard. Stir into first mixture. Cook, stirring constantly, until thickened.

Sauerbraten

Makes 6 servings.

1½ pounds 1-inch beef cubes
1 tablespoon vegetable oil
1 envelope brown gravy mix
2 cups water
1 tablespoon minced onion
2 tablespoons white wine vinegar
2 tablespoons brown sugar
½ teaspoon salt
¼ teaspoon pepper
½ teaspoon ginger
1 teaspoon Worcestershire sauce
1 bay leaf
  Hot buttered noodles

Brown meat in hot oil; remove from skillet. Add gravy and water to skillet; bring to boil, stirring constantly. Stir in remaining ingredients except noodles. Return meat to skillet; simmer 1½ hours. Stir occasionally. Remove bay leaf. Serve over noodles.

Poultry

Roast Goose with Apples

- 1 8-pound goose, with giblets
- 2 cups bread crumbs
- 1 chopped onion
- 2 tablespoons vegetable oil
- ¼ teaspoon sage
- 1 teaspoon salt
  Pinch pepper

Cook giblets until tender. Chop and add to stuffing made by mixing bread crumbs, onion, oil, sage, and seasoning. After cleaning the goose thoroughly, stuff and sew the neck and back. Roast 15 minutes at 450°; reduce heat to 350° and cook 3 hours. Serve with hot Baked Apples.

Baked Apples

- 6 to 8 apples, washed and cored
- ¼ cup brown sugar
- 3 sweet potatoes, cooked, mashed and seasoned

Sprinkle apples with brown sugar; stuff with sweet potatoes. Bake at 350° until tender.

Poultry Stuffing Casserole

- 2 cups chicken broth
- 1 10¾-ounce can cream of mushroom soup
- ½ cup milk
- ¼ cup butter
- 5 cups seasoned bread cubes
- 2 eggs, beaten
- 2½ cups cut-up chicken

Heat broth, soup, milk, and butter in a saucepan until butter melts. Pour over bread cubes. Add eggs and chicken; mix well. Pour into a casserole. Bake at 350° for 35 minutes.

Party Chicken

- 1 4-ounce jar dried beef
- 8 slices bacon
- 4 whole, boned chicken breasts
- 1 10¾-ounce can mushroom soup
- 1 cup sour cream

Separate beef and layer in the bottom of a greased 8-inch square pan. Wrap bacon around chicken breasts; place on beef slices. Mix soup and sour cream; pour over chicken breasts. Refrigerate overnight. Bake at 350° for 2 hours.

Spicy Chicken

- 1 cup plain yogurt
- 1½ teaspoons salt
- 1 small clove garlic, crushed
- ½ teaspoon ground cardamom
- ½ teaspoon chili powder
- ¼ teaspoon ground cinnamon
- ¼ teaspoon ground ginger
- 1 2½- to 3-pound frying chicken, quartered
- 2 teaspoons flour

Combine first 7 ingredients in a shallow dish. Add chicken and marinate at least 4 hours or overnight. Place chicken, skin-side up, in a baking pan. Combine flour with marinade. Spoon over chicken. Bake in a preheated 350° oven 1½ hours or until tender, basting occasionally with the marinade.

Roast Turkey

- 1 10- to 12-pound turkey
- 8 cups stuffing
- 1 cup butter or margarine, melted

Preheat oven to 325°. Fill dressed, cleaned bird with Wild Rice Stuffing. Skewer or sew openings. Truss and arrange on a rack in a shallow roasting pan. Roast, uncovered, until tender, 3½ to 4 hours. When turkey begins to brown, cover lightly with a tent of aluminum foil. Remove foil and baste occasionally with butter during roasting.

Wild Rice Stuffing

Makes enough for a 10-pound turkey.

- 1 cup raw wild rice
- 3 cups chicken broth or bouillon
- 1 cup diced celery
- ¼ cup minced onion
- ½ cup butter, melted
- 1 4-ounce can mushrooms
- ½ teaspoon salt
- ¼ teaspoon black pepper
- ¼ teaspoon sage

Add rice to boiling broth. Cover and let simmer slowly 30 to 45 minutes until broth is absorbed. Sauté celery and onion in butter 2 or 3 minutes. Combine all ingredients.

Chicken Kiev

Makes 6 chicken rolls.

- ½ cup butter or margarine
- 1 tablespoon chopped parsley
- 1 clove garlic, minced
- ¼ teaspoon crushed rosemary
  Dash pepper
- 3 chicken breasts (2½ pounds), split, skinned and boned
- 1 egg, lightly beaten
- ½ cup fine dry bread crumbs

Blend together butter, parsley, garlic, rosemary, and seasoning. Form a pattie ¾-inch thick; freeze until firm. Flatten chicken with edge of heavy saucer to ¼ inch thick. Cut butter mixture into 6 equal pieces; place 1 piece in center of each breast. Tuck in ends and roll tightly. Secure with toothpicks. Dip in egg and then in bread crumbs. Deep fry 2 chicken rolls at a time in 350° fat for 10 to 12 minutes until well browned. Drain. Serve with Sauce.

Sauce

- 2 tablespoons butter or margarine
- 2 tablespoons chopped onion
- 1 tablespoon chopped parsley
- 1 10¾-ounce can cream of chicken soup
- ⅓ cup milk
- 2 tablespoons sherry

Melt butter in a saucepan; sauté onion and parsley until tender. Blend in remaining ingredients. Heat, stirring occasionally.

Holiday Duck

- 1 4½- to 5-pound duckling
  Salt
- ⅔ cup orange marmalade
- ½ cup barbecue sauce

Clean duckling and rub with salt. Place on a rack in a shallow roasting pan, breast side up. Cover loosely with aluminum foil and bake at 425° for 45 minutes. Prick skin occasionally. Reduce heat to 325° and bake 1½ hours. Pour off drippings; remove foil. Continue roasting 45 minutes to 1 hour, or until tender. Brush often with a mixture of the orange marmalade and barbecue sauce. Serve on rice, if desired.

Chicken Newburg

- ⅓ cup butter
- ½ cup sliced fresh mushrooms
- ¼ cup flour
- 2 cups milk
- 1½ cups cooked, sliced chicken
- ¾ cup shredded Cheddar cheese
- 1 tablespoon chopped pimiento
- 1 teaspoon salt
- ¼ cup cooking sherry
- 1 teaspoon minced onion
- ¼ teaspoon black pepper
- ½ cup toasted slivered almonds

In a skillet, melt butter and sauté mushrooms for 2 minutes. Stir in flour until smooth. Add milk, stirring constantly. Add chicken and remaining ingredients, except almonds. Top with almonds just before serving. Serve with rice or in patty shells.

Duckling a l'Anglaise

- 1 4- to 5-pound duckling
  Salt and pepper to taste
- 3 cups bread crumbs
- 1 tablespoon minced onion
- ¼ cup minced celery
  Thyme to taste
  Softened butter

Clean and prepare duck for roasting. Rub with salt. Combine remaining ingredients except butter; stuff duckling. Sew securely. Rub outside with butter and place in a shallow pan. Bake at 375°. Allow 30 to 35 minutes per pound.

Glazed Chicken

- ½ cup butter
- 1 frying chicken, quartered
- 1½ teaspoons salt
- 1 cup plum jam
- 1 tablespoon catsup
- 2 teaspoons grated lemon rind
- 5 teaspoons lemon juice

Melt butter in a skillet. Add chicken; brown on both sides. Add salt. Place chicken in a shallow baking pan. Combine remaining ingredients and pour over chicken. Bake in a preheated 375° oven 30 to 40 minutes.

Butterhorns

- 2 envelopes dry yeast
- 1 cup warm milk
- 1 cup butter, melted
- ½ cup sugar
- 2 eggs, beaten
- 4½ cups flour
  Melted butter
  Confectioners' Sugar Frosting (Recipe on this page)
  Almond or orange extract
  Finely chopped nuts

Dissolve yeast in the warm milk. Add butter, sugar, eggs, and salt. Add 2 cups of the flour. Beat with an electric mixer until well blended. Add the rest of the flour to make a stiff dough; knead 10 minutes. Place in a greased bowl and grease top of dough. Cover and let rise until double in bulk. Roll dough; brush with melted butter. Cut in pie-wedges and roll each piece, starting from the wide end. Place on a greased baking sheet, turn each to form a crescent shape, brush with melted butter, cover, and let rise until double in bulk. Bake at 375° about 20 minutes or until lightly browned. Frost while still warm with a well blended combination of Confectioners' Sugar Frosting and almond or orange extract. Top with nuts.

Sweet Fruit Loaf

- 1 package dry yeast
- ½ cup lukewarm water (110 to 115°)
- ½ teaspoon salt
- ¼ cup sugar
- ½ cup lukewarm water
- 1 egg, beaten
- ¼ cup shortening, melted
- 2 cups plus 2 tablespoons sifted flour
- ½ teaspoon ground nutmeg
- 1 cup fruit mix (chopped raisins and chopped candied cherries)

Soften yeast in ½ cup lukewarm water; add the next 4 ingredients and beat well. Add shortening, flour, and nutmeg; beat well. Fold in fruit mix. Let rise until double in bulk. Punch down and place in a greased loaf pan. Let rise until double in bulk. Bake at 375° for 45 minutes.

Confectioners' Sugar Frosting

- 3 tablespoons margarine
- 2 cups confectioners' sugar
- ⅛ teaspoon salt
- 1 teaspoon vanilla extract
- 3 tablespoons warm milk

Cream margarine with sugar and salt; mix thoroughly. Add vanilla and milk. Beat until fluffy.

Swiss Christmas Bread

Makes 2 loaves.

- 5 cups sifted flour
- 2 packages dry yeast
- 1 cup milk, scalded
- ½ cup hot water
- ¼ cup sugar
- 1 teaspoon salt
- ½ teaspoon ground nutmeg
- ½ teaspoon mace
- ¼ teaspoon ground cloves
- 1 egg, lightly beaten
- ¼ cup butter, melted
- ½ cup raisins
- ½ cup chopped candied cherries
- ¼ cup chopped citron
- ¼ cup chopped nuts

Combine 2 cups of the flour with the yeast in a bowl. Cool milk to lukewarm. Blend yeast mixture, milk, and next 7 ingredients; beat 3 minutes. Add butter, raisins, cherries, citron, and nuts; mix. Gradually add the remaining 3 cups flour; knead until smooth. Place in a lightly greased bowl. Grease surface of dough lightly. Cover and let rise in a warm place until double in bulk, about 30 minutes. Turn out onto a lightly floured board. Punch down; divide into 2 equal parts and mold each part into a loaf. Put each loaf into a greased loaf pan. Cover and let rise in a warm place until double in bulk, about 30 minutes. Bake in a preheated 375° oven about 40 minutes.

Cranberry Casserole Bread

- 2 cups flour
- ¾ cup sugar
- 2 teaspoons baking powder
- ½ teaspoon baking soda
- 1 teaspoon salt
- ¼ cup shortening
- ¾ cup orange juice
- 1 tablespoon grated orange rind
- 2 eggs, well beaten
- 1 cup coarsely chopped cranberries
- ½ cup chopped candied green cherries
- 1 tablespoon flour

Combine flour, sugar, baking powder, baking soda, and salt. Cut in shortening until mixture resembles coarse cornmeal. Combine orange juice, grated rind, and eggs. Pour all at once into dry ingredients, mixing just enough to dampen. Dust chopped cranberries and cherries with flour; carefully fold into batter. Spoon into a well greased 1½-quart casserole. Bake at 350° for 1 hour, or until a toothpick inserted in center comes out clean. Cool 10 minutes. Frost with Confectioners' Sugar Frosting (Recipe on page 25).

Almond Coffee Cake

Makes 2 cakes.

- 1 cup milk
- ½ cup butter
- 1 package dry yeast
- ½ cup sugar
- ½ teaspoon salt
- 3 eggs, beaten
- 4½ cups flour
- ½ cup butter, softened
- 1 can almond paste filling for cakes
- Slivered almonds

Scald milk and pour over ½ cup butter in a large mixing bowl. Cool to lukewarm; add yeast and stir until dissolved. Add sugar and salt to beaten eggs; add to milk mixture. Stir in flour to make a stiff dough. Place in a greased bowl, cover and let

rise in a warm place until doubled in bulk, about 1½ hours. Divide dough in half and knead until smooth and elastic. On a lightly floured board, roll out each piece to a 12 x 8-inch rectangle. Spread each rectangle with half the softened butter and half of the almond paste. Roll up as for a jelly roll. Curve in a ring, overlapping ends to seal. Place in greased round cake pans. With scissors, make cuts at 1-inch intervals, cutting two-thirds through the ring. (Start at the outside and cut toward the center.) Turn each section on its side. Cover and let rise again until doubled in bulk, 30 to 45 minutes. Bake in a 350° oven 45 minutes. When slightly cooled, ice and sprinkle with almonds.

Icing

- 1 tablespoon butter or margarine, softened
- 1 cup confectioners' sugar
- 1½ tablespoons milk
- ¼ teaspoon almond extract

Combine all ingredients. Beat until smooth and of spreading consistency.

Pumpkin Bread

Makes 2 loaves.

- 2⅔ cups sugar
- ⅔ cup shortening
- 4 eggs, beaten
- ⅔ cup water
- 2 cups cooked or canned pumpkin
- 3½ cups flour
- ½ teaspoon baking powder
- 2 teaspoons baking soda
- 1½ teaspoons salt
- 1 teaspoon ground cinnamon
- ½ teaspoon ground cloves
- ⅔ cup chopped nuts
- ⅔ cup raisins
- ⅔ cup chopped dates

Combine sugar and shortening; add eggs, water, and pumpkin. Sift dry ingredients; combine with first mixture. Add nuts, raisins, and dates. Bake at 350° for 1 hour.

Cakes

Hot Milk Cake

- 1 cup milk
- 2 tablespoons butter
- 2 cups sugar
- 4 eggs
- 2 teaspoons baking powder
- 2 cups flour
- 1 teaspoon vanilla extract

Heat milk and butter in a saucepan until butter melts. Beat sugar and eggs until creamy. Add baking powder and flour to the sugar and egg mixture; add milk and butter; mix. Add vanilla. Pour into a tube pan and bake at 350° for 45 to 50 minutes. Do not open oven door during the first 30 minutes of baking. Cake is done when a toothpick inserted in center of cake comes out clean. Cool cake and frost.

Icing

- 1 8-ounce package cream cheese, softened
- ½ cup margarine, softened
- 1 pound confectioners' sugar

Blend cream cheese and margarine. Add sugar. To color add a few drops of red or green food coloring, if desired.

Cranberry Cake

- 1 package yellow cake mix
- 1 package fluffy white frosting mix

Prepare and bake cake as directed on package; cool. When cool, cut the layers in half horizontally. Spread cooled Cranberry Filling between layers. Place top layer of cake top-side down. Prepare frosting mix as directed on package; frost entire cake.

Cranberry Filling

- ⅓ cup cornstarch
- 2 16-ounce cans whole cranberry sauce
- 1 tablespoon lemon juice
- 1 cup chopped blanched almonds

Combine cornstarch and cranberry sauce in a saucepan. Cook and stir over medium heat until thickened, boiling 2 minutes. Remove from heat; add lemon juice and almonds, stirring well. Cool.

Fruit Cupcakes

Makes 3 dozen cupcakes.

- 1 14-ounce package date bar mix
- ⅓ cup sifted flour
- ¾ teaspoon baking powder
- 1 teaspoon pumpkin pie spice
- 2 eggs, beaten
- 2 tablespoons honey
- ½ cup thick applesauce
- ½ cup moist mincemeat
- ½ cup light raisins
- 1 cup chopped walnuts
- 1½ cups chopped mixed candied fruit and peels

Grease and flour cupcake pans. Combine date bar mix, flour, baking powder, and spice in a large mixing bowl; stir to blend. Add eggs, honey, applesauce, mincemeat, and raisins; beat well. Stir in walnuts and candied fruits. Spoon into prepared pans, filling about two-thirds full. Bake at 375° for 25 minutes or until toothpick inserted in center of cupcake comes out clean.

Gumdrop Cake

- 4 cups flour
- ½ teaspoon salt
- 1 teaspoon ground cinnamon
- 1 teaspoon ground nutmeg
- 1 cup shortening
- 2 cups sugar
- 2 eggs, beaten
- 1½ cups cooked applesauce
- 2 pounds colored gumdrops, chopped and floured
- 1 cup chopped nuts
- 1 pound white raisins
- 1 teaspoon vanilla extract
- 1 teaspoon orange extract
- 1 teaspoon baking soda dissolved in
  - 1 tablespoon water

Sift together flour, salt, and spices; set aside. Cream shortening. Add sugar and eggs; beat well. Add applesauce, gumdrops, nuts, raisins, flavorings, and baking soda; mix well. Gradually stir in dry ingredients. Place greased paper in bottom of pan; pour in batter. Bake at 350° for 1 hour.

Mincemeat Fruitcake

1 18-ounce jar mincemeat, with rum and brandy
1 cup broken pecans
1 cup white raisins
½ cup margarine, melted
1 cup sugar
3 eggs, separated
1 teaspoon baking soda
1 tablespoon boiling water
2 cups sifted flour
1 teaspoon vanilla extract
8 ounces candied fruit, optional

Combine first 5 ingredients in a mixing bowl. Add the egg yolks and baking soda dissolved in the boiling water. Gradually add flour. Fold in stiffly beaten egg whites and vanilla. Add candied fruit, if desired. Pour into a greased and floured bundt pan; bake at 300° for 1½ hours.

Christmas Pound Cake

2 cups sugar
1 cup margarine, softened
6 eggs
2 cups flour
1 teaspoon vanilla extract
4 teaspoons lemon extract
8 ounces candied pineapple
8 ounces candied cherries
1 cup chopped pecans
2 tablespoons flour

Combine sugar and margarine; cream well. Add eggs, flour, and flavorings; mix thoroughly. Add fruits and nuts that have been dredged in the 2 tablespoons flour. Pour into a lightly greased tube or bundt pan. Bake at 325° for 1 hour. Cool cake for 8 minutes. Pierce the surface of the cake with a fork; pour Glaze over cake. Cool before cutting.

Glaze

¼ cup margarine
1½ cups sugar
½ cup lemon juice
½ tablespoon grated lemon rind

Combine all ingredients in a saucepan; heat until sugar dissolves.

Apple-Raisin Rum Cake

½ cup butter, softened
1 cup white sugar
½ cup brown sugar
2 eggs
2 cups flour
1½ teaspoons baking powder
1 teaspoon salt
½ teaspoon baking soda
1 teaspoon ground cinnamon
½ teaspoon ground nutmeg
1 cup evaporated milk
2 tablespoons rum
2 cups chopped apples
1 cup raisins
Chopped nuts, optional

In a bowl cream butter and sugars; beat until light and fluffy. Beat in the eggs. Sift together the flour, baking powder, salt, baking soda, cinnamon, and nutmeg. Add dry ingredients alternately with the evaporated milk and rum to the creamed mixture. Mix in the chopped apples, raisins, and nuts. Pour into a greased 9 x 13-inch baking pan. Bake at 350° for 40 minutes or until cake springs back when touched.

Toffee Cake

2 cups flour
½ cup butter
1 cup brown sugar
½ cup white sugar
1 cup buttermilk
1 teaspoon baking soda
1 egg
1 teaspoon vanilla extract

Blend flour, butter, and sugars. Set aside ½ cup of the mixture. To remaining mixture add buttermilk, baking soda, egg, and vanilla. Blend well. Pour into a greased 10 x 14-inch pan. Prepare Topping and sprinkle over batter. Bake at 350° for 40 minutes.

Topping

6 chocolate toffee bars
½ cup chopped pecans

Crush candy bars; blend with nuts. Add to the ½ cup reserved mixture.

Whipped Cream Cake

    1 cup whipping cream, whipped
    3 egg whites, stiffly beaten
    2 cups flour
    1 cup sugar
    ¼ teaspoon salt
    2 teaspoons baking powder
    ½ cup water
    1 teaspoon vanilla extract
    ½ cup chopped walnuts, optional

In a large mixing bowl, fold whipped cream into stiffly beaten egg whites. Sift flour, sugar, salt, and baking powder 3 times and add alternately with water and vanilla to the whipped cream mixture. Fold in walnuts. Pour into a medium-size loaf pan. Bake in a preheated 350° oven for about 30 minutes.

Holiday Date Cake

    1 tablespoon butter, softened
    1 cup sugar
    1 egg
    ½ cup chopped nuts
    1 teaspoon vanilla extract
    1 teaspoon baking soda
    1 cup chopped dates
    1 cup boiling water
    1¼ cups flour

Cream butter and sugar. Add egg, nuts, and vanilla; set aside. Sprinkle baking soda over dates; pour boiling water over dates and baking soda. Cool. Add dates to butter and sugar mixture. Gradually add flour; mix well. Pour into a large loaf pan. Bake at 350° for 40 to 50 minutes.

White Fruitcake

    1½ cups flour
        Pinch salt
    1 teaspoon baking powder
    1 cup butter, softened
    1 cup sugar
    4 eggs
    1 cup chopped candied fruit
    1 tablespoon flour
    1 lemon, juice and grated rind

Combine flour, salt, and baking powder. Blend in butter and sugar. Add 2 of the eggs; beat 10 minutes. Add remaining eggs and beat another 10 minutes. Mix in candied fruit, the 1 tablespoon flour, lemon juice and rind. Pour into a greased and floured bundt cake pan. Bake at 350° for 1 hour or until done.

Holiday Mint Angel Cake

    8 egg whites
    ¼ teaspoon salt
    1 teaspoon cream of tartar
    1 teaspoon almond extract
    1 teaspoon vanilla
    1¼ cups sugar
    1 cup cake flour
    3½ cups whipped topping
    ½ cup coarsely crushed, hard mint candies

Beat egg whites in a small mixing bowl until foamy. Add salt and cream of tartar; beat until soft peaks form. Fold in almond extract and vanilla. Gradually beat in sugar; continue beating until stiff. Sift flour into egg whites and gently fold in. Bake in an ungreased 10-inch tube pan at 325° for 50 to 60 minutes. Invert pan on a rack or place center over a soft drink bottle to cool thoroughly. Remove from pan and slice horizontally into 3 layers. Place 1 layer on a cake plate. Drizzle about 2 tablespoons Mint Syrup over the bottom layer. Spread on ½ cup of the whipped topping. Sprinkle on about 1 tablespoon crushed mints. Add second layer and repeat the procedure. Invert the top layer; sprinkle with remaining Mint Syrup. Place right-side-up on second layer. Spread entire cake with remaining whipped topping and sprinkle with remaining crushed mints. If desired, place scoops of vanilla ice cream on top. Place in freezer until ready to serve.

Mint Syrup

    ¼ cup hard mint candies
    ¼ cup water

Place mints in a blender and blend at high speed until coarsely crushed. Add water and blend until thick.

Tortes

For a simple way of making thin-layered tortes, use double-thick sheets of aluminum foil to form two long pans in which the batter can be thinly spread. The cake bakes very quickly in these foil pans and is soft and tender. The same delicate sponge cake baked in a jelly roll or layer cake pan is likely to dry out and get hard around the edges.

Each long cake is cut into squares to form the 8 layers needed. The layers are assembled with a frosting between layers, on top, and sides.

Since tortes need to be refrigerated several hours before serving, a chilling and serving tray can be made by covering a piece of heavy cardboard with aluminum foil.

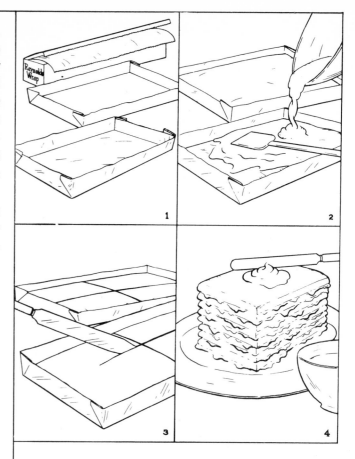

Schaum Torte

    8 egg whites
    ¼ teaspoon salt
    2 cups sugar
    1 tablespoon vinegar
    1 teaspoon vanilla extract
      Fresh or frozen berries
      Whipped cream

Beat egg whites and salt about 10 minutes until stiff but not dry. Gradually add sugar. Add vinegar and beat 10 to 15 minutes. Add vanilla. Pour into a springform pan. Preheat oven to 400°; place pan in oven and turn oven off. Leave torte in oven until oven is cool, 2 to 3 hours. Serve with berries and whipped cream.

Peppermint Candy Torte

    1 chiffon or angel food cake
    ⅓ cup confectioners' sugar
    1 cup crushed peppermint stick candy
    2 drops red food coloring
    1½ cups whipping cream, whipped
      Strawberries

Cut cake into 2 layers. Fold sugar, candy, and food coloring into the whipped cream. Spoon whipped cream mixture between layers, on top, and on sides of cake. Garnish with strawberries.

Cranberry Torte

Makes 12 servings.

    3 cups graham cracker crumbs
    ½ cup butter, softened
    2 cups sifted confectioners' sugar
    1 egg
    1 medium apple, ground
    1 cup raw cranberries, ground
    1 12-ounce can crushed pineapple, drained
    1 cup sugar
    1 teaspoon vanilla extract
    1 pint whipping cream, whipped

Pat graham cracker crumbs into a 12 x 7-inch pan. Reserve ½ cup of the crumbs for topping. Cream butter; gradually add confectioners' sugar and beat until fluffy. Add egg; mix well. Pour into crumb-lined pan. Combine apple, cranberries, pineapple, and sugar; spread over butter mixture. Add vanilla to whipped cream; spread over fruit mixture. Sprinkle reserved crumbs over top. Chill.

Cream Cheese Refrigerator Torte

Makes 12 to 14 servings.

- 2 cups graham cracker crumbs
- ⅓ cup sugar
- ½ cup butter or margarine, melted
- 1 teaspoon ground cinnamon

Combine ingredients. Pat into a buttered 9-inch springform pan. Bake at 425° for 5 minutes. Cool. Pour Filling into crust; refrigerate 8 hours. Top with pie filling.

Filling

- 1 3-ounce package lemon-flavored gelatin
- 1 cup hot water
- ¼ cup pineapple juice
- 1 8-ounce package cream cheese, softened
- ½ cup sugar
- 1 large can evaporated milk, chilled
- 2 teaspoons vanilla extract
- 1 20-ounce can crushed pineapple, drained
  Canned cherry or pineapple pie filling

Soften gelatin in hot water. Add pineapple juice; let cool until it begins to thicken. Blend cream cheese and sugar. Whip chilled milk in a large, cold bowl until stiff. Fold cheese mixture and whipped milk into gelatin. Add vanilla and pineapple.

Empire Torte

Makes 10 to 12 servings.

- 1 cup sifted flour
- 1 teaspoon baking powder
- ¾ cup sugar
- 4 eggs, separated
- ½ teaspoon salt
- ½ teaspoon cream of tartar
- ⅓ cup sugar
- ¼ cup water
- 1 teaspoon vanilla extract
- 1 teaspoon orange extract
  Walnuts, chopped and whole

Following instructions on page 32, form 2 16 x 10-inch pans; set aside. Sift together flour, baking powder, and the ¾ cup sugar in a small mixing bowl. In a large mixing bowl beat egg whites, salt, and cream of tartar until soft mounds form. Gradually add the ⅓ cup sugar, beating until stiff peaks form. Do not underbeat. Combine egg yolks, water, and flavorings. Add to dry ingredients; beat 1 minute at medium speed of electric mixer. Fold batter into beaten egg whites. Pour into the two foil pans. Spread batter evenly. Bake at 375° for 10 to 12 minutes. (Cakes may be baked one at a time.) Cool 10 minutes. Cut each cake into quarters. Remove from foil pans. Cover tightly with aluminum foil until ready to frost. Stack the 8 layers, spreading 2 to 3 tablespoons Chocolate Frosting between each layer. Frost sides and top. Garnish sides with walnuts. Chill at least 2 hours.

Chocolate Frosting

- 1 cup butter or margarine, softened
- 2 squares (2 ounces) unsweetened chocolate, melted and cooled
- 1 teaspoon vanilla extract
- ½ teaspoon maple flavoring
- 2 cups sifted confectioners' sugar

Cream butter until fluffy. Add chocolate, flavorings, and sugar; blend. Beat at high speed of electric mixer until of spreading consistency.

Eggnog Torte

- 1 envelope unflavored gelatin
- ¼ cup cold water
- ¾ cup butter, softened
- 1 cup confectioners' sugar
- 4 eggs, separated
- ⅓ cup dark rum or brandy
- ¾ cup chopped, toasted, salted almonds
- ¼ teaspoon salt
- 1 cup whipping cream, whipped
- 1 10-inch angel food cake, broken into small pieces
  Slivered almonds, optional

Soften gelatin in the cold water about 5 minutes. Dissolve over hot water. Cream butter; gradually add sugar. Add egg yolks, one at a time, beating well after each addition. Add rum and nuts; mix. Fold in slightly cooled gelatin. Add salt to egg whites and beat until stiff but not dry. Fold egg whites and whipped cream into first mixture. Pour over angel food cake pieces. Blend lightly. Pour into an ungreased 10-inch springform pan. Refrigerate 2 to 3 hours. Serve with whipped cream and sprinkle with slivered almonds.

Pies

Grasshopper Pie

Makes 1 9-inch pie.

- 1⅓ cups graham cracker crumbs
- ¼ cup sugar
- ¼ cup cocoa
- ¼ cup margarine, melted
- ¼ cup green creme de menthe
- 1 9-ounce jar marshmallow creme
- 2 cups whipping cream, whipped

Combine first 4 ingredients thoroughly. Press into a 9-inch pie plate; reserve 2 tablespoons of mixture for topping. Bake at 375° for 8 minutes. Gradually add creme de menthe to marshmallow creme; beat until well blended. Fold whipped cream into marshmallow mixture; pour into crust. Sprinkle reserved crumbs around the edge and center of the pie. Freeze until firm.

Eggnog Wreath Pie

Makes 1 9-inch pie.

- 1¼ cups graham cracker crumbs
- ¼ cup packed light brown sugar
- ⅓ cup butter or margarine, melted

Combine cracker crumbs, brown sugar, and butter. Evenly press into a 9-inch pie plate. Bake at 400° for 8 minutes. Remove to wire rack to cool. Prepare Filling and spoon into cooled crust. Refrigerate until set. Decorate by arranging the 6 apricot halves upside-down on top of the pie in a circular wreath pattern. Make leaves by slicing cherries lengthwise into quarters. Place leaves next to apricot halves. Spoon or pipe whipped cream into center of wreath. Garnish with cherry pieces.

Filling

- 1 30-ounce can apricot halves, drained
- 1½ cups eggnog
- 2 eggs, separated
- 1 envelope unflavored gelatin
  Dash salt
  Dash ground nutmeg
- 2 tablespoons brandy
- ¼ cup sugar
- ½ cup whipping cream, whipped
  Red and green candied cherries

Reserve 6 apricot halves for garnish. Place remaining drained apricots into a blender and puree until smooth. In top of a double boiler, combine pureed apricots, eggnog, egg yolks, gelatin, salt, and nutmeg. Cook, stirring constantly, over simmering water until gelatin dissolves and mixture coats spoon. Remove from heat; stir in brandy. Refrigerate apricot mixture in a bowl until mixture mounds when dropped from a spoon. Beat egg whites until soft peaks form. Add sugar, 1 tablespoon at a time; continue beating until stiff peaks form. Stir ¼ of this egg white mixture into apricot mixture. Gently fold in remaining egg whites.

Hot Water Whipped Piecrust

Makes 2 9-inch crusts.

- ¼ cup boiling water
- 1 tablespoon milk
- ¾ cup vegetable shortening
- 2 cups flour
- 1 teaspoon salt

In a mixing bowl add boiling water and milk to shortening. Beat with rapid strokes until mixture is creamy and holds soft peaks. Sift flour and salt together; add to mixture and stir until dough holds together. Roll out between waxed paper.

Fruit Turnovers

- 2 cups flour
- 1 cup margarine
- 1 cup small curd cottage cheese
  Fruit-flavored jam or canned fruit

Cream flour, margarine, and cottage cheese. Chill 4 hours. Drop by teaspoonfuls onto floured board and roll to 3-inch circles. Place 1 teaspoon of the fruit filling in center. Fold over sides, making a triangle. Pinch edges together at top. Bake at 425° until dough becomes "freckled" (from the cottage curds). Serve warm.

Sweet Potato Pie

Makes 1 9-inch pie.

1¼ cups cooked, mashed sweet potatoes
3 eggs, beaten
½ cup brown sugar
1 tablespoon honey
1 teaspoon mace
1 teaspoon salt
1 cup milk
1 9-inch unbaked piecrust

Combine all ingredients for filling; blend well. Pour into piecrust. Bake at 425° for 20 minutes. Reduce heat to 350° and bake 25 to 30 minutes.

Special Chocolate Pie

Makes 1 9-inch pie.

3 squares unsweetened chocolate
3½ cups milk
¾ cup sugar
⅔ cup sifted cake flour
¾ teaspoon salt
1 egg or 2 egg yolks, lightly beaten
2 tablespoons butter
1½ teaspoons vanilla extract
1 9-inch baked piecrust
½ cup whipping cream, whipped
1 cup chopped raisins or dates
¼ cup chopped nuts

Add chocolate to milk and heat in a double boiler. When chocolate is melted, beat with a rotary egg beater until blended. Combine sugar, flour, and salt. Add a small amount of chocolate mixture, stirring until smooth. Return to double boiler and cook until thick, stirring constantly. Continue cooking 10 minutes, stirring occasionally. Add a small amount of mixture to the egg, stirring vigorously. Return to double boiler and cook 2 minutes, stirring constantly. Remove from heat. Add butter and vanilla. Cool slightly and turn into piecrust; chill. Before serving, cover with whipped cream to which raisins or dates have been added. Top with nuts.

Graham Cracker Crust

Makes 1 9-inch crust.

⅓ cup butter or margarine
2 tablespoons sugar
1¼ cups graham cracker crumbs

Stir butter and sugar together in a saucepan over low heat until butter is melted. Blend in cracker crumbs. Press evenly into a 9-inch pie pan. Chill.

Christmas Pie

Makes 1 9-inch pie.

1 3-ounce package raspberry-flavored gelatin
1 cup boiling water
1 16-ounce can whole cranberry sauce
1 cup crushed pineapple, drained
1 9-inch Graham Cracker Crust, chilled (Recipe on this page)
2 cups miniature marshmallows
¼ cup milk
½ teaspoon vanilla extract
   Green food coloring
1 cup whipping cream, whipped

Dissolve gelatin in boiling water; refrigerate until slightly thickened. Fold in cranberry sauce and pineapple. Pour into crust and chill until firm. In a double boiler, melt marshmallows and milk; stir until smooth. Add vanilla and a few drops of the green food coloring. Chill until thickened. Fold in whipped cream. Spread over pie filling. Chill pie until firm.

Different Pecan Pie

3 egg whites
1 cup sugar
1 teaspoon baking powder
1 cup graham cracker crumbs
1 cup chopped pecans

Beat egg whites until stiff; beat in the sugar and baking powder. Stir in cracker crumbs and nuts. Pour into a greased pan and bake at 350° for 30 minutes. Serve topped with whipped cream, if desired.

Mincemeat Pie

Makes 1 9-inch pie.

- 1½ cups flour
- 1 teaspoon salt
- ⅔ cup shortening
- 5 to 6 tablespoons ice water

Sift flour and salt into a bowl. Cut in shortening with a pastry blender until mixture resembles fine cornmeal. Add ice water, tossing lightly until dough holds together in a ball. Roll out on a floured board into a 10-inch circle. Fit into the pan; trim off excess dough. Pour in the Filling. Top with bits of butter; sprinkle with ground nutmeg. Add the top crust, making slits to let steam escape. Fold top edge under lower crust; pinch edges to seal. Sprinkle top crust with sugar and drops of milk to make a brown glaze. Bake at 425° for 35 minutes.

Filling

- 2 cups mincemeat
- ½ cup orange marmalade
- 2 tablespoons flour
- 1 tablespoon lemon juice
- ¼ teaspoon ground nutmeg

Combine all ingredients; mix well.

Holiday Pie

Makes 1 9-inch pie.

- ⅓ cup shortening
- 2 tablespoons cold water
- ¼ teaspoon salt
- 1 cup sifted flour

Cream shortening; add water and salt. Stir with a fork until well mixed. Add flour all at once, mixing lightly with a fork until well blended. Press into a ball and roll out to a ⅛ inch thick circle. Fit into a 9-inch pie pan; flute edge. Cut some dough into the shape of a bell. Place on baking sheet. Bake shell and cut-out bell at 450° until golden brown. Spoon cooled Filling into baked piecrust. Top with the bell cutout.

Filling

- 6 apples, peeled, cored, and cut into thick slices
- 1 cup cranberries
- ½ cup raisins
- ½ cup chopped dates
- 3 tablespoons flour
- 1¼ cups sugar
- ¾ cup water
- ½ cup chopped nuts

Combine apple slices with cranberries, raisins, and dates. Sprinkle with flour. Bring sugar and water to boil in a saucepan. Lower heat and add fruit mixture. Simmer 10 minutes or until fruit is soft, adding more water if it becomes too dry. Cool slightly; stir in nuts.

Nesselrode Pie

Makes 1 8-inch pie.

- 3 eggs, separated
- 1 cup milk
- ¼ teaspoon salt
- ⅔ cup sugar
- 1 tablespoon unflavored gelatin
- 2 tablespoons cold water
- ½ cup whipping cream, whipped
- ¼ cup chopped maraschino cherries
- 2 tablespoons rum extract
- 1 8-inch baked piecrust
  Grated chocolate

In the top of a double boiler, place the slightly beaten egg yolks, milk, salt, and ½ cup of the sugar. Set over simmering water, stirring constantly, until thick. Soak gelatin in the water; stir into the hot mixture until dissolved. Chill until syrupy. Whip egg whites until stiff peaks form. Gradually add remaining sugar. Fold whipped cream into egg whites. Stir cherries and rum extract into gelatin mixture; fold in whipped cream and egg whites. Pile into baked piecrust; garnish with grated chocolate. Chill until firm.

Puddings

Steamed Carrot Pudding

Makes 4 to 5 servings.

- ½ cup chopped suet
- 1 cup flour
- ½ cup currants or raisins
- ½ cup sugar
- 2 teaspoons salt
- 1 teaspoon ground cinnamon
- 1 cup grated raw carrots
- 1 teaspoon butter

Combine all ingredients, except butter, in a bowl; mix well. Brush a mold or double boiler with butter and spoon in carrot mixture. Boil 2 hours. Serve hot with a lemon sauce or Hard Sauce.

Hard Sauce

- ½ cup butter, softened
- 1 teaspoon flavoring
  Confectioners' sugar

Combine butter, flavoring, and as much confectioners' sugar as the butter will absorb; cream well. Cover and refrigerate. Keeps well several months.

Christmas Pudding

- ¼ pound suet, butter or margarine
- ½ cup brown sugar
- 1 large egg
- 1 cup grated raw carrots
- ½ cup seeded raisins
- ½ cup currants
- 1¼ cups flour
- 1 teaspoon baking powder
- ½ teaspoon salt
- 1 tablespoon warm water
- ½ teaspoon baking soda
- ½ teaspoon ground cinnamon
- ½ teaspoon ground nutmeg or ½ teaspoon ground allspice

Combine first 3 ingredients; mix well. Add carrots, raisins, and currants. Sift together the flour, baking powder, and salt; stir into first mixture. Combine warm water and baking soda in a small bowl; stir into the flour and carrot mixture. Add spices; stir to blend. Pour into a greased mold. Cover or tie aluminum foil over mold. Place mold on a rack in a pan with a tight-fitting cover; add enough water to the pan to reach within ¼ inch of cover of mold. Cover. Steam 1½ hours. Remove from water and cool. Bake 10 minutes at 350°. Remove from mold and place on a platter. Decorate with sprigs of holly; serve with Hard Sauce.

Hard Sauce

- ½ cup butter or margarine, softened
- 1 cup brown sugar
- ¼ cup cream
- ½ teaspoon lemon juice
  Chopped nuts, optional

Cream together butter and sugar. Add cream, lemon juice, and nuts; mix well.

Cranberry Steamed Pudding

- 1½ cups flour
- 2 teaspoons baking soda
- 2 cups fresh cranberries, halved
- ½ cup molasses
- ⅓ cup hot milk
- ½ cup chopped nuts

Sift flour with baking soda. Stir in cranberries. Combine molasses and milk; stir into cranberry mixture until well blended. Stir in nuts. Pour into a 6-cup buttered mold. If mold has a lid, butter the inside and cover mold or cover with buttered aluminum foil pressed tightly over mold and secured with a string. Place mold on a rack in a pan with a tight-fitting cover. Pour about 1 inch of water into the pan. Bring water to a boil and cover; reduce heat to simmer. Steam for 2 hours. Cool 10 minutes; unmold.

Sauce

- ½ cup butter
- 1 cup sugar
- ½ cup light cream
- 1 teaspoon vanilla extract

In a 1-quart saucepan melt butter. Stir in sugar and cream until sugar dissolves. Bring to a boil, stirring constantly. Stir in vanilla. Serve hot on pudding.

Desserts

Marble Brownies

Makes 2 dozen.

    1   4-ounce bar sweet chocolate
    5   tablespoons butter
    1   3-ounce package cream cheese
    1   cup sugar
    3   eggs
    ½   cup plus 1 tablespoon unsifted flour
    2   teaspoons vanilla extract
    ¼   teaspoon salt
    ½   teaspoon baking powder
    ¼   teaspoon almond extract
    ½   cup chopped nuts

Melt chocolate and 3 tablespoons of the butter over low heat; stir. Cool slightly. Combine cream cheese and remaining 2 tablespoons butter; cream until smooth. Gradually add ¼ cup sugar. Blend in 1 egg, 1 tablespoon flour, and 1 teaspoon vanilla. In a separate bowl beat 2 eggs until light in color. Add ¾ cup sugar and beat well. Add ½ cup flour, salt, and baking powder. Blend in chocolate mixture, 1 teaspoon vanilla, almond extract and nuts. Spoon half of the chocolate mixture in a greased 8-inch square pan. Spoon white batter on top. Zigzag knife through batter to give marble effect. Bake at 350° for 40 minutes or until done.

Boule de Neige

    ¼   cup rum, brandy or kirsch
    1   cup mixed candied fruit
    1   quart vanilla ice cream, softened
    1   cup whipping cream, whipped
    2   tablespoons sugar
    1   teaspoon vanilla extract
        Toasted flaked coconut

Add liquor to the candied fruit; let stand several hours, stirring occasionally. Line a 1½-quart bowl with aluminum foil, allowing for enough foil to fold over top. Fold fruit into ice cream; quickly pack mixture into bowl. Cover with foil; freeze. To serve, loosen ice cream from bowl by pulling on foil. Unmold on cold plate; remove foil. Whip cream; add sugar and vanilla. Frost ice cream with whipped cream. Top with toasted coconut. slice in wedges.

Peppermint Ice Cream

    ½   cup crushed peppermint stick candy
    12 large marshmallows
    ¼   teaspoon salt
    1   cup milk, scalded
    1   cup whipping cream, whipped

Add ¼ cup crushed candy, marshmallows, and salt to the scalded milk; stir until dissolved. Pour into a freezer tray; freeze until firm about 2 hours. Place in a chilled bowl and beat until smooth. Fold in remaining candy and whipped cream. Return to tray and freeze until firm, 3 to 4 hours.

Mincemeat Bars

    2   cups ground rolled oatmeal
    1¾   cups sifted flour
    1   cup brown sugar
    1   cup butter or margarine
    2   cups mincemeat pie filling

Mix oatmeal, flour, and sugar in a mixing bowl. Cut in butter until mixture is crumbly. Divide into 2 parts. Pack 1 part firmly in the bottom of a greased 9 x 13-inch baking pan. Spread the mincemeat evenly over the bottom layer; add remaining mixture and pack. Bake at 350° for 40 minutes. Cool thoroughly and cut into strips or bars.

Heavenly Rice Pudding

Makes 8 servings.

    ½   cup cooked white rice, chilled
    1   8¾-ounce can pineapple chunks, drained,
        reserve syrup
    1   cup miniature marshmallows
    10 maraschino cherries, halved (⅓ cup)
    1   package whipped topping mix
    2   tablespoons maraschino cherry juice

In a large bowl, combine rice, pineapple, marshmallows, and cherries; stir until well combined. Refrigerate, covered, overnight. Prepare whipped topping mix according to package directions. Stir reserved pineapple syrup and cherry juice into rice mixture. Fold in whipped topping just until combined. Refrigerate 1 hour before serving.

Cherry Bars

¾ cup butter, softened
⅓ cup brown sugar
1½ cups sifted flour
2 tablespoons unflavored gelatin
½ cup cold water
2 cups white sugar
½ cup hot water
½ cup drained, quartered maraschino cherries or candied cherries
½ teaspoon almond extract or cherry juice
2 drops red food coloring
½ cup chopped walnuts or almonds, optional

Beat butter until creamy. Gradually add brown sugar, beating after each addition. Stir in flour. Press firmly into a 9 x 13-inch pan and bake at 325° until golden brown. Cool. Sprinkle gelatin over cold water and allow to soften. Combine white sugar and hot water in a saucepan. Place over high heat, stir and bring to a boil. Boil 2 minutes. Remove from heat and add softened gelatin. Beat with an electric mixer until very stiff. Fold in cherries, almond extract, coloring, and nuts. Spoon over cooled cake layer; cool. Cut into squares.

Pumpkin Squares

Makes 18 servings.

2 cups pumpkin
1 cup sugar
1 teaspoon salt
1 teaspoon ground ginger
1 teaspoon ground cinnamon
½ teaspoon ground nutmeg
1 cup chopped, toasted pecans
½ gallon vanilla ice cream, softened
36 gingersnaps

Combine pumpkin, sugar, salt, ginger, cinnamon, nutmeg, and chopped nuts. In a chilled bowl fold pumpkin mixture into the ice cream. Line bottom of a 9 x 13-inch pan with half of the gingersnaps. Top with half of the ice cream mixture. Cover with another layer of gingersnaps; add remaining ice cream mixture. Freeze until firm, about 5 hours. Cut into squares. Garnish with whipped cream and pecan halves.

Christmas Custard

Makes 8 servings.

½ cup sugar
3 eggs, well beaten
1 quart milk, scalded
½ teaspoon vanilla extract
⅛ teaspoon salt
⅛ teaspoon ground nutmeg
1 cup crushed pineapple, drained
Whipped cream, toasted coconut or maraschino cherries

Add sugar to the beaten eggs; beat until sugar is dissolved. Slowly add milk. Cook in top of a double boiler until mixture coats a spoon. Add vanilla, salt, and nutmeg. Stir in crushed pineapple; cool. If custard separates, smooth with further beating. Garnish with whipped cream, toasted coconut, or a maraschino cherry.

Note: Custard keeps well in refrigerator several days.

Chocolate and Apricot Crepes

Makes 12 to 14 crepes.

2 eggs
¼ cup sugar
1 teaspoon salt
1 1-ounce square unsweetened chocolate, melted
¼ teaspoon ground cinnamon
1 cup water
½ cup light cream
¾ cup flour
Apricot jam
Confectioners' sugar
1 cup whipping cream, whipped

Beat eggs until thick and light. Gradually add sugar and salt, beating well. Blend in melted chocolate and cinnamon. Combine water with cream; alternately add to chocolate mixture with flour. Pour 2 tablespoons at a time into a hot, well-buttered 8-inch skillet; cook, turning once, until lightly browned. Set crepes aside. Repeat until batter is used up. Spread each warm crepe with 1 tablespoon apricot jam. Roll up and sprinkle with confectioners' sugar. Top with whipped cream.

Chestnut Soufflé

Makes 6 servings.

- ½ pound fresh chestnuts
- ¼ cup sugar
- 1 cup cream or milk
- 3 eggs, separated
- 1 teaspoon vanilla extract
  Whipped cream

Pierce shells of chestnuts; boil or steam 20 minutes. Cool. Remove skins, peel, and force through a chopper. Add sugar and stir. Heat cream and add to chestnut mixture. Beat egg yolks until creamy; stir into mixture. Whip egg whites until stiff; fold into mixture. Add vanilla. Pour into a greased baking dish. Bake at 350° for 40 minutes. Serve with whipped cream.

Flaming Peaches

Makes 8 servings.

-   Brown sugar
- 8 peach halves
-   Butter, softened
- 4 cubes of sugar, halved
-   Lemon extract

Sprinkle brown sugar in hollows of peach halves in baking dish. Dot with butter. Broil slowly until sugar crusts. Soak sugar cubes in lemon extract for 20 minutes. Place ½ sugar cube in the center of each peach half; ignite the sugar and serve.

Cherry Cheesecake Parfait

Makes 8 servings.

- 1 3-ounce package instant vanilla pudding
- 2 cups sour cream
- 1 8-ounce package cream cheese, softened
- ¼ cup sugar
- 2 teaspoons almond flavoring
- 1 teaspoon vanilla extract
- 1 21-ounce can cherry pie filling
- 1 3½-ounce can flaked coconut

Combine pudding mix, sour cream, and cream cheese; beat until smooth. Slowly stir in sugar and flavorings. Spoon into 8 parfait glasses, filling each half full. Add 1 tablespoon pie filling to each glass. Spoon remaining pudding over and top with another spoonful of pie filling. Garnish with coconut.

Winter Snowballs

- ½ cup butter, softened
- 1 cup sugar
- 2 eggs, separated
- 1 cup crushed pineapple, well drained
- ½ cup chopped nuts
- 1 box butter cookies
- 2 envelopes whipped topping
  Coconut

Combine butter, sugar, and egg yolks; cream well. Add pineapple and nuts. Beat egg whites until stiff; fold into mixture. Spread between individual butter cookies and stack until 4 inches high. Refrigerate overnight. Before serving, cover with whipped topping, prepared according to package directions, and sprinkle with coconut. Tint coconut for added color, if desired.

Frozen Yule Log

Makes 12 to 14 servings.

- 1 20-ounce can sliced pineapple, drained, reserve ¼ cup syrup
- 1 cup quartered maraschino cherries
- ⅔ cup slivered almonds, toasted
- ¼ cup honey
- 1 cup mayonnaise
- 2 cups whipping cream, whipped
  Almonds
  Mint leaves

Combine reserved pineapple syrup with cherries, almonds, honey, and mayonnaise. Fold in whipped cream. In a 2-pound coffee can, layer pineapple and whipped cream mixture. Cover with plastic wrap and freeze. To unmold, run spatula around the inside of can, cut around bottom of can and push log out. Sprinkle with additional almonds and garnish with mint leaves.

Chocolate-Fudge Fondue

- 1 can hot fudge topping
- 1 square baking chocolate

Warm hot fudge topping. Melt chocolate and stir into hot fudge topping. Serve as dipping sauce with cubed angel food cake, well-drained pineapple chunks, banana slices, fresh whole strawberries, and marshmallows.

Date Log

1 cup brown sugar
½ cup butter, melted
1 8-ounce box dates, chopped
2 cups crisp rice cereal
1 cup pecans
  Confectioners' sugar

Add sugar to melted butter and stir together over medium heat. Add dates. Boil 5 minutes and stir until sugar is melted. Remove from heat. Add rice cereal and pecans; mix well. Cool slightly. Form into the shape of a log. Roll in confectioners' sugar. Place on waxed paper. Slice and serve.

Cream Puff Wreath

1 cup water
½ cup butter
1 cup sifted flour
4 eggs

Place water and butter in a saucepan; bring to a boil. Gradually add flour to form a soft ball. Beat in eggs, one at a time; continue beating until smooth. Drop by spoonfuls onto ungreased baking sheet according to size desired. Bake in a preheated 400° oven for 45 minutes. Cool, cut off tops, and fill with whipped cream, ice cream, or a favorite filling. Arrange cream puffs around a bowl of chocolate sauce; drizzle sauce over puffs before serving.

Mincemeat Cobbler

Makes 9 servings.

1 18-ounce jar mincemeat with rum and brandy
1 14½-ounce package coconut-pecan snack cake mix
1 egg
2 tablespoons butter, softened
  Whipped cream

Spread mincemeat in an 8-inch square pan. Mix together dry cake mix, egg, and butter until crumbly. Sprinkle over mincemeat. Bake at 325° for 45 to 50 minutes or until light brown. Serve warm. Garnish with whipped cream.

Charlotte Russe

Makes 6 servings.

8 ladyfingers, split
1 envelope unflavored gelatin
½ cup sugar
1 cup milk, scalded
½ cup water
4 egg yolks, beaten
1 teaspoon vanilla extract
1 teaspoon lemon juice
2 cups prepared whipped topping

Place ladyfingers on bottom and around sides of a 6-cup mold or bowl or a 9 x 5-inch loaf pan. Combine gelatin and sugar in a saucepan. Stir in milk and water. Cook and stir over medium heat until mixture comes to a boil. Pour a small amount of hot mixture into egg yolks, stirring quickly to blend. Return to saucepan, cook and stir 1 minute. Chill until slightly thickened. Blend in vanilla, lemon juice, and whipped topping. Pour into lined mold. Chill until firm, at least 2 hours. Invert onto serving dish. Top with sweetened fruit, if desired.

Frozen Fruit Mold

Makes 8 servings.

1 cup sour cream
½ 4½-ounce container frozen whipped topping, thawed
½ cup sugar
2 tablespoons lemon juice
1 teaspoon vanilla extract
1 13-ounce can crushed pineapple, drained
2 bananas, sliced or diced
½ cup sliced red candied cherries
½ cup sliced green candied cherries
½ cup chopped walnuts
  Lettuce
  Candied cherries

In a mixing bowl, blend sour cream, whipped topping, sugar, lemon juice, and vanilla. Fold in fruit and nuts. Pour into a 4½-cup ring mold. Freeze overnight. Unmold onto a lettuce-lined plate. Garnish with additional candied cherries. Let stand 10 minutes before serving.

Plum Good Party Mold

2 17-ounce cans greengage plums, drained, pitted, reserve syrup
2 tablespoons cornstarch
2 tablespoons lemon juice
5 drops green food coloring
½ gallon vanilla ice cream, softened

Sieve plums into a saucepan. Blend a few tablespoons syrup into cornstarch to make a smooth paste. Stir cornstarch mixture, remaining syrup, lemon juice, and food coloring into plums. Cook, stirring constantly, until thick and clear. Chill. Set aside ¼ cup sauce for garnish. Pour ½ cup sauce into mold; freeze. Fill mold, alternating layers of ice cream and sauce. Freeze. To serve, unmold and spoon reserved sauce over mold.

Brandied Fruit

Into a 2- or 3-gallon crock or jar with a cover, pour 1 pint of brandy. For each pint of fruit, add 1 pint of sugar. Add only fresh fruit in season. Do not use plums or canned or frozen fruit. Allow at least 1 week intervals between each addition of fruit and sugar. Store container, covered, in a dark, cool, dry place. For best flavor, allow fruit to set 4 months after last addition before using.

Peach Melba

Makes 6 servings.

6 peach halves
1 quart vanilla, peach or pistachio ice cream

Place 1 peach half in each serving dish. Top with a large scoop of ice cream. Spoon Melba Sauce over ice cream.

Melba Sauce

1½ teaspoons cornstarch
1 10-ounce package frozen raspberries, thawed
½ cup currant jelly

Blend cornstarch with 1 tablespoon juice from raspberries to make a smooth paste; set aside. In a saucepan heat raspberries with jelly. Stir in cornstarch mixture. Cook, stirring constantly, until thick and clear. Cool.

Sugar Plum Ring

1 package dry yeast
¼ cup lukewarm water (110 to 115°)
½ cup milk, scalded
⅓ cup sugar
⅓ cup shortening
1 teaspoon salt
3¾ cups flour
2 beaten eggs
¼ cup butter, melted
¾ cup sugar
1 teaspoon ground cinnamon
½ cup whole blanched almonds
½ cup whole candied red cherries
⅓ cup dark corn syrup

Soften yeast in warm water. Combine scalded milk, the ⅓ cup sugar, shortening, and salt; cool to lukewarm. Stir in 1 cup flour; beat well. Add yeast and eggs. Add remaining flour or enough to make soft dough. Place in a greased bowl turning once to grease surface. Cover and let rise until double in bulk. Punch down. Let rest 10 minutes. Divide dough into 4 parts. Cut each part into 10 pieces; shape into balls. Dip balls in melted butter. Combine the ¾ cup sugar and cinnamon; sprinkle on balls to coat. Arrange ⅓ of the balls in a well-greased tube pan. Sprinkle with ⅓ of the almonds and candied cherries. Repeat 2 more layers. Mix the corn syrup and butter left from dipping balls; drizzle over top. Cover and let rise until double in bulk. Bake at 350° for 35 minutes. Cool 15 minutes.

Peppermint Fluff

2 tablespoons finely crushed peppermint candy
1 pint peppermint ice cream, softened
4 cups milk
1 cup whipping cream
Peppermint ice cream
Crushed peppermint candy

In a large mixing bowl, beat the 2 tablespoons crushed candy into the 1 pint ice cream. Gradually blend in milk and whipping cream. Beat until frothy. Pour into chilled glasses. Top each with a scoop of ice cream. Sprinkle on crushed candy for garnish.

Filled Cookies

      4 cups brown sugar
      ¾ cup butter or margarine, softened
      4 eggs
      1 teaspoon cream of tartar
      1 teaspoon baking soda
      6 cups flour
      1 teaspoon vanilla extract

Blend sugar and butter. Add eggs one at a time; mix well after each addition. Sift together cream of tartar, baking soda, and flour; add to sugar and butter. Beat well. Add vanilla. Roll out on a floured surface; cut into circles. Place about 1 tablespoon of the Filling in the center of a circle. Place a second circle on top of Filling; press dough together. Bake on a greased baking sheet at 350° for 8 to 10 minutes.

Filling

    2½ cups raisins
      2 tablespoons cornstarch
      2 tablespoons water
      1 cup sugar
      1 cup chopped nuts

Place raisins in a saucepan; add enough water to cover raisins. Simmer until tender. Combine cornstrach and water to make a paste. Add paste and sugar to raisins; mix well. Stir in nuts.

Gingerbread Cookies

      2 cups flour
      1 teaspoon baking powder
      ¼ teaspoon baking soda
      1 teaspoon ground cinnamon
      ½ teaspoon ground ginger
      ⅓ cup sugar
      ½ cup shortening
      ½ cup molasses
      3 tablespoons hot water

Combine all ingredients in a large bowl; blend well. Chill dough 1 hour. Roll out on a floured surface to ⅛-inch thickness. Use gingerbread man cookie cutter. Place on ungreased baking sheets. Bake at 400° for 8 to 10 minutes. Cool and decorate.

Almond Crescents

Makes 40 cookies.

      1 cup butter or margarine, softened
      ½ cup plus 1 tablespoon confectioners' sugar
      1 egg yolk
      1 teaspoon vanilla extract
      1 teaspoon almond extract
      2 cups sifted flour
      1 cup finely chopped nuts
         Confectioners' sugar

Cream butter and sugar; beat well. Add egg yolk and flavorings; beat to blend. Gradually add flour, mixing until moistened. Add nuts and blend. Form into crescents about 2½ inches long. Bake on ungreased baking sheets at 350° for 20 minutes or until slightly golden. Remove from oven. Sprinkle with confectioners' sugar while still warm.

Springerle

Makes 3 dozen.

      2 eggs
      1 cup sugar
      2 cups sifted flour
      ¼ teaspoon salt
      1 teaspoon baking powder
      1 teaspoon anise extract or anise seed

Beat eggs at high speed in a small bowl of an electric mixer until thick and light colored. Add sugar gradually; turn mixer to low and beat until sugar is dissolved about 10 minutes. Fold in sifted dry ingredients and anise. Place a small portion of dough at a time on a well floured board; coat dough with flour and pat with palms of hands to ⅓-inch thickness. Dust springerle rolling pin with flour; press on dough to emboss the designs and get a clear imprint. Working quickly, cut out the squares, place on greased baking sheets and allow to dry at room temperature for 4 to 6 hours. Bake at 350° for 10 to 12 minutes. Cool. Store in a covered container to mellow and soften.

Christmas Candle Cookies

- 2 cups sugar
- 1 cup margarine
- 2 eggs
- 1 cup milk
- 7 cups flour
- 2 tablespoons baking powder
- 1 teaspoon salt
- 2 teaspoons vanilla extract

Combine all ingredients; mix well. Roll to ½ inch thick; cut with a cookie cutter or make desired pattern with cardboard. Place cut cookies on lightly greased baking sheets. Bake at 375° for 7 to 10 minutes or until edges are lightly browned. Frost.

Icing

- 2 tablespoons shortening
- 2 tablespoons light corn syrup
- Flavoring to taste
- Milk
- Confectioners' sugar

Combine shortening, syrup, and flavoring. Add enough milk and sugar for desired consistency.

Note: This recipe can also be used to make jam tarts by cutting rounds, placing a teaspoonful of jam on one round, covering with another, and sealing the edges. Increase baking time by 2 to 3 minutes.

Cathedral Window Cookies

- ½ cup butter or margarine
- 1 12-ounce package chocolate chips
- 2 eggs, well beaten
- ½ cup ground nuts, optional
- 1 10½-ounce package colored miniature marshmallows
- Confectioners' sugar

Slowly melt the butter and chocolate chips. Remove from heat; stir in eggs and nuts. Cool. Gradually add marshmallows, mixing well after each addition. Divide mixture into 3 rolls; roll each in confectioners' sugar, wrap in waxed paper, and refrigerate. Chill 3 to 4 hours or overnight. Slice and serve.

Cinnamon Krinkles

- 2⅔ cups sifted flour
- 2 teaspoons cream of tartar
- 2 teaspoons baking soda
- ½ teaspoon salt
- 1 cup butter
- 1½ cups sugar
- 2 eggs
- 2 tablespoons ground cinnamon
- 3 tablespoons sugar

Sift together flour, cream of tartar, baking soda, and salt; set aside. Cream butter and sugar. Add eggs, one at a time; beat well after each addition. Add dry ingredients. Refrigerate 1 hour. Drop by teaspoonfuls onto a greased baking sheet. Combine cinnamon and sugar; sprinkle on cookies. Bake at 350° for 12 to 15 minutes.

Sugar Cookies

Makes 6 dozen.

- 4 cups sifted cake flour
- 2½ teaspoons baking powder
- ½ teaspoon salt
- ⅔ cup shortening
- 1½ cups sugar
- 2 eggs
- 1 teaspoon vanilla extract
- 4 teaspoons milk

Sift together flour, baking powder, and salt; set aside. Mix shortening, sugar, eggs, and vanilla until light and fluffy. Alternately add flour mixture and milk; blend well. Refrigerate dough until easy to handle. On a floured surface, roll ⅓ of the dough at a time, keeping the remaining dough refrigerated. For crisp cookies roll dough thin. Cut into desired shapes. Arrange ½ inch apart on a greased baking sheet. Decorate with white or colored sugar, chopped nuts, flaked coconut, cinnamon, or candied fruit. Bake at 400° for 9 minutes.

Note: Clean strings may be pressed into the cookies to form a loop so cookies can be hung on the Christmas tree.

Christmas Drop Cookies

Makes 8 dozen.

1½ cups flour
½ pound blanched almonds, chopped
½ pound walnuts, chopped
½ pound Brazil nuts, chopped
1 pound dates, chopped
3 slices candied pineapple, cut up
½ cup butter
¾ cup brown sugar
1 large egg, beaten
½ teaspoon vanilla extract
½ teaspoon baking soda
¼ teaspoon salt

Combine ½ cup of the flour, the nuts, and fruit; mix thoroughly and set aside. Cream butter and sugar; add beaten egg and vanilla. Mix in the remaining 1 cup flour, baking soda, and salt. Add floured nuts and fruit; mix well. Drop by teaspoonfuls onto a greased baking sheet. Bake at 350° for 15 minutes. Cool and store in air-tight containers 1 week before using.

Glazed Lebkuchen

Makes 2 dozen.

¾ cup honey
½ cup granulated sugar
¼ cup packed brown sugar
2 eggs, beaten
2½ cups sifted flour
1 teaspoon baking soda
¼ teaspoon ground cloves
1¼ teaspoons ground cinnamon
⅛ teaspoon ground allspice
½ cup minced citron
½ cup minced candied lemon peel
¾ cup chopped blanched almonds
1 cup confectioners' sugar
3 tablespoons hot milk
¼ teaspoon vanilla extract
Candied cherries, citron

Bring honey to a boil in a saucepan; cool. Add sugars and eggs; beat well. Blend in sifted dry ingredients, fruit, and almonds. Spread into a greased 10 x 15 x 1-inch pan. Bake at 350° for about 25 minutes. Blend confectioners' sugar, milk, and vanilla; spread over warm cake. Decorate with fruits. Cut into bars.

Christmas Seed Cookies

Makes 8 dozen.

2½ cups sifted cake flour
½ teaspoon baking powder
⅛ teaspoon salt
1 cup sugar
1 cup butter, softened
2 egg yolks
1 teaspoon vanilla extract
Caraway, sesame or poppy seed

Sift the first 4 ingredients; cut in butter. Add egg yolks and vanilla; blend. Chill several hours. Roll to ⅛ inch thick and cut into desired shapes. Place on baking sheets; sprinkle with seed. Bake at 400° for about 8 minutes.

Pecan Balls

Makes 4 dozen.

1 cup margarine, softened
¼ cup sugar
2 cups sifted flour
2 cups pecans, broken into small pieces
Confectioners' sugar
Granulated sugar

Cream margarine, sugar, and flour; add pecans and mix well. Shape 1 tablespoon per cookie into balls; place on ungreased baking sheets. Bake at 300° for 45 minutes. Combine confectioners' and granulated sugars. Roll balls in sugars while still hot.

Chocolate Nut Puffs

Makes 3 dozen puffs.

1 cup (6-ounces) semisweet chocolate chips
2 egg whites
⅛ teaspoon salt
½ cup sugar
½ teaspoon vinegar
½ teaspoon vanilla extract
¾ cup chopped nuts

Melt chocolate over warm water; set aside. Beat egg white with salt until foamy. Gradually add sugar; beat until stiff peaks form. Beat in vinegar and vanilla. Fold in melted chocolate and nuts. Drop by teaspoonfuls on a greased baking sheet. Bake at 350° for about 10 minutes.

Raisin-Currant Bars

Makes 3½ dozen bars.

1½ cups sifted flour
1 teaspoon baking powder
1 cup firmly packed brown sugar
1½ cups quick-cooking rolled oats
¾ cup butter

Combine all ingredients; mix until crumbly. Pat ⅔ of the dough in a greased 9 x 13-inch baking pan. Spread with Fruit-Spice Filling. Cover with remaining crumbs. Bake at 350° for 35 minutes. Cool and cut into bars.

Fruit-Spice Filling

1 cup raisins
1 cup currants
1½ cups hot water
1 cup sugar
2 tablespoons flour
1 teaspoon ground cinnamon
½ teaspoon ground cloves
1 teaspoon vinegar
1 tablespoon butter

Combine all ingredients in a saucepan. Bring to a boil and cook until thick, stirring occasionally.

Snow-Covered Gingersnaps

¾ cup shortening, softened
1 cup sugar
¼ cup molasses
1 egg
2 cups flour
2 teaspoons baking soda
1 scant teaspoon salt
1 teaspoon ground cloves
1 teaspoon ground cinnamon
1 teaspoon ground ginger
Confectioners' sugar

Cream shortening; add sugar gradually, creaming well after each addition. Add molasses; mix well. Add egg; beat. Measure flour before sifting; add soda, salt, and spices. Stir into dough. Roll into balls the size of a walnut; roll in confectioners' sugar. Place 2 inches apart on an ungreased baking sheet. Bake at 350° for 10 to 12 minutes. Sprinkle with confectioners' sugar before removing from baking sheet.

Coconut Dainties

Makes 4 dozen.

1 cup butter or margarine, softened
¼ cup sifted confectioners' sugar
2 teaspoons vanilla extract
1 tablespoon water
2 cups sifted flour
1 cup chopped pecans
Confectioners' sugar
Finely shredded coconut

Thoroughly cream butter, sugar, and vanilla. Stir in water and flour; mix well. Stir in nuts. Shape into 1-inch balls. Place 1 inch apart on an ungreased baking sheet. Bake at 300° for 20 minutes or until firm. Dip cookies in confectioners' sugar and roll in coconut.

Cream Cheese Cookies

1 small package cream cheese, softened
¼ pound margarine, softened
1 egg yolk
2½ tablespoons sugar
3 ounces chocolate chips
1 cup flour

Mix ingredients together, adding flour last. Chill in refrigerator 2 hours or overnight. Use wax paper to form dough into roll. Refrigerate. Cut into ¼-inch slices to form cookies. Bake on ungreased baking sheets at 350° for 20 minutes or until light brown around edges.

Mother's Butterscotch Cookies

½ cup butter, softened
2 cups brown sugar
2 eggs
2 teaspoons vanilla extract
3 cups flour
2 teaspoons baking powder
½ teaspoon baking soda
⅛ teaspoon salt
½ cup chopped pecans or hickory nuts

Cream butter and sugar. Stir in unbeaten eggs. Add vanilla, sifted dry ingredients, and nuts; mix well. Knead into a roll and refrigerate several hours or overnight. Cut into very thin slices. Bake at 375° for 15 minutes.

Candies

Butter Toffee

2¼ cups sugar
  1 teaspoon salt
  ½ cup water
1¼ cups butter
1½ cups (½-pound) chopped, blanched almonds
  1 cup finely chopped walnuts
  ¼ pound milk chocolate, melted

Bring sugar, salt, water, and butter to a boil. Add half of the almonds. Cook, stirring constantly, to the hard-crack stage (290° on a candy thermometer). Remove from heat. Add remaining almonds and half of the walnuts. Pour into a greased, shallow 9 x 13-inch pan. Cool. Brush with melted chocolate and sprinkle with remaining walnuts. Let chocolate harden; then break into pieces.

Holiday Pralines

  1 cup brown sugar
  1 cup white sugar
  1 cup light cream
  ⅛ teaspoon salt
  3 tablespoons butter
  1 cup chopped pecans
  1 tablespoon maple syrup

Bring first 3 ingredients to a full boil for 1 minute. Add remaining ingredients and cook to soft-ball stage (234° on a candy thermometer). Quickly stir and drop by teaspoonfuls onto waxed paper. Cool.

Lemon Taffy

1½ cups sugar
  ¾ cup water
  ½ teaspoon cream of tartar
  ⅓ teaspoon lemon extract

Boil all ingredients without stirring until brittle when dropped in cold water (300° on a candy thermometer). Cool slightly. Butter hands. Pull with tips of fingers and thumbs until taffy is light and creamy. Set aside to harden; break into chunks. Store in air-tight containers.

Fairy Food

Makes 1 pound.

  1 cup sugar
  1 cup light corn syrup
  1 tablespoon vinegar
1½ tablespoons baking soda
  1 6-ounce package semisweet chocolate chips, melted

Mix sugar, syrup, and vinegar in a 3-quart saucepan; cook to hard-crack stage (300° on a candy thermometer). Remove from heat. Add baking soda; mix quickly. Pour into a greased 11 x 7-inch pan. Cool. Invert on a tray and spread with melted chocolate. Break into chunks.

Frosties

20 large marshmallows
  ¼ cup evaporated milk
1½ cups shredded coconut

Cook 8 marshmallows and evaporated milk in the top of a double boiler, stirring constantly, until marshmallows dissolve. Remove from heat but leave mixture over hot water. Cut 12 marshmallows in half and dip, one at a time, into mixture. Roll in shredded coconut; place on waxed paper. The coconut may be toasted a light brown, if desired.

Hard Candy

1¾ cups sugar
  ½ cup light corn syrup
  ½ cup water
  1 teaspoon flavoring
    Food coloring

Combine sugar, corn syrup, and water in a saucepan. Bring to a boil over medium heat until mixture reaches 300° on a candy thermometer. Remove from heat; add flavoring and a few drops of food coloring. For variety, divide mixture in half and add ½ teaspoon each of different flavorings and colors. Pour onto a marble slab to cool. Cut with scissors or break with a knife into strips. Store in glass jars.

Tiny Tim Oranges

Makes 40 oranges.

>   Peel of 4 medium oranges
>   2 cups sugar

Place orange peel in a saucepan; cover with cold water and simmer until tender. Drain well. Reserve 1 cup of the water in which the peel was cooked. Put orange peel through a food chopper, using coarse blades. Combine sugar and 1 cup reserved orange liquid. Stir over low heat until sugar dissolves. Cook to 238° on a candy thermometer, or until a little of the mixture forms a soft ball when dropped in cold water. Add orange peel, simmer 10 minutes or until most of the liquid has evaporated. Spread in a buttered shallow pan. When cool enough to handle, form into ¾-inch balls. Roll in granulated sugar to which orange food coloring has been added.

Maple Butternut Candy

>   6 cups sugar
>   4 cups maple syrup
>   ¼ cup butter
>   2 cups chopped butternuts or pecans

Combine sugar, syrup, and butter; cook to soft-ball stage (about 236° on a candy thermometer). Remove from heat. Add nuts; stir until thick enough so that nuts do not rise to the top. Pour into 2 greased 9 x 13-inch pans.

Candy Strawberries

>   1 pound shredded coconut
>   2 6-ounce packages wild strawberry-flavored gelatin
>   1 can sweetened condensed milk
>   1 teaspoon almond extract
>   Red crystal sugar
>   Strawberry stems or green crystal sugar

Grind coconut in a blender. Mix all ingredients together. Shape into strawberries. Roll in red sugar. Insert strawberry stems, if available from a cake decorating shop. If stems are unavailable, dip top part of strawberry in green sugar.

Christmas Pudding Candy

>   3 cups sugar
>   1 cup light cream
>   1 tablespoon butter
>   1 teaspoon vanilla extract
>   1 pound dates, cut up
>   1 pound figs, cut up
>   1 pound raisins
>   1 pound flaked coconut
>   1 or 2 cups chopped nuts

Cook sugar, cream, and butter to soft-ball stage (about 236° on a candy thermometer). Add vanilla; beat until creamy. Add fruit, coconut, and nuts; mix well. Roll into a loaf. Wrap in dampened cloth, then in waxed paper; store in a cool place for 2 weeks. Slice in desired shapes when ready to use.

Marzipan

>   ¼ cup margarine, softened
>   ¼ cup light corn syrup
>   ¼ teaspoon salt
>   ½ teaspoon lemon or vanilla extract
>   1 pound confectioners' sugar
>   1 cup almond paste
>   Food coloring

Cream margarine, syrup, salt, and flavoring. Add sugar, ⅓ at a time, and mix well after each addition. Knead in almond paste. Color with a few drops of food coloring. Mold into small shapes of fruits and vegetables or use as the center of candied cherries, dates, and prunes.

Caramel Turtles

>   1 cup pecan halves
> 36 light caramels
>   ½ cup sweet chocolate, melted

Arrange pecans, flat-side-down, in clusters of 4 on a greased baking sheet. Place 1 caramel on each cluster of pecans. Heat at 325° until caramels soften, 4 to 8 minutes. Remove from the oven; flatten caramel with buttered spatula. Cool slightly and remove from pan to waxed paper. Swirl melted chocolate on top.

Maple Seafoam

    3 cups firmly packed light brown sugar
    ¾ cup water
    1 tablespoon maple syrup
    2 egg whites
    ⅛ teaspoon salt
    1 teaspoon vanilla extract
    1 teaspoon maple flavoring
    1½ cups broken walnuts, optional

Mix sugar, water, and maple syrup in a saucepan; bring to a boil. Cook to soft-ball stage (about 236° on a candy thermometer). Beat egg whites with the salt until stiff. Pour sugar syrup over egg whites in a thin stream, beating constantly. Continue beating until thick and creamy. Add flavorings and nuts. Drop from teaspoon onto a well-greased pan.

Peanut Brittle

    2 cups sugar
    1 cup light corn syrup
    ½ cup water
    ¼ teaspoon salt
    1 teaspoon butter
    2 cups raw Spanish peanuts
    2 teaspoons baking soda

Using a large saucepan, boil first 4 ingredients together until mixture reaches thread stage (238° on a candy thermometer). Add butter and peanuts. Cook, stirring constantly until golden brown. Remove from heat; add baking soda. (Mixture will bubble up.) Mix well. Pour onto a well-greased baking sheet. As it cools, pull as thin as possible. When cool, break into pieces. Store in an airtight container.

Tan Fudge

    2 cups sugar
    1 cup milk
    1 7-ounce jar marshmallow creme
    1 12-ounce jar crunchy peanut butter
    1 teaspoon vanilla extract

Combine sugar and milk in a large, heavy saucepan. Slowly bring to a boil. Cook, stirring, to soft ball stage (238° on a candy thermometer). Remove from heat; add remaining ingredients. Beat until blended. Pour into a buttered 9-inch pan; cool. Cut into squares.

Rainbow Popcorn Balls

    ½ cup unpopped corn
    ¼ cup plus 2 tablespoons salad oil
    1½ cups salted peanuts, coarsely chopped
    1 cup light corn syrup
    ½ cup sugar
    1 3-ounce package strawberry- or lime-flavored gelatin
      Red or green food coloring

To pop corn, heat oil over medium heat. Add popcorn in a single layer. Heat until all corn is popped. Turn into a bowl; add peanuts to popcorn and toss to mix. Set aside. In a 1-quart saucepan combine corn syrup and sugar. Cook, stirring with a wooden spoon, until sugar dissolves. Without stirring, bring mixture to a full rolling boil. Remove from heat and add gelatin. Stir until dissolved and add food coloring. Pour over popcorn and mix. Butter hands and form into balls.

No-Cook Chocolate Fudge

Makes about 2 pounds.

    1 pound confectioners' sugar
    2 eggs, well beaten
    1 cup broken nuts
    1 teaspoon vanilla extract
    6 squares unsweetened chocolate
    2 tablespoons butter

Sift sugar; add to the eggs. Mix until smooth. Add nuts and vanilla. Melt chocolate slowly in the top of a double boiler, stirring constantly. Add butter to melted chocolate and blend. Add chocolate mixture to nut mixture; mix well. Quickly pour into a 10 x 6-inch well-greased pan. Let harden. When firm, cut into pieces.

Maple Seafoam, Tan Fudge,
No-Cook Chocolate Fudge,
Rainbow Popcorn Balls,
Peanut Brittle

New Year's Eve Buffet

Lemon Champagne Sparkler

- 2 12-ounce cans frozen lemonade concentrate
- 2 12-ounce cans frozen pineapple juice
- 1½ quarts water
- 2 quarts ginger ale, chilled
- 1 quart sparkling water, chilled
- 1 bottle (⅘-quart) dry champagne, chilled

Mix concentrated lemonade, pineapple juice, and water. Chill, covered. Before serving add ginger ale and sparkling water; pour into a large punch bowl. Add ice cubes. Pour champagne over punch and stir.

New Year's Herring Dip

- 1 8-ounce package cream cheese, softened
- 2 tablespoons chopped pimiento
- 1 8-ounce jar herring fillets in wine sauce, drained
- 1 cup cottage cheese

Combine cream cheese and pimiento. Cut herring into small pieces. Fold herring and cottage cheese into cream cheese. Heat mixture over low heat until hot and bubbly. Transfer to a chafing dish; keep warm. Add herring liquid as needed for dipping consistency. Serve with assorted crackers.

Pickled Shrimp

Makes 12 servings.

- ½ clove garlic
- 1 teaspoon salt
- ½ cup cider vinegar
- ¼ cup salad oil
- 4 drops Tabasco sauce
- 2 tablespoons chopped stuffed olives
- 3 tablespoons minced parsley
- 2 tablespoons chopped dill pickle
- 2 pounds jumbo shrimp, cooked and cleaned

Mash garlic and salt together. Add all ingredients and place in a quart jar; shake well. Place in refrigerator at least 24 hours before serving. Serve with slices of pumpernickel bread.

Ham and Cheese Specials

Makes 8 open-face sandwiches.

- 2 3-ounce packages cream cheese, softened
- 2 teaspoons ground cinnamon
- 1 16-ounce can brown bread, cut into 8 slices
- 8 slices boiled ham
- 2 8-ounce cans sliced pineapple in unsweetened juice, drained, reserve 5 tablespoons juice
- 1 10½-ounce can chicken gravy

Combine cream cheese and cinnamon. Spread about 1 tablespoon on each slice of bread. Top with ham and pineapple. Broil 4 inches from heat for 5 minutes or until hot. In a saucepan blend gravy and reserved pineapple juice into the remaining cream cheese mixture. Heat, stirring occasionally. Spoon over sandwiches.

Gourmet Meat Roll

Makes 8 servings.

- 2 eggs, beaten
- ¾ cup soft bread crumbs
- ½ cup tomato juice
- ¼ cup sherry
- 2 tablespoons chopped parsley
- 1 small clove garlic, chopped
- ½ teaspoon salt
- ¼ teaspoon black pepper
- 2 pounds ground beef
- 8 thin slices boiled ham
- 1½ cups shredded mozzarella cheese
- 3 slices mozzarella cheese, halved diagonally

Combine eggs, bread crumbs, tomato juice, sherry, parsley, garlic, salt, and pepper. Stir in ground beef, mixing well. On foil or waxed paper, pat meat to a 12 x 10-inch rectangle. Arrange ham slices on top of meat, leaving a small margin around edges. Sprinkle shredded cheese over ham. Starting from short end, roll up meat, using foil to lift. Seal edges and ends. Place roll seam-side-down in a 13 x 9-inch pan. Bake at 350° for 1 hour and 15 minutes. Place cheese wedges over top of roll, return to oven for 5 minutes until cheese melts.

Orange Eggnog Punch

 2 pints raspberry, orange or lime sherbet
 2 cups pineapple juice
 2 cups orange juice
 1 quart dairy eggnog

In a mixing bowl, place all but 1 cup of the sherbet; beat until smooth. Add juices and blend thoroughly. Gradually add eggnog. Pour into a punch bowl. Float small scoops of sherbet on top.

Fruit Salad

 1 can mandarin oranges, drained, reserve juice
 1 can pineapple chunks, drained, reserve juice
 1 package vanilla pudding
 1 package vanilla tapioca pudding
 1 tablespoon (heaping) frozen orange juice concentrate, thawed
 1 banana, sliced

Add enough water to reserved fruit juices to measure 3 cups. Cook puddings with the 3 cups liquid and orange juice concentrate. Cool slightly; add fruits and gently toss. Refrigerate.

Stuffed Mushrooms

 1 pound mushrooms
 1 tablespoon chopped onion
 ½ cup butter
 1 10-ounce package frozen spinach, cooked and drained
   Ground nutmeg
   Salt and pepper
 ⅓ cup grated Cheddar cheese

Twist out mushroom stems and chop. Sauté chopped stems and onion in half of the butter. Remove from skillet and set aside. Add remaining butter to skillet; gently sauté mushroom caps. Remove and set aside on absorbent paper. Put spinach, sautéed onion, and mushroom stems in blender. Add seasonings. Puree. Fill mushroom caps with teaspoonfuls of mixture. Sprinkle each with grated cheese. Bake on a cookie sheet at 375° for 15 minutes.

Note: These may be made ahead and refrigerated to bake just before serving.

Sausage and Oyster Casserole

 1 pound pork sausage, cut into 1-inch pieces
 1 small can button mushrooms
 ½ cup chopped onion
 2 10¾-ounce cans cream of celery soup
 1 cup milk
1½ teaspoons salt
 ¼ teaspoon black pepper
 ½ cup chopped parsley
 1 pint oysters
 3 cups cooked elbow macaroni

Fry sausage in a skillet until lightly browned. Remove sausage to paper towels using a slotted spoon. Pour off half of the fat. Add mushrooms and onion to remaining fat; sauté until onion is transparent. Stir in soup, milk, seasoning, and parsley. Cook until thoroughly heated. Add oysters and half of the browned sausage; mix. Heat thoroughly. In a greased 3-quart casserole, alternately layer macaroni and sausage-oyster mixture. Top with remaining sausage. Bake at 350° for 30 minutes.

Snowball Cake

2½ packages unflavored gelatin
 5 tablespoons water
 1 cup boiling water
2½ cups sliced pineapple, drained
 1 cup sugar
 1 tablespoon lemon juice
 5 packages whipped topping
 1 angel food cake
 1 cup chopped pecans
 ½ teaspoon vanilla extract
 1 can flaked coconut

Dissolve gelatin in the 5 tablespoons water. Add the 1 cup boiling water, pineapple, sugar, and lemon juice to gelatin and mix. Refrigerate until thick. Prepare 4 packages of the whipped topping. Break cake into bite-size pieces; add to the whipped topping. Add nuts and vanilla. Combine cake mixture and gelatin mixture. Spoon into a buttered tube pan. Refrigerate overnight to set. Prepare remaining 1 package of whipped topping and frost cake. Sprinkle with flaked coconut.

Gifts from the Kitchen

Coconut Christmas Cookie Tree

Makes 1 cookie tree.

1½ cups butter or margarine
1 cup sugar
2 eggs
4½ cups sifted flour
1 teaspoon vanilla extract
1 teaspoon almond extract
2 cups flaked coconut
¼ cup hot milk
1 pound unsifted confectioners' sugar
  Green food coloring, optional
  Flaked coconut

Cut star-shaped patterns from heavy paper 9, 8, 7¼, 6½, 5½, 4¾, 4, and 3 inches in diameter, measuring from point to point. Cut two round patterns, 2½ and 1½ inches in diameter.

Cream butter until soft; gradually add sugar, beating until light and fluffy. Add eggs and beat well. Add flour, a small amount at a time, mixing well after each addition. Blend in vanilla, almond extract, and the 2 cups flaked coconut. Divide dough into 2 equal portions, wrap in waxed paper and chill 30 minutes or until firm enough to roll. Roll dough ⅛ inch thick on a lightly floured board. Cut 2 cookies from each star pattern, making a total of 16 cookies. Cut 12 cookies from the 1½-inch round pattern and 20 cookies from the 2½-inch round pattern. With a large drinking straw, cut a hole in the center of each cookie. Place on ungreased baking sheets. Bake at 350° for 8 minutes, or until edges are lightly browned. Cool. Gradually add hot milk to the confectioners' sugar, using just enough milk for a spreading consistency. Tint green with food coloring, if desired. Spread on each star-shaped cookie. Sprinkle flaked coconut on edges.

To Assemble Tree

Place a 12- to 15-inch stick or thin candle in a candle holder; secure with paper. Slip 2 of the larger round cookies over the stick. Slip on largest star cookie and continue to stack cookies in decreasing size, placing 2 round cookies between star-shaped cookies. Top with a rosette of frosting or a small candle. Decorate with silver dragées or small candles, if desired.

Nut Roll

Makes about 5 pounds.

1 7½-ounce jar marshmallow creme
1 teaspoon vanilla extract
3½ cups confectioners' sugar
1 pound caramels
9½ cups chopped nuts

Combine marshmallow creme and vanilla; add sugar gradually. Shape into rolls about 1 inch in diameter. Wrap in plastic wrap and freeze for at least 6 hours. Melt caramels over hot water; keep warm. Dip candy rolls in caramels and roll in nuts until well coated. Cool and store in an airtight container.

Striped Cookies

Makes about 5½ dozen.

2½ cups sifted cake flour
1 teaspoon baking powder
½ teaspoon salt
½ cup butter or margarine, softened
⅔ cup sugar
1 egg
1 tablespoon milk
1 square unsweetened chocolate, melted
  Milk

Sift together flour, baking powder, and salt; set aside. Cream butter and sugar; beat until light and fluffy. Add egg and milk, blend well. Add flour mixture, a small amount at a time, beating well after each addition. Divide dough in half. Blend chocolate into one half. If necessary chill or freeze both parts of dough until firm enough to roll. Roll each portion of dough on a lightly floured board into a 9 x 4½-inch rectangle. Brush chocolate dough lightly with milk; place plain dough on top. Using a long, sharp knife, cut rectangle lengthwise into 3 equal strips 1½ inches wide. Brush each layer with milk. Stack strips, alternating colors, and press together lightly. Carefully wrap in waxed paper. Freeze until firm enough to slice, or refrigerate overnight. Cut into ⅛-inch slices, using a very sharp knife. Place on greased baking sheets. Bake at 400° for 6 to 8 minutes or just until white portions begin to brown.

Cranberry Claret Jelly

Makes 4 cups.

3½ cups sugar
1 cup cranberry juice cocktail
1 cup claret wine
3 ounces liquid fruit pectin

Combine sugar, cranberry juice cocktail, and wine in a large saucepan. Stir over medium heat, bringing mixture to just below the boiling point. Continue stirring until the sugar is dissolved, about 5 minutes. Remove from heat. Stir in fruit pectin; mix well. Skim off foam and pour quickly into glasses. Seal with paraffin.

Holiday Conserve

Makes 6 cups.

2 30-ounce cans apricot halves, drained, reserve 1½ cups syrup
1 cup candied mixed fruits
½ cup quartered red candied cherries
1½ cups sugar
¼ teaspoon salt
¼ teaspoon ground nutmeg
1 tablespoon grated lemon peel
1 tablespoon grated orange peel
1½ cups finely chopped pecans

Coarsely chop the apricots. Place all ingredients except pecans in a Dutch oven. Bring to a boil, stirring occasionally. Reduce heat; simmer, uncovered, 25 minutes or until thickened. Stir in pecans. Ladle into hot sterilized jars; seal with lid or cover with paraffin.

Stuffed Dates

Fill centers of pitted dates with 1 or more of the following: walnuts, pecans, peanut butter mixed with chopped peanuts, plain fondant or fondant mixed with chopped candied fruits. Roll in confectioners' sugar or finely grated coconut. Store in an air-tight container in the refrigerator.

Mini-Fruitcakes

Makes 3 dozen.

3 cups unsifted flour
1⅓ cups sugar
1 teaspoon salt
1 teaspoon baking powder
2 teaspoons ground cinnamon
1 teaspoon ground nutmeg
½ cup orange juice
½ cup brandy or water
1 cup vegetable oil
4 eggs
¼ cup light corn syrup
1 cup dark seedless raisins
2 cups diced, dried California apricots
2 cups mixed candied fruits
2 cups pecan halves
⅓ cup light corn syrup

In a large mixing bowl, combine all ingredients except fruits, nuts, and ⅓ cup corn syrup. Blend for ½ minute on low speed, scraping bowl constantly. Beat 3 minutes on high speed, scraping bowl occasionally. Stir in fruits and nuts. Spoon batter into 3 dozen 2½-inch muffin pans lined with paper baking cups. Bake at 275° for 65 to 70 minutes or until toothpick comes out clean when inserted in center of fruitcake. Cool fruitcakes in pans for 5 minutes; remove to cooling rack. Cool thoroughly. Heat corn syrup in a small pan; brush over tops of cakes. Place cupcakes in container; cover with cheesecloth soaked in brandy. Cover tightly; store in a cool place for up to 2 weeks. For longer storage, freeze in tightly covered containers.

Meltaway Maple Crisps

½ cup butter, softened
¼ cup sugar
1 teaspoon maple flavoring
2 cups sifted cake flour
¾ cup chopped pecans

Cream butter; add sugar gradually. Add flavoring and beat until fluffy. Stir in flour; mix well. Fold in pecans; press into a ball. Pinch off small pieces of dough and place on an ungreased baking sheet. Flatten cookies with a glass dipped in sugar. Bake at 350° for 7 minutes.

Candied Orange Coffee Cake

¾ cup sugar
¼ cup butter or margarine, softened
1 egg
½ cup milk
1½ cups sifted flour
2 teaspoons baking powder
½ teaspoon salt
4 teaspoons minced candied orange peel
1 tablespoon grated orange rind

Blend sugar, butter, and egg until light and fluffy. Alternately add milk and dry ingredients. Add orange peel and rind, stirring until just combined. Pour into a greased mold. Sprinkle with the Topping. Bake at 375° for 25 to 30 minutes.

Topping

½ cup sugar
⅓ cup flour
1 tablespoon grated orange rind
¼ cup chopped candied orange peel
¼ cup butter or margarine

Combine all ingredients; mix until crumbly.

Note: To freeze, cool, and tightly cover. To serve, heat at 350° for 20 minutes if frozen; 10 minutes if thawed.

Nut Stollen

Makes 2 stollens.

1 package dry yeast
¼ cup lukewarm water (110 to 115°)
1 teaspoon sugar
¾ cup shortening or margarine
2 cups flour
2 eggs, beaten
Poppy or prune cake filling

Dissolve yeast in water; add the sugar. Cut shortening into flour until crumbly; add eggs and the yeast mixture. Divide dough into 2 parts. Roll out each part into a rectangle. Spread with poppy or prune filling or use your own favorite filling. Roll up jelly-roll style from long side; seal edges. Place on a greased baking sheet. Make 3 slashes crosswise or 1 long cut through center. Bake at 350° for 30 minutes.

Marmalade Nut Bread

2½ cups unsifted flour
⅓ cup sugar
3½ teaspoons baking powder
1 teaspoon salt
1 cup coarsely chopped walnuts
1 egg
1 cup orange marmalade
1 cup orange juice
3 tablespoons vegetable oil

In a large mixing bowl, thoroughly stir together flour, sugar, baking powder, and salt. Add walnuts; toss to coat evenly. In a medium bowl, beat egg slightly; stir in marmalade, orange juice, and vegetable oil. Add to flour mixture; stir only until dry ingredients are moistened. Divide batter evenly between 2 well-greased 9 x 5-inch loaf pans. Bake at 350° for 1 hour or until toothpick inserted in center comes out clean. Cool in pans on rack 10 minutes; remove from pans; cool thoroughly on rack. Wrap tightly and let stand several hours before serving.

Spicy Applesauce Cake

2 cups sifted flour
1½ teaspoons baking soda
½ teaspoon salt
½ teaspoon each: ground cinnamon, cloves, nutmeg and allspice
½ cup butter or margarine, softened
1 teaspoon vanilla extract
1 cup firmly packed light brown sugar
½ cup white sugar
2 eggs, lightly beaten
1½ cups sweetened applesauce
¾ cup each: chopped dates, raisins, broken walnuts
Confectioners' sugar

Line an ungreased 9 x 5-inch loaf pan with aluminum foil. Sift flour with soda, salt, and spices. Cream butter, vanilla, and sugars until light and fluffy. Add eggs; continue beating until very light. Add flour mixture alternately with the applesauce, stirring until just blended. Combine dates, raisins, and nuts; fold in lightly. Spoon into loaf pan. Bake at 325° for 1 hour or until cake is firm and springy when touched. Cool and sprinkle with confectioners' sugar.

Cranberry-Orange Relish

Makes 2 pints.

- **4 cups (1-pound) cranberries**
- **2 oranges, seeds removed**
- **2 cups sugar**

Put cranberries and oranges, including rind, through a food chopper. Add sugar; mix well. Chill.

Maple Squash

Makes 8 servings.

- **1 3-pound butternut squash, cut into eighths, seeds and pulp removed**
- **¼ cup butter or margarine**
- **¼ cup maple syrup**
- **½ teaspoon salt**
  Ground nutmeg to taste
  Black pepper to taste

Place squash in boiling salted water; cover. Heat to boiling and cook 15 minutes or until tender. Drain, pare, and mash. Combine remaining ingredients with squash and heat thoroughly.

Cornish Game Hens with Wild Rice

- **4 ounces fresh mushrooms**
- **½ cup butter or margarine**
- **½ cup walnut halves**
- **4 1- to 1¼-pound Cornish game hens**
- **¾ cup wild rice**
- **1 teaspoon instant minced onion**
- **2 cups water**
- **4 chicken bouillon cubes**
  Garlic salt and black pepper to taste

Clean mushrooms; remove and slice stems. Melt 2 tablespoons butter in an electric skillet. Add mushrooms and walnuts; sauté lightly. Remove from skillet and set aside. Clean birds inside and out; dry with absorbent paper. Truss legs to body of bird. Add remaining butter to skillet; brown birds on all sides at 300°. Wash rice and place in a bowl with the onion, water, and bouillon cubes.

Reduce skillet temperature to 200°. Add rice mixture; spread evenly under and around birds. Cover and cook for 45 minutes or until birds are tender. Remove birds. Crisp birds, breast-side-up, 4 to 5 inches from broiler, if desired. Add mushrooms and walnuts to rice.

Upside-Down Pear Gingerbread Cake

- **¼ cup butter**
- **½ cup firmly packed light brown sugar**
- **2 tablespoons finely chopped maraschino cherries**
- **2 cups thinly sliced fresh pears**
  Orange or lemon juice
- **1 package gingerbread mix**
  Vanilla ice cream

Melt butter in an 8-inch square baking pan; stir in sugar. Sprinkle cherries over butter and sugar. Dip pear slices in juice to prevent darkening. Arrange pear slices in rows over cherries; set aside. Prepare gingerbread according to package directions. Pour over pears and bake according to package directions. Cool in pan on wire rack 5 minutes. Invert onto serving plate. Serve warm topped with vanilla ice cream.

Prune Pudding

- **1 pound cooked prunes, reserve ½ cup prune juice**
- **⅔ cup cornstarch**
- **2 cups sugar**
  Juice of 1 lemon
- **1 cup chopped nuts**
- **1 teaspoon ground cinnamon**
  Whipped cream

Pit and chop the prunes. Blend the reserved ½ cup prune juice with the cornstarch until smooth. Combine prunes, sugar, lemon juice, and cornstarch mixture in a saucepan; simmer until thick and clear. Cool slightly; add nuts and cinnamon. Chill. Serve with whipped cream.

Cornish Game Hens
with Wild Rice

Index

Book II

All Holidays
COOKBOOK

Introduction

Holidays and entertaining go together, and this cookbook provides you with new and interesting food ideas to make those special occasions even more memorable. Ranging from picnic simplicity to party elegance, the recipes and suggestions are equally good anytime.

There are tips for giving a successful party as well as varied and unique menu plans. Foods for all the major holidays throughout the year are featured such as Valentine's Day, Easter, Mother's Day, Father's Day, Thanksgiving, and Christmas. Also included are recipes for seasonal celebrations including a springtime luncheon, summer cookout and harvest get-together, as well as party ideas for youngsters. You'll never have to wonder again what to prepare for that special luncheon, Sunday brunch, or graduation party. Your guests will ask for the recipes!

Enjoy entertaining family and friends with tasty and attractive fare and await with confidence the compliments that are sure to follow.

Contents

New Year Party

Lemon Champagne Punch

Makes 50 servings.

- 4 6-ounce cans frozen lemonade concentrate
- 4 6-ounce cans frozen pineapple juice
- 1½ quarts water
- 2 quarts ginger ale, chilled
- 1 quart sparkling water, chilled
- 1 bottle (⅘ quart) dry champagne, chilled

Combine juices and water. Chill, covered. Before serving, add ginger ale and sparkling water; pour over ice cubes in a large punch bowl. Pour chilled champagne over punch and stir gently.

New Year's Eve Party Cheese Ball

- 2 8-ounce packages cream cheese
- ¼ pound blue cheese
- ½ pound extra-sharp Cheddar cheese, grated
- 1 tablespoon Worcestershire sauce
- 1 teaspoon cayenne pepper
- ½ teaspoon salt
- ½ teaspoon onion powder
- ½ teaspoon garlic powder
- 1 cup chopped pecans

Allow cheeses to reach room temperature; combine in a mixing bowl. Beat until well blended. Add Worcestershire sauce, cayenne pepper, salt, onion powder, and garlic powder. Add ½ cup of the chopped pecans. Chill. Shape into a ball and roll ball in remaining pecans. Chill thoroughly. Serve with assorted crackers and fresh fruits such as seedless grapes, apple and pear slices. Freeze, if desired.

Holiday Spinach Salad

- 5 slices bacon, fried and crumbled, reserve 2 tablespoons fat
- 3 tablespoons lemon juice
- 2 tablespoons salad oil
- 1 tablespoon sugar
- ½ teaspoon salt
- ½ teaspoon ground tarragon
- 1 pound spinach, washed and torn into bite-size pieces
- 1 cup sliced green onions
- 1½ cups celery slices
  Sliced orange sections

In a jar combine the bacon, 2 tablespoons bacon fat, lemon juice, salad oil, sugar, salt, and tarragon. Shake vigorously until all ingredients are well combined. Combine spinach, onions, celery, and orange sections. Pour dressing over all; toss until well coated.

Note: If desired, use half the amount of spinach and add other salad greens and tomatoes.

Auld Lang Syne Casserole

Makes 6 servings.

- 3 pounds chicken, cooked and cut up
- 1 cup chopped celery, cooked in chicken broth
- 1 cup rice, cooked in chicken broth
- 2 tablespoons minced onion
  Salt to taste
- 1 10¾-ounce can cream of chicken soup
- ¾ cup mayonnaise
- ½ cup slivered almonds
- 1 cup cornflakes, crushed
- 4 tablespoons margarine, melted

Mix all ingredients together, except cornflakes and margarine, in a casserole. Cover with cornflakes; drizzle on margarine. Bake at 350° for 30 minutes.

Peach Delight

- 3 egg whites
- 1 cup sugar
- ¼ teaspoon baking powder
- 1 teaspoon vanilla extract
- ½ cup pecans, finely chopped
- ½ cup finely crushed soda crackers

Beat egg whites stiff. Fold in sugar, baking powder, vanilla, pecans, and soda crackers. Pour into a buttered 11 x 7-inch pan. Bake at 325° for 30 minutes. Cool.

Topping

- ½ pint whipping cream, whipped
- 1 tablespoon confectioners' sugar
- 1 large can sliced peaches, well drained

Add sugar to whipped cream. Fold in peaches. Pour over cracker mixture and refrigerate overnight.

French Chocolate

Makes 4 servings.

2½ squares bitter chocolate
1 cup water
½ cup sugar
  Salt to taste
1 teaspoon vanilla extract
1 cup whipping cream, whipped
4 cups heated milk

Cook the chocolate with water until thick, stirring to prevent sticking. Add sugar and salt. Bring to a boil; remove from heat. Cool. Add vanilla. Fold in whipped cream. Makes about 2½ cups sauce. Place a generous spoonful of sauce in each of 4 serving cups. Refrigerate additional sauce for future use. Add hot milk to fill cup. Stir until mixed.

Nibble Mix

½ pound butter, melted
3 tablespoons Worcestershire sauce
4 cups each Rice Chex, Wheat Chex, Cheerios
4 cups pretzel sticks
1 can mixed nuts
1 teaspoon garlic salt
1 teaspoon onion salt

Place butter in a baking dish; stir in Worcestershire sauce. Add dry cereals, pretzel sticks, and nuts. Sprinkle with the garlic and onion salts; mix well. Bake at 225° for 1 hour, stirring occasionally.

Sombrero Snacks

2 ounces Cheddar cheese
1 mild chili pepper, diced
24 taco-flavored tortilla chips
  Bean dip

Cut cheese into 24 pieces. Arrange tortilla chips on a baking sheet. Place 1 teaspoon bean dip on each chip and top with cheese and chili pepper. Place 4 to 6 inches from the broiler; broil until cheese begins to melt.

Guacamole Dip I

2 ripe avocados, peeled, pitted and mashed
1 4-ounce container whipped cream cheese
  Seasoned salt

Mix avocado with cream cheese and season to taste. Cover and refrigerate until serving time.

Snow Ice Cream

½ cup sugar
1 cup cold evaporated milk
1 teaspoon vanilla extract
1 teaspoon maple extract

Beat above ingredients well with a spoon. Add clean snow, a little at a time, until creamy and the consistency of ice cream.

Party Cookies

Makes 100 cookies.

½ cup shortening, softened
½ cup butter, softened
2 cups brown sugar
2 cups applesauce
2 eggs, lightly beaten
3½ cups flour
2 teaspoons baking soda
1 teaspoon baking powder
2 teaspoons ground cinnamon
1 teaspoon ground cloves
2 teaspoons ground nutmeg
1 teaspoon salt
2 cups rolled oats
2 cups chopped nuts
1 12-ounce package chocolate chips

Cream first 5 ingredients thoroughly. Sift together flour, baking soda, baking powder, cinnamon, cloves, nutmeg, and salt. Add to creamed mixture. Add remaining ingredients; mix. Drop by teaspoonfuls onto a greased baking sheet. Bake at 375° for 12 to 15 minutes.

Valentine's Day

Valentine Cream Puff Heart

- 1 cup water
- ½ cup butter
- 1 cup sifted flour
- 4 eggs
- 1 10-ounce package frozen strawberries, drained
  Confectioners' sugar

Mark a heart-shaped outline with pencil on a baking sheet. Grease sheet lightly. Bring water and butter to boiling. Reduce heat. Add flour. Stir vigorously over low heat until mixture forms a ball, about 1 minute. Remove from heat. Beat in eggs, one at a time, beating until smooth after each addition. Drop mixture by spoonfuls, with sides touching, onto heart outline on baking sheet. Bake at 400° for 45 minutes. Cool on a rack. Cut off top. Fill shell with cream filling; top with strawberries. Replace top. Dust with confectioners' sugar. Serve at once.

Cream Filling

- 1 3¼-ounce package vanilla pudding
- 1½ cups milk
- 1 cup heavy cream, whipped
- 1 teaspoon vanilla

Combine pudding and milk in a medium saucepan. Cook, stirring constantly, over medium heat until mixture comes to a full rolling boil. Remove from heat. Cover surface of pudding with waxed paper. Cool. Fold in whipped cream and vanilla.

Strawberry Divinity

Makes 2¼ pounds.

- 3 cups sugar
- ¾ cup light corn syrup
- ¾ cup water
- 2 egg whites
- 1 package strawberry-flavored gelatin
- ½ cup flaked coconut
- 1 cup chopped pecans

Combine sugar, corn syrup, and water in a 2-quart saucepan and heat to boiling, stirring constantly. Continue cooking, stirring occasionally, until a small amount of the mixture forms a hard ball when tested in cold water (252° on a candy thermometer). Beat egg whites until foamy, add gelatin, beating until mixture forms peaks. Slowly pour hot syrup into beaten egg whites, beating constantly on high speed of electric mixer. Beat until candy begins to hold its shape. Fold in coconut and nuts; place in a greased 9-inch square pan. Cool and cut into squares.

Pretty Pink Gelatin Salad

- 1 small package mixed fruit-flavored gelatin
- 1 cup boiling water
- 1 cup creamed cottage cheese
- 1 8-ounce can crushed pineapple, drained
- 72 colored miniature marshmallows
- ½ pint whipping cream, whipped

Dissolve gelatin in boiling water. Chill until it thickens. Fold in cottage cheese and pineapple. Allow to thicken. Fold in marshmallows and whipped cream. Fill a 5-cup mold; chill until set.

Split Seconds

- 2 cups sifted flour
- ½ teaspoon baking powder
- ⅔ cup sugar
- ¾ cup butter or margarine, softened
- 1 egg, beaten
- 2 teaspoons vanilla extract
- ⅓ cup red jelly or jam

In a mixing bowl, sift together first 3 ingredients. Blend in butter, egg, and vanilla to form a dough. Place on a lightly floured board. Divide dough into four parts. Shape each into a roll 13 inches long and ¾ inch thick. Place on ungreased baking sheets 4 inches apart and 2 inches from edge of sheet. With a knife handle make a depression ¼ to ⅓ inch deep lengthwise down the center of each. Fill depressions with jelly. Bake at 350° for 15 to 20 minutes until golden brown. While warm, cut diagonally into bars and sprinkle with confectioners' sugar.

Mardi Gras

Mardi Gras Carrot Loaf

Makes 2 loaves.

1¼ cups vegetable oil
2 cups sugar
2 eggs
2 cups grated carrots
1 8-ounce can crushed pineapple and juice
3 cups flour
1 teaspoon baking soda
3 teaspoons ground cinnamon
1 teaspoon salt
2 to 3 teaspoons vanilla extract
1 cup chopped nuts

Blend cooking oil and sugar with eggs. Add carrots and pineapple and juice. Sift dry ingredients; add with vanilla and nuts. Grease and flour 2 loaf pans. Bake at 350° for 1 hour.

Cranberry Cream Cheese Mold

Makes 10 to 12 servings.

1 3-ounce package strawberry-flavored gelatin
1 cup boiling water
1½ cups raw cranberry relish

Dissolve gelatin in boiling water. Cool to room temperature and stir in cranberry relish. Pour into individual molds or 1 large mold. Chill until firm.

Top Layer

1 3-ounce package lemon-flavored gelatin
1½ cups boiling water
2 cups miniature marshmallows
1 cup crushed pineapple
1 3-ounce package cream cheese, softened
½ cup mayonnaise
½ cup whipping cream, whipped

Dissolve lemon gelatin in boiling water. Add marshmallows immediately. Stir until marshmallows dissolve. Add pineapple; chill mixture until partially set. Blend cheese with mayonnaise; stir into second mixture. Fold in whipped cream. Pour onto cranberry layer. Chill. Unmold and serve with salad greens, if desired.

Gourmet Shrimp Cocktail

¼ cup catsup
¼ cup chili sauce
2 teaspoons Worcestershire sauce
4 teaspoons horseradish
1 cup mayonnaise
1 teaspoon salt
½ teaspoon pepper
2 tablespoons chopped chives
¼ cup brandy
2 pounds cooked shrimp

Combine all ingredients except brandy and shrimp. Gradually stir in brandy. Chill in a serving bowl. Arrange the shrimp on a lettuce-lined tray surrounding the bowl of sauce.

Sardine-Stuffed Eggs

6 hard-cooked eggs, cut lengthwise in half
1 4⅜-ounce tin boneless, skinless, oil-packed sardines, drained
¼ cup mayonnaise
2 teaspoons lemon juice
Seasoned salt to taste

Carefully scoop out egg yolks. Mash the yolks and mix well with the other ingredients. Refill the whites. These eggs may be prepared 1 to 2 days in advance, wrapped with plastic wrap, and refrigerated.

Vegetable Ice

1 tablespoon lemon juice
¼ teaspoon Tabasco sauce
6 cups vegetable juice cocktail
Lemon slices, optional
Mint sprigs, optional

Combine ingredients and pour into freezer trays; freeze. Remove from freezer 15 minutes before serving. Spoon into sherbet glasses and garnish with a lemon slice and sprig of mint.

Cheese Puffs

Makes 4 dozen puffs.

- ½ cup butter
- 1 cup boiling water
- 1 cup sifted flour
- ½ teaspoon salt
- 4 eggs
- ½ cup grated Parmesan cheese

Melt butter in water in a saucepan. Add flour and salt all at once. Cook over medium heat, stirring constantly, until mixture leaves the side of the pan. Remove from heat and allow to cool 1 minute. Add eggs, one at a time, beating well until smooth and glossy. Add cheese and mix well. Drop dough by teaspoonfuls onto a greased baking sheet. Bake at 425° for 18 to 20 minutes.

Note: The unbaked dough may be refrigerated, covered, up to 3 days.

Paprika Steak

Makes 6 servings.

- 2 tablespoons flour
- ½ teaspoon paprika
- ¼ teaspoon leaf thyme
- Dash pepper
- 1½ pounds round steak
- 2 tablespoons shortening
- 1 medium onion, sliced
- 1 clove garlic, minced
- 1 10¾-ounce can cream of vegetable soup
- ½ soup can water
- ½ cup sour cream

Combine flour, paprika, thyme, and pepper. Pound into steak with a meat hammer or the edge of a heavy saucer. Cut meat into 6 pieces. Melt the shortening in a skillet; brown meat, onion, and garlic. Blend soup and water; pour over meat. Cover and simmer for 1½ hours, occasionally spooning sauce over meat. Remove meat from pan to heated platter. Stir in sour cream; heat for a few minutes. Pour over meat. Sprinkle with additional paprika.

Double-Quick Dinner Rolls

Makes 1 dozen rolls.

- 1 package dry yeast
- ¾ cup warm water
- ¼ cup sugar
- 1 teaspoon salt
- 2¼ cups flour
- 1 egg
- ¼ cup butter, softened

Dissolve yeast in the warm water. Add sugar, salt, and half of the flour. Beat for 2 minutes. Add egg and butter. Beat with mixer at medium speed until batter is smooth, about 2 minutes. Add the rest of the flour and stir by hand until flour disappears. Scrape sides of bowl. Cover with waxed paper and let stand until double in bulk, about 40 to 50 minutes. Stir down batter in 20 to 25 strokes. Spoon into greased muffin tins, filling half full. Let rise again for about 30 minutes or until batter reaches top of muffin cups. Bake at 425° for 10 to 15 minutes.

Poor Man's Mille-Feuilles

- 1 package graham crackers
- 1 large box vanilla pudding, prepared and cooled
- 1 tablespoon sugar
- 1 teaspoon vanilla extract
- ½ pint whipping cream, whipped

Spread whole graham crackers on the bottom of a 7½ x 10½-inch pan. Cover with a layer of pudding. Add sugar and vanilla to the whipped cream. Spread a layer of whipped cream over pudding layer. Cover with a second layer of whole graham crackers.

Icing

- Milk
- ½ pound confectioners' sugar
- 1 teaspoon vanilla extract
- 1 square baking chocolate, melted

Add enough milk to sugar and vanilla to make a thin frosting. Spread evenly over graham crackers. Drizzle chocolate over icing. Chill 6 hours; serve within 24 hours.

Patriotic Greetings on WASHINGTON'S BIRTHDAY!

Washington's Birthday

Sour Cherry Cake

Makes 1 8-inch cake.

1¼ cups sugar
½ cup butter, softened
2 eggs
2 cups flour
1 teaspoon baking soda
¼ teaspoon salt
1 teaspoon cinnamon
¾ cup sour milk
1 cup sour cherries

Grease and flour 2 8-inch cake pans. Cream together sugar and butter. Beat in eggs, one at a time. In a separate bowl sift flour, baking soda, salt, and cinnamon. Add butter mixture to flour mixture alternately with milk, beating after each addition. Fold in cherries. Bake at 350° for about 30 minutes.

Sour Cherry Frosting

1 tablespoon butter, softened
1 tablespoon shortening
2½ cups confectioners' sugar
1 teaspoon vanilla extract
Cherry juice

Combine ingredients with enough cherry juice to obtain a spreading consistency. Mix until smooth; frost cake.

Note: To make cherry juice when using fresh sour cherries, cook a small amount of cherries in a little water and sugar to form a syrup. Strain.

Washington Cherry Cheesecake

2 cups graham cracker crumbs
1½ sticks margarine, melted
1¼ cups sugar, divided
2 8-ounce packages cream cheese, softened
2 eggs
1 can cherry pie filling

Combine graham cracker crumbs, margarine, and ¼ cup of the sugar. Line baking pan with crumb mixture; set aside. Beat together cream cheese, remaining 1 cup of sugar, and eggs until smooth and creamy. Pour cheese filling into graham cracker-lined pan; bake at 375° for 15 minutes. Cool. Spread pie filling over top.

Cherries in the Snow

1 small angel food cake
1 1-pound can cherry pie filling
½ pint heavy cream, whipped

Break cake into small pieces. Use half to cover the bottom of a shallow 2-quart glass baking dish. Spread half of the cherry pie filling over cake pieces, smoothing into an even layer with the back of a spoon. Spoon half of the whipped cream over this, smoothing again. Repeat layers, ending with whipped cream. Smooth the cream to cover the entire top of mixture. Cover dish tightly with plastic wrap and refrigerate for 24 hours. Cut into squares.

Bing Cherry Salad

1 cup pitted bing cherries, drain and reserve juice
1 cup crushed pineapple, drain and reserve juice
1 3-ounce package black cherry-flavored gelatin
1 cup chopped pecans or walnuts
1 cup marshmallows, chopped fine

Combine fruit juices and bring to a boil. Add to gelatin; stir until gelatin dissolves. Cool. Stir in fruit, nuts, and marshmallows. Pour into a 5-cup mold. Chill until firm. Unmold onto a lettuce bed and top with cream cheese or salad dressing, if desired.

Fruit Salad Dressing Supreme

2 tablespoons flour
¾ cup sugar
2 eggs, lightly beaten
2 tablespoons butter
2 tablespoons lemon juice
1 cup pineapple juice

Combine all ingredients in the top of a double boiler. Cook, stirring constantly, over boiling water until slightly thickened. Remove from heat and chill. Serve as dressing for fruit salad or gelatin salad.

Sunday Brunch

Orange Blossom Punch

- 1 4-ounce jar maraschino cherries, drained
- 1 8-ounce can pineapple chunks, drained
- 1 24-ounce bottle champagne
- ½ gallon orange juice

Fill a 6-cup ring mold with water. Drop in the cherries and pineapple. Freeze. At serving time pour orange juice and champagne into punch bowl. Unmold ice ring by dipping into 2 inches hot water; slide ice ring into punch.

Salmon Ball

- 1 16-ounce can red salmon, drained, remove skin and bones
- 1 8-ounce package cream cheese, softened
- 1 small onion, minced
- 2 tablespoons lemon juice
- ½ cup minced parsley
- ¼ cup chopped nuts

Flake salmon into a bowl. Add cream cheese; blend well. Add onion and lemon juice. Mix well. Shape into a ball and wrap in waxed paper; refrigerate until firm. Sprinkle parsley and nuts on waxed paper; mix well. Roll salmon ball in mixture until coated. Refrigerate until serving time. Place in center of platter and surround with crackers to serve.

Cheese and Egg Brunch

Makes 8 servings.

- 6 slices bread, cubed
- 1 large can mushrooms
- ½ cup sliced, stuffed olives
- ¾ cup grated sharp Cheddar cheese
- ¾ cup grated Swiss cheese
- 4 eggs, beaten
- 2 cups milk
- ½ teaspoon dry mustard
- ½ teaspoon salt

Place half of the bread cubes in a buttered 3-quart casserole. Layer with the mushrooms, olives, and cheeses. Top with the remaining bread cubes. Combine eggs, milk, mustard and salt; pour over all. Refrigerate overnight. Bake, uncovered, at 350° for 1 hour. Let stand 10 minutes before serving. Serve with sausage or bacon, hot rolls or sweet rolls.

Baked Canadian Bacon

- 3 pounds Canadian bacon
- 1 orange, cut into thin slices
  Whole cloves
- ½ cup molasses
- ¼ cup water
- ½ cup orange juice
- ¼ cup sugar
- ¼ teaspoon dry mustard

Remove casing from bacon and place, fat-side up, in an open pan. Bake at 325° for 2 hours. Remove from the oven and attach orange slices to bacon with cloves. Mix remaining ingredients. Pour over bacon and bake, basting often, at 325° for 30 minutes.

Fruit Medley

- 1 cup cubed cantaloupe
- 1 cup raspberries
- 1 cup pineapple chunks
- ½ cup sugar syrup

Combine fruits in a large bowl. Mix lightly. Pour sugar syrup over fruit mixture. Chill 30 minutes.

Sugar Syrup

- ½ cup sugar
- 1 cup water

Combine sugar and water. Boil 5 minutes. Cool.

Blueberry Muffins

- ½ cup sour milk
- 1 teaspoon baking soda
- 1 cup brown sugar
- ½ cup shortening
- 2 eggs
- ½ teaspoon salt
- 2½ cups sifted flour, divided
- 1 pint blueberries

Combine sour milk and baking soda; stir until baking soda dissolves; set aside. Cream sugar and shortening. Add eggs, 1 at a time. Combine salt and 2 cups of the flour. Alternately add sour milk and flour to sugar mixture. Mix the ½ cup flour and blueberries; fold into batter. Pour into greased muffin tins. Bake at 350° for approximately 25 minutes until light brown.

Special Luncheon

Claret Cup

Makes 8 to 10 servings.

- 1 quart claret wine
- 1 ounce Maraschino liqueur
- 2 ounces curacao liqueur
- 2 tablespoons granulated sugar

Combine all the ingredients in a pitcher. Serve over ice in tall glasses. Garnish each glass with a long toothpick skewered with a slice of orange, a chunk of pineapple, and a sprig of fresh mint, if desired.

Refrigerator Rolls

- 1 package dry yeast
- 1 cup warm water (110 to 115°)
- 1 tablespoon salt
- 2 tablespoons (heaping) shortening
- ½ cup sugar
- 2 cups boiling water
- 8 cups flour
- 3 eggs, beaten

Dissolve yeast in warm water; set aside. Combine salt, shortening, and sugar in a large bowl. Stir in boiling water. Cool to warm. Add enough flour to slightly thicken. Add yeast mixture; beat well. Add the eggs and remainder of the flour. Knead dough until smooth. Let rise until double in bulk. Punch down and place in a well-greased bowl. Cover and refrigerate. When ready to use, cut off desired amount of dough, shape and let rise about 3 hours. Bake at 375° for 20 minutes. Punch down any remaining dough and refrigerate until needed.

Lemoned Carrots

- 1 1-pound can diced carrots, reserve ¼ cup liquid
- 1 teaspoon sugar
- 1 teaspoon lemon juice
- 2 teaspoons butter
- ½ teaspoon grated lemon peel

Combine all ingredients including carrot liquid and heat. Sprinkle on lemon peel.

Imperial Crab

Makes 4 servings.

- ¼ cup butter
- 1 cup half and half
- 1 teaspoon dry mustard
- 1 teaspoon lemon juice
- 2 teaspoons Worcestershire sauce
- 1 teaspoon salt
- ¾ teaspoon pepper
- 1 egg, lightly beaten
- 1 pound crabmeat
  Cracker crumbs

Melt butter in a double boiler. Mix in half and half, mustard, lemon juice, Worcestershire sauce, salt, pepper, and egg, stirring constantly. Add crabmeat. Fill individual casseroles with mixture. Sprinkle on cracker crumbs. Bake at 400° for 30 minutes until golden brown.

Strawberry Dream

Makes 12 to 14 servings.

- 1 cup butter
- ½ cup brown sugar
- 2 cups flour
- 1 cup chopped nuts

Combine ingredients and place in a 9 x 13-inch pan. Bake at 400° for 15 minutes, stirring occasionally. When brown press half of the mixture into an oblong pan. Spread on Filling; top with remaining crumb mixture. Freeze overnight until ready to use.

Filling

- 1 10-ounce package frozen strawberries, thawed
- 2 egg whites
- 1 cup sugar
- 1 tablespoon lemon juice
- 1 teaspoon vanilla extract
- ½ pint whipping cream, whipped

Place all ingredients, except whipped cream, in a large mixing bowl. Beat with an electric mixer for 20 minutes. Fold in the whipped cream.

"May the roads rise
with you,
And the wind be always
at your back;
And may the Lord hold
you in the hollow of His
hand."
OLD GAELIC BLESSING

St. Patrick's Day

Emerald Salad

Makes 8 to 10 servings.

- 1 16-ounce can sliced peaches, drained, reserve syrup
- 2 3-ounce packages lime-flavored gelatin
- 2 cups boiling water
- 1 cup cold water
- 1 red maraschino cherry
- 1 cup grapes, halved and seeded (or 1 8¾-ounce can grapes, drained)
  Lettuce
  Cottage cheese

Add enough water to syrup to make 1 cup. Dissolve gelatin in the boiling water. Add the 1 cup water and the peach syrup. Chill until partially set. Place 1 cup of gelatin mixture in a 6-cup mold. Press 12 peach slices into gelatin, forming a sunburst. Place cherry in center. Dice remaining peaches. Add peaches and grapes to remaining gelatin. Pour into mold; chill until firm. Unmold onto chilled serving plate. Surround with lettuce cups filled with cottage cheese.

Shamrock Rolls

Refrigerater Rolls dough (Recipe on page 13)

Shape the dough into small balls; brush with melted butter. Arrange 4 balls in each cup of a greased muffin tin. Allow dough to rise and bake according to recipe directions.

Scalloped Tomatoes

Makes 4 servings.

- 6 medium tomatoes, peeled and quartered
- ¾ cup water
- 2 slices toast, buttered and cubed
- 8 soda crackers, broken
- 1 teaspoon butter
- ½ teaspoon dried parsley
  Salt and pepper to taste

Cook tomatoes in the water until mushy. Add buttered toast and 6 of the broken soda crackers. Add butter and parsley; salt and pepper to taste. Before serving, top with remaining crackers.

Corned Beef and Cabbage

- 1 4-pound corned beef brisket
- 1 head cabbage

Wash brisket; place in a kettle and cover with cold water. Bring water to a boil; cover and simmer 30 minutes. Drain. Cover with fresh boiling water and simmer until meat is tender. Chop cabbage into wedges. About 20 minutes before meat is done, add cabbage. Cook uncovered for 10 to 15 minutes. Do not overcook the cabbage.

Irish Bread

- 4 cups flour
- 4 teaspoons baking powder
- ¼ teaspoon baking soda
- ½ tablespoon salt
- 2 tablespoons shortening
- 1 tablespoon butter
- 2 eggs, lightly beaten
  Buttermilk
  Raisins, citron or currants, optional

Mix dry ingredients. Cut in shortening and butter until mixture is crumbly. Add eggs and buttermilk. Add raisins, citron, or currants as desired. Bake at 350° about 1 hour.

Pistachio Cake

- 1 16-ounce box almond-flavored cake mix (or use white cake mix and 1 teaspoon almond extract)
- 1 3-ounce package pistachio instant pudding
  Green food coloring, optional
- ¾ cup cold water
- ¾ cup vegetable oil
- 1 teaspoon almond extract, optional
- 4 eggs

Blend cake mix and pudding. If more color is desired, add a few drops of green food coloring to the water. Add water and oil to the cake mixture. Add extract and eggs, one at a time, using low speed of mixer. Beat 5 minutes. Oil a large angel food cake or bundt pan. Bake at 350° for 45 to 50 minutes. Cool before removing from pan.

Note: This cake freezes well.

Springtime Favorites

Springtime Avocado Salad

- 1 avocado, sliced
- 1 can mandarin oranges, drained
- ¼ cup chopped red onion
- ½ cup Creamy French Dressing

Combine fruits and the onion. Add dressing. Refrigerate to mix flavors.

Creamy French Dressing

- ¾ cup sugar
- 1 teaspoon salt
- 1 teaspoon dry mustard
- ½ teaspoon paprika
  - Dash pepper
- 2 egg yolks, well beaten
- ½ cup vinegar
- 2 cups salad oil
- ¼ cup boiling water

Combine dry ingredients. Add to egg yolks. Blend in vinegar alternately with small amounts of oil. Stir in water. Store in refrigerator.

Blender Instructions: Beat egg yolks; add dry ingredients, vinegar, and oil. Blend well. Pour in boiling water.

Pork Croquettes

Makes 4 servings.

- 2 tablespoons flour
- 2 tablespoons butter or margarine
  - Pinch salt
- 1 cup milk
- 2 cups ground cooked pork
- 1 egg, lightly beaten
  - Cracker crumbs

Blend first 3 ingredients in a saucepan; add milk. Stir over low heat until thick. Stir in pork. When cool enough to handle, shape mixture into cylinders. Chill in refrigerator for several hours or overnight. Dip in egg and crumbs; deep fry until golden.

Note: May be served with a white sauce. If desired, shape into flat, round patties and fry in skillet.

Lettuce and Dandelion Salad

- 2 cups fresh dandelion greens, washed
- ½ head lettuce, torn into bite-size pieces
- 1 cup thinly sliced onion
  - French dressing
- 1 hard-cooked egg, sliced
  - Grated Parmesan cheese
  - Paprika

Rinse dandelion greens in ice water to crisp. Drain well on paper towels. Place lettuce, dandelion greens and onion slices in a garlic-rubbed salad bowl. Pour French dressing over all. Toss lightly until ingredients are coated. Garnish with egg slices, grated cheese and paprika.

Dill Dip

- 1 cup mayonnaise
- 1 cup sour cream
- 1 teaspoon seasoned salt
- 1 tablespoon chopped parsley
- 1 tablespoon dillweed
- 1 tablespoon dry onion flakes
  - Lemon juice to taste

Combine all ingredients; chill. Serve with raw vegetables.

Surprise Coconut Pie

Makes 2 9-inch pies.

- 4 eggs
- 1¾ cups sugar
- 2 cups milk
- 1 teaspoon vanilla
- ½ cup flour
- ¼ cup margarine, melted
- 1 7-ounce package flaked coconut

In a large mixing bowl, beat together eggs, sugar, milk, vanilla, flour, and margarine until well combined and fold in the coconut. Pour into 2 greased and floured 9-inch pie pans. Bake in a preheated 350° oven for 40 minutes or until golden brown. Crust forms as pie bakes.

Ham-Asparagus Rolls au Gratin

Makes 8 rolls.

     3 tablespoons butter or margarine
     3 tablespoons flour
    ¾ teaspoon salt
     2 cups milk
     1 cup shredded pasteurized process Swiss cheese
    1⅓ cups cooked rice
     8 ¼-inch slices cooked ham
    24 to 32 slender asparagus spears, cooked and drained
    ¼ cup shredded Parmesan cheese

Melt butter in a saucepan. Blend in flour and salt. Add milk and cook, stirring constantly, until thick. Add cheese and stir until melted. Blend 1 cup sauce into rice. Spoon an equal amount of rice mixture onto end of ham slice. Top each slice with 3 or 4 asparagus spears and roll ham around filling. Arrange rolls in shallow 2-quart baking dish. Pour remaining sauce over rolls. Sprinkle with Parmesan cheese. Bake at 350° until hot, about 25 to 30 minutes.

Crab Louis

Makes 6 servings.

     1 head lettuce, torn into bite-size pieces
     1 cup crabmeat, more if desired
     2 avocados
     1 small can julienned beets, drained
     1 small can pitted olives, drained
     2 hard-cooked eggs
     2 tomatoes
    ½ cup sliced green onion
    ½ green pepper, sliced

Place lettuce on serving plates. Arrange remaining ingredients on lettuce. Pour Louis Dressing over all.

Louis Dressing

    ¼ cup chili sauce
    ½ pound sour cream
    ¼ cup minced green pepper
    ¼ cup minced green onion
     1 cup mayonnaise
     1 teaspoon lemon juice
       Salt to taste

Blend all ingredients thoroughly.

Lima Beans in Sour Cream

     1 pound baby lima beans
     3 teaspoons salt
    ½ cup butter, softened
    ¾ cup brown sugar
     1 tablespoon dry mustard
     1 tablespoon molasses
     1 cup sour cream

Cook lima beans until tender; rinse with hot water. Place in a large casserole dish. Combine remaining ingredients and stir into beans. Bake at 350° for 1 hour.

Frozen Strawberry Jam

     4 cups sugar
     2 cups strawberries, crushed
    ¾ cup water
     1 box pectin

Add sugar to fruit; mix well. Combine water and pectin in a saucepan. Bring to a boil; boil 1 minute, stirring constantly. Stir into fruit mixture. Continue stirring 3 minutes. A few sugar crystals will remain. Quickly ladle into jars; cover at once with tight lids (no paraffin is necessary). Set at room temperature 24 hours. Store in the freezer. Jam is ready to eat after 3 weeks.

Rhubarb Cake

Makes 12 servings.

    1½ cups brown sugar
    ½ cup shortening, softened
     1 egg
     1 cup sour milk or buttermilk
     2 cups flour
     1 teaspoon baking soda
     1 teaspoon vanilla extract
    1½ to 2 cups chopped rhubarb
    ½ cup sugar
     1 teaspoon ground cinnamon

Cream together the brown sugar and shortening. Add the egg, sour milk, flour, soda, vanilla, and rhubarb. Stir to blend all ingredients. Place in a 9 x 13-inch greased and floured pan. Mix sugar and cinnamon; sprinkle over top. Bake at 350° for 35 minutes.

Easter

Champagne and Strawberries

1 pint fresh strawberries, washed and hulled
1 bottle champagne or sparkling Burgundy

Divide berries among champagne or sherbet glasses. Pour chilled champagne over berries.

Melon Ball Treat

Watermelon
Cantaloupe
Honeydew melon

Scoop out melon balls. Place in fruit cups. Garnish with lime wedges, if desired.

Party Avocado Salad

1 avocado, cubed
1 medium tomato, cut up
1 small onion, minced
1 teaspoon lemon juice
Salt and pepper to taste
Mayonnaise

Mix all ingredients with enough mayonnaise to moisten.

Fresh Vegetable Casserole

1½ pounds mushrooms, sliced or ¾ pound
  mushrooms and ¾ pound carrots
1 onion, sliced
1 tomato, sliced
1 tablespoon butter
1 tablespoon flour
½ cup sour cream
  Juice of ½ lemon
1½ ounces brandy
½ teaspoon salt
⅛ teaspoon pepper
1 tablespoon chopped parsley

Layer vegetables in a 2-quart casserole dish. Make a white sauce with the butter, flour and sour cream. Add lemon juice and brandy to the sour cream mixture. Pour over vegetables. Add salt and pepper. Sprinkle parsley over all. Cover. Bake at 350° for 45 minutes.

Stuffed Leg of Lamb

1 5- to 6-pound leg of lamb
½ pound ground raw veal
½ pound ground cooked lean ham
½ pound dry bread crumbs
½ pound fresh mushrooms, minced
1 egg
1 small clove garlic, crushed
1 tablespoon Worcestershire sauce
1 tablespoon orange marmalade with rind
  Salt, pepper, oregano to taste

Bone lamb, leaving 3 inches of shank bone. Preheat oven to 325°. Mix remaining ingredients until smooth and compact. Pack into cavity of lamb. Sew opening securely with heavy string. Place lamb, fat side up, on a rack in a roasting pan. Roast for 30 to 35 minutes per pound. Serve with mint jelly or spiced peaches.

Ice Cream Parfait

Fill parfait glasses with alternate layers of mint ice cream and cold fudge sauce. Top with whipped cream and a sprig of mint. This can be frozen.

Coconut Cookies

1 cup shortening
1 cup brown sugar
2 eggs
1 teaspoon vanilla extract
2½ cups flour
1 teaspoon baking soda
½ teaspoon baking powder
½ teaspoon salt
2 cups bran flakes
2 cups coconut

Cream shortening, sugar, and eggs; add vanilla. Sift flour, baking soda, baking powder, and salt together. Put bran flakes and coconut in a bowl. Mix well with flour mixture, add liquid mixture and mix to soft dough. Form into small balls; flatten on a baking sheet about 2 inches apart. Bake at 400° until done.

Hot Cross Buns

    1 package dry yeast
    2 tablespoons warm water (110 to 115°)
    1 cup scalded milk
    ¼ cup sugar
    1½ teaspoons salt
    ½ teaspoon ground cinnamon
    ¾ cup currants
    2 eggs, well beaten
    4 cups sifted flour
    ½ cup butter, melted

Soften yeast in the warm water. In a separate bowl, combine the scalded milk, sugar, salt, cinnamon, and currants. Cool to lukewarm. Add yeast mixture and eggs. Add 2 cups of the flour and mix. Add the melted butter and beat well. Add remaining flour gradually. Mix but do not knead. Place dough in a greased bowl, turning to grease top of dough. Cover and chill until firm enough to handle. Divide dough into 18 to 20 portions and shape into buns. Set aside until double in bulk. Place on greased baking sheet. Bake at 400° for 10 to 15 minutes. Using the Frosting form a cross on each bun.

Frosting

    3 cups sifted confectioners' sugar
    3 tablespoons butter, melted
    3 tablespoons milk
    1 tablespoon vanilla extract

Combine all ingredients; mix until smooth.

Apple Rolls

Makes 12 servings.

    2 cups flour
    4 teaspoons baking powder
    ¼ teaspoon salt
    6 tablespoons shortening
    ¾ cup milk
    6 to 8 apples, peeled and diced
      Ground cinnamon
    ¼ cup sugar
    1½ cups sugar
    2 cups water

Mix the flour, baking powder, and salt. Cut in shortening with pastry cutter. Add milk and mix until mixture resembles coarse crumbs. Roll out about ¼ inch thick on a floured board. Spread apples over dough. Sprinkle with cinnamon and the ¼ cup sugar. Roll up as for a jelly roll. Cut into 12 slices. Place in a 9 x 13-inch pan. Boil the 1½ cups sugar and 2 cups water. Pour over apple rolls. Bake at 375° until brown. Serve with whipped cream.

Easter Egg Bread

    5 eggs
    1 cup flour
    ¼ cup sugar
    1 teaspoon salt
    1 package dry yeast
    ⅔ cup milk
    2 tablespoons butter
    2 eggs
    1¼ to 2 cups flour

Dip the 5 uncooked eggs in food coloring to dye shells. In a large bowl, thoroughly mix next 4 ingredients. Combine milk and butter in a saucepan. Heat until warm, not melted. Gradually add to dry ingredients; beat 2 minutes at medium speed with an electric mixer. Add the 2 eggs and ½ cup of the flour. Beat 2 minutes at high speed. Stir in remaining ¾ to 1½ cups flour to make a soft dough. Turn out onto a lightly floured board. Knead 8 to 10 minutes until smooth and elastic. Place in a greased bowl, turning to grease top. Allow to rise in a warm place, covered, until double in bulk, about 1 hour. Punch down dough. Divide dough into 2 equal balls. Let stand, covered, for 10 minutes. Roll each ball into a long roll about 36 inches long and 1 to 1½ inches thick. Using the 2 long pieces of dough, form a loosely braided ring, leaving spaces for the 5 colored eggs. Place on a buttered 15½ x 12-inch baking sheet. Place colored eggs into spaces in the braid. Cover loosely with a towel. Set dough aside in a warm place until double in bulk. Brush bread with melted butter and sprinkle with tiny multicolored decorations. Bake at 350° for 50 to 55 minutes.

Tossed Green Salad

Select several varieties of fresh, crisp greens. In addition to lettuce (romaine, bibb, iceberg, or Boston), try spinach, mustard greens, watercress, curly endive, or chicory. Wash and drain the greens thoroughly. Tear into bite-size pieces, place in a salad bowl and chill in the refrigerator several hours. Toss with dressing just before serving. Top with croutons, bacon bits, anchovies, crumbled cheese, minced chives, or whatever you prefer.

Onion Dressing

    1 medium onion, grated
1¾ cups sugar
    1 teaspoon celery seed
    2 teaspoons salt
    1 teaspoon dry mustard
  ¾ cup cider vinegar
    1 pint salad oil

Mix first 5 ingredients together. Slowly stir in vinegar and salad oil alternately.

Ham de Mullich

    1 thick center cut ham slice
      Mustard and red pepper to taste
    1 onion, sliced
    1 cup water
    2 potatoes, peeled, quartered and parboiled

Sear ham on both sides in a hot skillet. Place in a shallow roasting pan. Spread with mustard; sprinkle on red pepper. Add onion on top of ham; pour in water. Cover and bake at 350° for 30 minutes. Add potatoes and bake until slightly brown, adding more water if necessary.

Baked Pineapple

2½ cups crushed pineapple
  ½ cup sugar
  ¼ pound butter or margarine, melted
    4 eggs, beaten
    5 slices bread, torn into small pieces

Combine all ingredients in a baking dish. Bake at 350° for 45 minutes.

Note: This is good served with ham or lamb.

Spiced Orange Pot Roast

Makes 6 to 8 servings.

    4 to 5 pounds beef chuck roast
    1 tablespoon shortening or bacon drippings
  ½ cup minced onion
    1 clove garlic, minced
    1 8-ounce can tomato sauce
    2 cups orange sections
    2 tablespoons sugar
    1 tablespoon grated orange rind
1½ teaspoons salt
  ½ teaspoon ground nutmeg
  ½ teaspoon ground cinnamon
  ¼ teaspoon ground cloves
      Dash pepper
      Orange slices, optional
      Watercress or parsley, optional

Brown meat slowly on both sides in hot shortening. Add onion and garlic. Cover and cook 20 minutes. Pour tomato sauce, orange sections, sugar, and grated orange rind over meat. Sprinkle with salt and spices. Cover and cook slowly until meat is tender, about 2 hours. Garnish with orange slices and watercress or parsley, if desired.

Baked Corn

    1 16-ounce can cream-style corn
    1 cup milk
    1 egg, well beaten
  ¾ teaspoon salt and pepper
    1 cup cracker crumbs
  ½ cup buttered cracker crumbs

Heat corn and milk. Gradually stir in egg. Add seasonings and 1 cup cracker crumbs. Place in a buttered baking dish. Sprinkle buttered crumbs on top. Bake at 350° for 1 hour.

Creamy Uncooked Cherry Pie

    1 medium can cherry pie filling
    1 prepared graham cracker piecrust
    2 cups (heaping) whipped cream
  ½ cup finely chopped pecans

Pour cherry pie filling onto piecrust. Spread with whipped cream. Sprinkle on nuts. Chill 2 hours. Serve.

Mother's Day

French Silk Chocolate Pie

- ¾ cup butter, softened
- 1 cup sugar
- 3 eggs, beaten
- 2 ounces chocolate, melted
- 1 teaspoon vanilla extract
- 1 9-inch pie shell, baked

Cream butter thoroughly; add sugar, mixing well. Add eggs and blend. Add cooled chocolate; beat until smooth. Add vanilla and pour into pie shell. Top with whipped cream and nuts, if desired.

Whipped Cream Substitute

- ½ cup flour
- 2 cups milk
- 1 pound butter or margarine, softened
- 2 cups sugar
- 2 teaspoons vanilla extract

Cook flour and milk until thick; cool. Cream butter, sugar and vanilla until fluffy. Beat in cooled flour mixture.

Forgotten Cookies

Makes 2 dozen.

- 2 egg whites, room temperature
- ⅔ cup sugar
-   Pinch salt
- 1 teaspoon vanilla extract
- 1 cup chopped pecans
- 1 cup chocolate bits or cornflakes or crisp rice cereal
- 1 cup coconut, optional

Beat egg whites until foamy. Gradually add sugar; continue beating until stiff. Add salt and vanilla; mix well. Add pecans and remaining ingredients. Preheat oven to 350°. Drop cookies by the spoonful on ungreased foil-covered baking sheets. Place cookies in oven and immediately turn off oven. Leave cookies in closed oven overnight. Do not open oven door until the end of baking time.

Bran Muffins

- 1 cup boiling water
- 3 cups all-bran cereal
- ½ cup vegetable shortening, softened
- 1½ cups white sugar
- 2 eggs, beaten
- 2 cups buttermilk
- 2½ cups flour
- 2½ teaspoons baking soda
- ¼ teaspoon salt
- ⅓ cup currants, optional

Pour the boiling water over the bran cereal. Set aside. Cream shortening and sugar. Add beaten eggs and buttermilk. Sift flour, soda, and salt together. Add to shortening mixture. Fold in bran. Add currants, if desired. Do not stir or beat. Spoon gently into greased muffin tins. Bake at 400° for 15 to 18 minutes.

Note: This muffin batter will keep in the refrigerator for 6 weeks.

Yummy Cake

- 1 package yellow cake mix
- 1 package pineapple or vanilla instant pudding
- ¾ cup vegetable oil
- 4 eggs, well beaten
- 10 ounces lemon-lime soda

Combine all ingredients except soda; add soda and beat well. Bake in a 13 x 9-inch greased and floured pan at 350° for 40 minutes. Pour Icing over cake while still hot.

Icing

- 3 eggs, beaten
- 1½ cups sugar
- 2 tablespoons flour
- ½ cup margarine
- 1 cup crushed pineapple, drained
- 1 small can coconut

Combine eggs, sugar, flour, and margarine in a saucepan. Cook over medium heat until thick. Add pineapple and coconut.

Father's Day

Curried Fruit

3½ cups canned peach halves, drained
3½ cups canned pear halves, drained
3½ cups canned pineapple chunks, drained
⅓ cup butter or margarine, melted
½ cup light brown sugar
½ teaspoon curry powder
Maraschino cherries

Arrange fruits in baking dish. Mix butter, sugar, and curry powder; spoon over fruit. Bake, uncovered, at 350° for 1 hour. Refrigerate at least 24 hours. Add a maraschino cherry to each peach and pear half. Heat at 350° for 30 to 40 minutes. Serve warm.

Clear Mushroom Soup

Makes 4 servings.

1 pound mushrooms
4 cups consommé
4 teaspoons sherry

Chop mushrooms. Add to consommé and simmer, tightly covered, for 30 minutes. Strain and reheat. Add sherry.

Sweet Potato Souffle'

2 cups cooked or canned, mashed sweet potatoes
1¼ cups granulated sugar
6 tablespoons butter or margarine
1 cup milk (if canned potatoes are used, use only ½ cup milk)
½ teaspoon ground nutmeg
½ teaspoon ground cinnamon

Mix all ingredients. Pour into casserole and bake at 400° for 20 minutes. Cover with Topping. Bake for 10 minutes.

Topping

¾ cup crushed cornflakes
½ cup pecans, chopped
½ cup brown sugar
6 tablespoons butter, melted

Combine all ingredients; mix well.

Sweet and Sour Spareribs

Makes 4 servings.

2 pounds spareribs
2 small cloves garlic, minced
¼ cup brown sugar
¼ cup soy sauce
2 tablespoons vinegar
2 cups canned pineapple chunks, reserve juice
2 tablespoons cornstarch

Cut spareribs in 1½-inch pieces. Combine all ingredients except pineapple and cornstarch. Simmer 1 hour. Set aside for a few minutes. Pour off excess fat. Place meat in a separate bowl. Heat liquid. Add pineapple juice to liquid; bring to a boil. Add cornstarch; cook until thick. Pour sauce over spareribs. Arrange pineapple chunks on top. Serve hot.

Hash-Brown Potatoes

2 tablespoons shortening
6 potatoes, grated
1 onion, minced
1 egg, lightly beaten
Salt and pepper to taste

Melt shortening in a skillet. Mix all other ingredients together; spread evenly in skillet. Sauté until golden. Turn and brown other side. Cut into wedges and serve immediately.

Broccoli Casserole

⅓ cup margarine, melted
1 teaspoon salt
1 cup grated sharp cheese
1 egg, beaten
1 cup milk
1 small onion, diced
1 cup cooked rice
1 10-ounce package frozen chopped broccoli, cooked and drained

Combine margarine, salt, cheese, egg, milk, and onion. Blend with rice. Add broccoli. Pour into buttered casserole and bake at 350° for 1 hour.

Tomato Casserole

- 8 slices bread
- ½ pound Velveeta cheese, sliced
- 1 16-ounce can stewed tomatoes
- 2 eggs, beaten
- 1 cup milk
- ½ teaspoon salt
- Pepper to taste

Place bread slices in buttered baking dish. Top with thin slices of cheese. Cover with layer of tomatoes. Repeat three times. Beat eggs; add milk, salt, and pepper. Pour into baking dish and bake at 325° for 30 minutes.

Banana Nut Bread

Makes 2 loaves.

- 1 cup sugar
- ½ cup margarine, softened
- 2 eggs, beaten
- 3 bananas, mashed
- 3 cups flour
- 1 teaspoon baking soda
- 1 teaspoon vanilla extract
- 1 cup chopped walnuts

Cream sugar and margarine; add eggs and bananas. Combine and stir in remaining ingredients. Place in greased bread pans and bake at 325° for 45 minutes.

Note: This bread freezes well.

Crown-of-Gold Meat Loaf

Makes 6 to 8 servings.

- 1½ cups fine, soft bread crumbs
- 1½ pounds lean ground beef
- 4 egg yolks
- 1½ teaspoons salt
- 1½ tablespoons prepared horseradish
- 2 tablespoons minced onion
- 2 tablespoons prepared mustard
- 3 tablespoons minced green pepper
- ⅓ cup catsup

Mix bread crumbs with meat. Combine remaining ingredients; blend into meat-bread mixture. Pack lightly into a 9-inch casserole and bake at 325° for 30 minutes. Remove from oven and cover with Topping. Return to oven and bake 20 to 25 minutes longer or until tipped with brown.

Topping

- 4 egg whites
- ¼ teaspoon cream of tartar
- ¼ cup prepared mustard

Beat egg whites until foamy; add cream of tartar and beat until very stiff. Gently fold in the mustard.

Golden Sugar Cookies

- 2½ cups sifted flour
- 1 teaspoon baking soda
- 1 teaspoon cream of tartar
- ¼ teaspoon salt
- 1 cup butter, softened
- 1 teaspoon vanilla extract
- ½ teaspoon lemon extract
- 2 cups sugar
- 3 egg yolks

Sift together flour, soda, cream of tartar, and salt; set aside. Cream butter and extracts until smooth. Gradually add sugar, creaming until fluffy. Add egg yolks one at a time, beating well after each addition. Add dry ingredients slowly to the creamed mixture. Beat until blended. Form dough into 1-inch balls and place 2 inches apart on an ungreased baking sheet. Bake at 350° for 10 minutes or until golden brown.

Sour Milk Chocolate Cake

Makes 1 8-inch cake.

- 5 teaspoons cocoa
- 1 cup sugar
- Pinch salt
- ½ cup shortening, softened
- 1 teaspoon baking soda
- 1 cup sour milk
- 2 cups flour
- 1 teaspoon vanilla extract

Mix cocoa with water to make a paste. Cream sugar, salt, and shortening. Add baking soda to milk in a small bowl. Add to shortening mixture; add flour, then vanilla and cocoa paste. Bake at 350° for 30 to 35 minutes.

Vegetable Dippers

Use the following relishes with a favorite dip:

Radishes
Celery hearts
Cucumber petals
Carrot crinkles
Cauliflowerets
Green onions
Broccoli buds
Cherry tomatoes

Guacamole Dip II

Makes 1 cup.

1 cup mashed avocado
1 tablespoon lemon juice
1 teaspoon salt
1½ teaspoons grated lemon

Combine all ingredients and mix well. Chill several hours. Serve with chips or crackers.

Note: For variety, add 1 or more of the following:

Dash Tabasco sauce
1 teaspoon curry powder
1 teaspoon Worcestershire sauce
½ teaspoon chili powder

Shrimp de Jonghe

Makes 8 servings.

1 cup butter, melted
2 cloves garlic, minced
⅓ cup chopped parsley
½ teaspoon paprika
Dash cayenne pepper
2 hard-cooked eggs, whites and yolks separated
⅔ cup cooking sherry
2 cups soft bread crumbs
5 to 6 cups cleaned, cooked shrimp
Chopped parsley

Mix butter, garlic, parsley, paprika, pepper, finely chopped egg white, and sherry. Add the bread crumbs and toss. Place shrimp in an 11 x 7 x 1½-inch baking dish. Spoon butter mixture over top. Bake at 325° for 25 minutes. Garnish with parsley and grated egg yolks.

Sweet and Sour Dressing

1 onion, chopped
½ cup vinegar
1 teaspoon salt
1 teaspoon dry mustard
1 teaspoon celery salt
1 cup sugar
1 cup salad oil

Place all ingredients, except oil, in a blender. Blend until onion is liquid. Add oil and beat again. Serve on lettuce or tossed salad.

Scalloped Corn

1 16-ounce can cream-style corn
1 cup milk
1 cup cracker crumbs
2 eggs, lightly beaten
Salt and pepper to taste

Mix all ingredients together. Spoon into a buttered 1½-quart casserole. Dot with butter. Bake at 350° for 45 minutes.

Pineapple Angel Dessert

Makes 15 servings.

1 cup cold water
1 cup boiling water
1 cup pineapple juice
2 envelopes unflavored gelatin
4 packages whipped topping
1 cup sugar
2 cups crushed pineapple, drained
1 large angel food cake
Coconut
Maraschino cherries

Add cold water, boiling water, and pineapple juice to the unflavored gelatin, mixing well. Allow to thicken. Combine 2 packages prepared whipped topping, sugar, and crushed pineapple. Fold into the gelatin mixture. Break the angel food cake into small pieces; line the bottom of a 9 x 13-inch baking pan with the pieces. Add a layer of pineapple mixture. Repeat with remaining cake and pineapple mixture. Prepare remaining 2 packages of the whipped topping. Spread over top, sprinkle with coconut and dot with maraschino cherries. Chill 3 hours.

New Homemaker

Fun Dip

  2 cups sour cream
  1 teaspoon salt
  1 teaspoon Worcestershire sauce
  4 drops Tabasco sauce
  ¼ teaspoon dry mustard
  1 teaspoon dry dillweed
  2 tablespoons minced pimiento, rinsed and drained

Combine all ingredients and refrigerate 2 hours to blend flavors. Serve with crisp vegetables such as whole radishes, cauliflower and broccoli flowerets, raw zucchini strips, and cherry tomatoes.

Speedy Rolls

  2 cups warm water (110 to 115°)
  ⅓ cup sugar
  2 packages dry yeast
  1 tablespoon salt
  6½ cups sifted flour
  2 eggs
  ⅓ cup shortening, softened

Place warm water, sugar, and yeast in a mixing bowl. Add salt and 2 cups of the flour. Beat 2 minutes. Add eggs and shortening. Beat 1 minute. Gradually add remaining flour. Stir until dough is formed. Allow dough to stand in bowl for 20 minutes for easy handling. Form dough into balls; place on a greased baking sheet. Bake at 350° for 25 to 30 minutes until done.

Note: The dough may be refrigerated for 1 or 2 days.

Five-Can Casserole

Makes 6 servings.

  1 10¾-ounce can mushroom soup
  1 10¾-ounce can chicken with rice soup
  1 small can evaporated milk
  1 can chow mein noodles
  1 can chicken, or 1 cup diced cooked chicken

Mix all ingredients together, place in casserole and top with crushed potato chips. Bake at 350° for 1 hour.

Oven Beef Stew

  2 pounds beef stew meat
  6 carrots, diced
  3 medium potatoes, diced
  3 ribs celery, diced
  1 large onion, diced
  1 teaspoon salt
  1 tablespoon sugar
  2 tablespoons tapioca
  ½ cup tomato sauce

Mix all ingredients. Spoon into a roaster pan and cover tightly. Bake at 250° for 4 hours. Do not remove cover during baking time.

Mushroom Scalloped Potatoes

  1 10¾-ounce can cream of mushroom soup
  ½ cup grated American cheese
  ¼ cup minced onion
  1 teaspoon salt
  ⅔ cup evaporated milk
  4 cups sliced potatoes
  ¼ cup grated American cheese

Combine soup, the ½ cup cheese, onion, salt, and milk. Add potatoes. Mix and put in a greased baking dish. Top with the ¼ cup cheese. Bake at 375° until potatoes are tender, about 1 hour and 15 minutes.

Super Baking Powder Biscuits

  2 cups flour
  ½ teaspoon salt
  4 teaspoons baking powder
  ½ teaspoon cream of tartar
  2 teaspoons sugar
  ½ cup shortening, softened
  ⅔ cup milk

Sift together dry ingredients. Cut in shortening. Add milk; mix until dough just sticks together. Roll out ½ inch thick, cut with biscuit cutter, and place on greased baking sheet. Bake at 400° for 10 to 12 minutes or until light brown.

Chili Con Carne

Makes 6 servings.

½ cup chopped onion
½ cup chopped green pepper
¼ cup chopped celery
1 clove garlic, minced
1 pound ground beef
2½ cups canned tomatoes
2 teaspoons sugar
2 teaspoons salt
1 tablespoon chili powder
2½ cups red kidney beans
15 sticks vermicelli, broken in small pieces

Sauté onion, green pepper, celery, and garlic until lightly browned. Add meat and sauté until brown, not dark. Add tomatoes, sugar, salt, and chili powder. Cover and bring to a boil. Simmer for 30 minutes. Add kidney beans and vermicelli. Cook for 15 minutes.

Twice-Baked Potatoes

4 baking potatoes
2 tablespoons hot cream
1 egg, well beaten
Butter to taste
Salt to taste

Bake potatoes at 425° for 45 minutes. Remove from oven. Cut lengthwise, scoop out centers and mash with remaining ingredients. Beat well. Spoon back into the potato shells. Brush with melted butter. Return to oven and bake 5 to 10 minutes.

Favorite Hamburgers

1 pound lean ground beef
1 egg
1 cup catsup or chili sauce
2 teaspoons prepared mustard
½ cup chopped onion
1 teaspoon salt
Pepper to taste

Combine ingredients and spread on bun halves. Bake at 375° for 20 minutes.

Oven-Baked Rice

Makes 8 servings.

1½ cups uncooked rice
3 teaspoons chicken broth
3 tablespoons vegetable oil
3½ cups boiling water

Combine rice, chicken broth, and vegetable oil in a 2-quart casserole. Pour boiling water over rice and stir with a fork. Cover. Bake at 350° for 40 minutes. To serve, fluff rice with fork.

Macaroni and Cheese

Makes 2 servings.

2 cups cooked macaroni
5 ounces sharp cheese
2 teaspoons butter or margarine
1 cup milk

Place macaroni in a buttered casserole. Break cheese into small pieces. Add cheese, butter, and milk to macaroni; mix well. Bake at 375° until cheese has melted.

All-In-One Dinner

Makes 6 servings.

1½ pounds ground beef
1 cup sliced raw onion
¼ cup chopped green pepper
2 cups sliced raw potatoes
1 cup chopped celery
Salt and pepper to taste
2 cups canned tomatoes
4 slices American cheese
Butter

Sauté ground beef until brown; drain. Place alternate layers of ground beef and fresh vegetables in a greased casserole dish in order listed. Add salt and pepper to each layer. Pour canned tomatoes over all. Top with cheese slices and dot with butter. Cover casserole. Bake at 350° for 1½ hours or until vegetables are done.

Cucumbers in Sour Cream

2 cucumbers, sliced thin
Sour cream

Soak cucumbers in salted water 20 to 30 minutes. Squeeze carefully to remove excess water. Do not mash. Put into a bowl, sprinkle with salt and pepper. Mix with enough sour cream to cover cucumbers.

Vegetable Soup

Makes 8 servings.

1½ pounds beef shank, plus soupbones
8 cups water
2½ tablespoons salt
¼ teaspoon pepper
2 tablespoons minced parsley
½ cup barley
1½ cups cubed carrots
¼ cup chopped onion
½ cup chopped celery
2 cups cooked tomatoes
1½ cups frozen peas

Cut meat into cubes and brown. Place meat, bones, water, seasonings, and parsley in Dutch oven. Cover and cook slowly for 1 hour. Add barley; cook 1 hour. Cool and skim off excess fat. Remove soupbones. Add carrots, onion, celery, and tomatoes. Cook 45 minutes. Add peas and continue cooking 15 minutes.

Butter Cake

Makes 1 9-inch layer cake.

2 cups sugar
¾ cup butter and shortening (half of each)
1 cup milk
4 eggs
2½ cups flour
2 teaspoons baking powder
Pinch salt
1 teaspoon vanilla extract

Put all ingredients into a mixing bowl. Mix 10 minutes at medium speed of electric mixer. Pour batter into 2 greased 9-inch pans and bake at 375° for approximately 40 minutes.

Fantastic Fruit Fluff

Makes 6 to 8 servings.

2 cups milk
1 8-ounce package cream cheese
1 package instant vanilla pudding
1 16-ounce can fruit cocktail, drained
1 cup miniature marshmallows

Gradually add ½ cup of the milk to the cream cheese. Blend in pudding and remaining milk. Beat slowly 1 minute. Stir in fruit and marshmallows. Chill.

Luscious Lemon Pie

1 cup sugar
1¼ cups water
1 tablespoon butter or margarine
¼ cup cornstarch
3 tablespoons cold water
6 tablespoons lemon juice
1 teaspoon grated lemon peel
3 egg yolks
2 tablespoons milk
1 egg white, stiffly beaten
1 baked pie shell

Combine sugar, water and butter. Cook until sugar dissolves. Add cornstarch that has been blended with the cold water. Cook slowly until clear, about 8 minutes. Add lemon juice and grated lemon peel. Cook 2 minutes. Slowly add the egg yolks beaten with the 2 tablespoons of milk. Bring to a boil. Cool. Fold the egg white into the filling. Pour mixture into pie shell. Top with Meringue.

Meringue

½ cup sugar
⅛ teaspoon salt
¼ cup water
⅛ teaspoon cream of tartar
2 egg whites, stiffly beaten
¼ teaspoon almond extract

Cook first 4 ingredients to thread stage (232°). Gradually pour this over egg whites, beating constantly. Continue beating until mixture holds shape. Add almond extract.

Party and Cooking Aids

You'll do the best entertaining and make your guests happiest when you do what you really like to do. So, first of all, decide what kind of party it will be. Formal or informal? Indoors or out? Large or small? What to serve: full-meal, light refreshments, late-evening buffet?

Follow a written plan. You'll save time if you take time to write everything down—from the guest list to the timetable for cooking.

Make a shopping list. Include everything you will need, from cocktail napkins to candles.

Pick a theme. Set the mood. Make your party a little different from anyone else's, whether it's celebrating a birthday, anniversary, job promotion, or just for the fun of it.

Choose guests carefully. They should share some mutual interests. Mix up talkers and listeners. Let the spirit of friendship prevail.

Get out invitations a week or two ahead. Telephone or write a note. In both cases be specific about time, date, place, anything out of the ordinary about dress (sport clothes, costume, black tie), and any special information about the occasion (if it's gift-giving, be explicit).

Plan what you'll serve. Your menu is all-important. No monochromatic menus, please! Get good color contrasts, but make sure foods in the same course do not clash. Contrast hot dishes with cold; soft foods with crisp; bland with strong-flavored. Vary the cooking method, for instance, no completely fried dinners. Enhance a colorless dish with a sauce or colorful garnish.

Choose food that suits the occasion. Be realistic about what you can prepare well. Use recipes that you have already tested. Plan foods that don't require a lot of last-minute fuss. Ideally, choose recipes that can be fully or partially prepared early in the day.

Plan variety. A creamy-sauced food needs something crisp and crunchy. You might add the crunch right in the sauce (with water chestnuts, slivered nuts, or celery); in the vegetable course, or, in a relish tray. Keep a texture contrast throughout the meal, as well as within each course. Top off a heavy meal with a light dessert, and vice versa.

Include both tart and sweet. Save the very sweetest foods for the end of the meal. One strong flavor or spiced dish is usually enough in one meal. Do not repeat flavors in the same meal (such as tomatoes, onions, or nutmeats).

Try new recipes using ingredients you know everyone likes. Even if you can get by serving the same old standbys—don't. Hamburger can be served as Swedish meatballs, individual meat loaves, spaghetti or lasagna. Combining foods is an easy way to create new dishes: mix two different cans of soup together; combine carrots with scallions, peas with dill, green beans with almonds.

Set a schedule for yourself. Plan to be ready one half hour ahead. This will give you time to catch your breath before the guests arrive.

Plan the table setting early. This is fun to do when you have enough time—and aren't polishing silver when you should be putting the finishing touches on the flowers for the centerpiece. Work out a theme or color scheme, and make sure you have all the dishes, linens, and silver to carry it out. Try to set the table in the morning or the night before.

Clear a counter for soiled dishes. Out of sight of guests, please.

COOKERY TERMS

Appetizer: Food served before the first course of a meal.

Brown: To make food a brown color by frying, sautéing, broiling or baking.

Cream: To blend butter and sugar by stirring or beating.

Dice: To cut into small pieces.

Garnish: To add decorative color to food.

Grease: To rub a baking pan with fat, butter or oil.

Knead: To work dough until smooth and pliable.

Marinate: To soak food in a seasoned liquid to flavor and tenderize.

Melt: To liquefy by heat.

Mince: To chop into fine pieces.

Sauté: To cook food quickly with fat, butter or margarine.

Scald: To bring liquid to a temperature just below the boiling point.

Whip: To beat rapidly.

EQUIVALENT AMOUNTS

Apples: 1 pound = 3 medium

Baking chocolate: 1 square = 1 ounce or 5 tablespoons grated

Bread: 1 pound loaf = 18 slices

Butter or margarine: 1 pound = 2 cups; 1 stick or ¼ pound = ½ cup

Cheese (American, Cheddar): 1 pound = 4 cups grated

Cottage cheese: 1 pound = 2 cups

Eggs: 5 whole = 1 cup; 8 whites = about 1 cup; 16 yolks = about 1 cup

Flour, all purpose: 1 pound = 4 cups

Flour, cake: 1 pound = 4¾ cups

Lemon juice: 1 medium lemon = 3 tablespoons juice

Lemon rind: 1 medium lemon = 1 tablespoon grated rind

Noodles: 1 cup raw = 1¼ cups cooked

Macaroni: 1 pound = 3 cups uncooked; 1 cup = 2 cups cooked

Meat: 1 pound = 2 cups diced

Milk, evaporated: 1 6-ounce can = ⅔ cup; 1 14½-ounce can = 1⅔ cups

Potatoes: 1 pound = 3 medium

Rice: 1 pound = 2⅓ cups uncooked; 1 cup raw = 3 cups cooked

Sugar:
Brown—1 pound = 2¼ cups firmly packed;
Confectioners'—1 pound = 3½ cups;
Granulated—1 pound = 2 cups

Tomatoes: 1 pound = 3 medium

Vegetable shortening: 1 pound = 2 cups

CONTENTS OF CANS

Size No.	Cup Amount
300	1¾
1 tall	2
303	2
2	2½
2½	3½
3	4
10	12-13

MEASUREMENTS

1 tablespoon = 3 teaspoons
1 fluid ounce = 2 tablespoons
¼ cup = 4 tablespoons
⅓ cup = 5⅓ tablespoons
½ cup = 8 tablespoons
⅔ cup = 10⅔ tablespoons
¾ cup = 12 tablespoons
1 cup = 16 tablespoons or 8 fluid ounces
1 pint = 2 cups
1 quart = 2 pints or 4 cups
1 pound = 16 ounces
¾ pound = 12 ounces
½ pound = 8 ounces
¼ pound = 4 ounces

Fourth of July

Deviled Eggs

6 hard-cooked eggs
¼ cup mayonnaise
1 teaspoon prepared mustard
½ teaspoon vinegar
¼ teaspoon salt
White pepper to taste
Paprika

Cut eggs in half lengthwise. Remove yolks. Mash yolks with remaining ingredients except paprika until mixture is smooth. Fill egg whites with mixture. Sprinkle with paprika.

Marinated Chicken

1 envelope Italian dressing
¼ cup lemon juice
½ cup salad oil
2 frying chickens, cut up
¼ cup instant onion flakes moistened
with mayonnaise
Salt, pepper and paprika to taste

Combine first 3 ingredients; pour over chicken and marinate for 4 to 5 hours. Line a baking sheet with foil; grease lightly. Brush meat with a generous coating of mayonnaise-onion mixture. Arrange meat on foil; meat should not touch. Sprinkle with salt, pepper, and paprika. Bake at 350° for 1 hour or until golden brown.

German-Style Potato Salad

Makes 12 servings.

5 pounds salad potatoes
6 slices bacon, diced
¼ cup flour
4 cups water
6 tablespoons sugar
1 teaspoon salt
⅛ teaspoon pepper
1 teaspoon celery salt
¾ cup vinegar
½ cup chopped onion
6 hard-cooked eggs, sliced

Boil potatoes in their skins in salted water until tender. Peel while still warm. Cool. Slice into a large bowl. Fry bacon until crisp. Remove from pan; set aside. Stir flour into bacon fat and blend with a wooden spoon. Add water gradually, stirring until smooth and thick. Add sugar, salt, pepper, and celery salt; simmer and stir until dissolved. Add vinegar and bring to a boil; pour over the sliced potatoes. Add bacon pieces, onion, and sliced eggs; fold until well blended. When cool, cover and refrigerate.

Firecracker Punch

Makes 30 servings.

4 cups cranberry juice
1½ cups sugar
4 cups pineapple juice
1 tablespoon almond extract
2 quarts ginger ale

Combine first 4 ingredients in a punch bowl. Stir until sugar is dissolved. Chill. Add ginger ale just before serving.

Lemon Picnic Cake

1 package yellow cake mix
¾ cup vegetable oil
¾ cup water
1 package instant lemon pudding
4 eggs

Combine all ingredients except eggs and beat 2 minutes. Add eggs, one at a time; beat thoroughly. Pour into greased and floured 9 x 13-inch pan. Bake at 350° for 40 minutes. While hot, prick entire top with a fork. Pour Glaze over cake.

Glaze

2 cups confectioners' sugar
⅓ cup orange juice
2 tablespoons butter, melted
2 tablespoons water

Combine all ingredients until smooth.

Summer Salads

Tomato and Cucumber Salad

Makes 6 servings.

- 5 medium tomatoes, sliced
- 1 cucumber, thinly sliced
- 1 green onion, thinly sliced
- 3 tablespoons olive oil
- 2 to 3 tablespoons red wine vinegar
- ½ teaspoon salt
- ½ teaspoon crushed oregano
- ¼ teaspoon crushed basil
-   Freshly ground pepper
- 1 tablespoon minced parsley

Place tomato, cucumber, and green onion in a mixing bowl. Combine remaining ingredients and pour over salad. Chill 1 hour before serving.

Lime Cottage Cheese Dressing

Makes 1 cup.

- ½ cup mayonnaise
- ½ cup small curd cottage cheese
- 2 tablespoons milk
- 1 tablespoon sugar
- ½ teaspoon grated lime rind
- 1 tablespoon lime juice

Combine all ingredients in a blender until smooth. Chill. Serve on a citrus fruit salad.

Smorgasbord Slaw

Makes 3 quarts.

- 2 cups sugar
- 1 cup vinegar
- ½ cup water
- 1 tablespoon salt
- 1 large cabbage, sliced thin
- 2 medium red peppers, chopped
- 2 medium green peppers, chopped
- ½ bunch celery, chopped
- 1½ teaspoons mustard seed
- 1½ teaspoons celery seed

Combine sugar, vinegar, and water in a saucepan; boil 5 minutes. Cool. Sprinkle salt over cabbage. Allow to stand 1 hour. Add peppers, celery, mustard seed, celery seed, and cooled vinegar mixture. Mix well. Chill.

Hot Chicken Salad

- 1 cup chopped celery
- 2 cups cubed, cooked chicken breast
- 1 cup cooked rice
- 1 10¾-ounce can cream of chicken soup, undiluted
- 1 teaspoon fresh minced onion
- 1 teaspoon lemon juice
- 1 teaspoon salt
- ¾ cup mayonnaise
- ½ cup sliced water chestnuts
- 1 cup crushed cornflakes
- ½ cup sliced almonds

Sauté celery for a few minutes. Mix all ingredients except cornflakes and almonds and place in a casserole. Sprinkle cornflakes and almonds over the top. Bake at 350° for 25 to 30 minutes.

Note: Make ahead and refrigerate until ready to use. Do not add the cornflakes and almonds until dish is ready for the oven. If salad is cold increase cooking time 20 to 30 minutes.

Pineapple-Mint Salad

- 1 3-ounce package lime-flavored gelatin
- ¼ cup sour cream
- 2 tablespoons sugar
- 2 teaspoons mint flavoring
- 2½ cups canned pineapple chunks, drained

Prepare gelatin according to package directions. Add sour cream, sugar, and mint. Allow to thicken slightly and stir in pineapple.

Pineapple-Marshmallow Salad

- 3 eggs
- ⅓ cup flour
- ½ cup pineapple juice
- ½ cup sugar
- ½ pint whipping cream, whipped
- 2 cups small marshmallows
- 2½ cups canned chunk pineapple, drained
-   Maraschino cherries

Combine eggs, flour, pineapple juice and sugar in top of a double boiler. Cook until thick. Cool. Add whipped cream. Fold in marshmallows, pineapple and cherries. Chill.

Marshmallow Waldorf Salad

Makes 4 to 6 servings.

     3 cups cubed apples
     1 tablespoon lemon juice
     1 cup miniature marshmallows
     1 cup chopped celery
    ¼ cup chopped walnuts
        Mayonnaise
        Lettuce

Sprinkle apples with lemon juice. Add marshmallows, celery, nuts and enough mayonnaise to moisten. Toss lightly. Serve on lettuce.

Zesty Coleslaw

Makes 6 to 8 servings.

     4 teaspoons vinegar
     2 teaspoons sugar
     1 teaspoon celery salt
     1 teaspoon dillweed
     4 cups shredded cabbage
     1 green pepper, minced, optional
     2 pimiento strips, minced, optional
    ½ cup mayonnaise or salad dressing

Mix all ingredients well; add more mayonnaise if necessary. Chill.

Mixed Vegetable Salad

     2 1¼-pound packages frozen mixed vegetables
     1 cup diced celery
     1 medium onion, diced
     1 medium green pepper, diced

Cook frozen vegetables until tender. Drain. Add remaining ingredients. Pour Dressing over vegetables and mix well.

Dressing

    1½ cups sugar
    ¾ cup white vinegar
    ¾ cup salad oil
     1 teaspoon paprika
     2 tablespoons water
        Salt to taste

Combine all ingredients in a saucepan; bring to a boil. Cool.

Lime Cucumber Salad

Makes 6 servings.

     1 package lime-flavored gelatin
     1 cup boiling water
    ¼ cup vinegar
     1 teaspoon salt
     1 teaspoon grated onion
     1 cup sour cream
     1 medium cucumber, coarsely grated
        Lettuce

Dissolve gelatin in the boiling water. Add vinegar, salt and onion. Chill until gelatin begins to thicken. Stir in sour cream and cucumber. Pour into 6 individual molds (or loaf pan about 12 x 5 x 3 inches). Chill until firm. Unmold onto lettuce bed.

Shrimp Potato Salad

    ½ pound canned shrimp, drained
     2 cups diced, cold cooked potatoes
    ⅔ cup chopped celery
    ¼ cup diced pickles
     3 hard-cooked eggs, diced
    ¼ cup shredded cheese
     2 tablespoons chopped onion
    ½ cup salad dressing
     1 teaspoon salt
        Dash pepper

Combine all ingredients; chill.

Creamed Ham Supreme

     4 tablespoons butter
     2 cups milk
    ¼ cup flour
     1 cup diced ham
     1 cup diced cheese
        Salt
        Paprika

Melt butter in a saucepan; blend in milk and flour and stir until smooth. Stir until mixture begins to thicken. Stir in ham, cheese, and salt to taste. Dust with paprika. Serve over poached eggs on toast or use over broccoli, asparagus or Brussels sprouts.

Weekend Cookout

Oregano Dip

    1 teaspoon crushed oregano
    ½ teaspoon grated onion
    ¼ teaspoon salt
      Few drops Tabasco sauce
    1 cup sour cream

Blend all ingredients into sour cream. Cover and chill.

Spiced Ice Tea

Makes 12 servings.

    1 cup sugar
    1 cup water
    1 whole nutmeg
    2 sticks cinnamon
    1 orange, studded with whole cloves
    2 cups orange juice
    ¼ cup lemon juice
    3 cups double-strength iced tea

Combine sugar, water, nutmeg, and cinnamon in a saucepan. Simmer 10 minutes. Add the orange. Cover; cool and strain. Add orange juice, lemon juice, and iced tea. Serve over ice cubes in tall glasses.

Garden Potato Salad

Makes 8 to 10 servings.

    2½ pounds small potatoes, cooked, peeled and sliced
    1 medium onion, chopped
    1 cucumber, peeled, chopped, seeds removed
    1 cup chopped celery
    1 cup chopped fresh tomatoes
    ½ cup sliced radishes
    5 hard-cooked eggs
    1 teaspoon salt
    ½ teaspoon pepper
      Garlic, celery salt and onion salt to taste
    1½ cups mayonnaise or salad dressing
    ½ cup milk
      Paprika

In a large bowl combine potatoes, the vegetables, 3 chopped, hard-cooked eggs, and seasonings. Combine mayonnaise with milk. Pour over vegetables; mix well. Garnish with the 2 remaining eggs, sliced, and paprika.

Charcoal-Broiled Sirloin Steak

    1 sirloin steak
    ⅓ cup salad oil
    ⅓ cup red wine vinegar
    2 cloves garlic, crushed
    1 teaspoon basil
    ½ teaspoon salt
    ½ teaspoon pepper

Trim excess fat from steak. Slash fat edge of steak at 1-inch intervals. Place steak in a pan large enough to allow steak to remain flat. Combine remaining ingredients. Mix and pour over steak. Cover. Chill 2 to 3 hours, turning several times. Start charcoal fire 30 to 40 minutes ahead of time, until coals are glowing and covered with gray ash. Rub hot grill with a bit of the fat trimmed from steak. Broil a 1½- to 2-inch steak 5 to 6 inches above coals. Place a 1-inch steak on a rack 4½ to 5 inches above coals. Broil first side, turn and brush with marinade, if desired. Broil second side until done.

Note: To test steak for degree of doneness, cut a small slash with a sharp knife in center of steak.

Fudge Treats

    1 cup flour
    1 cup sugar
    ½ teaspoon baking soda
    ½ teaspoon salt
    ½ teaspoon vanilla extract
    ¼ cup shortening, softened
    2 eggs
    2 squares baking chocolate
    ⅓ cup water
    ½ cup dairy sour cream
    1 cup (6-ounces) semisweet chocolate chips
    ½ cup chopped nuts

Combine all ingredients, except chocolate chips and nuts, in a mixing bowl. Beat at medium speed 2 minutes. Spread in a greased pan. Sprinkle chocolate chips and nuts on top. Bake at 350° for 25 to 30 minutes or until top springs back when touched in center. Cool. Sprinkle on confectioners' sugar.

SPICED ICED TEA

    2 quarts water
   12 single tea bags
    1 c. water
 1½ c. sugar
   ½ c. strained orange juice
    1 c. strained lemon juice
   12 cloves
    2 sticks cinnamon

Boil 2 quarts water. Add tea bags and steep 5 minutes. Remove tea bags. In a small pot bring 1 cup water and sugar to a boil. Remove from heat and add juices and spices. Add spiced mixture to steeped tea. Serve over ice in tall glasses.

Accompaniments

Corn Relish

Makes 6 pints.

- 12 large ears corn, uncooked
- 1 large cabbage, chopped
- 3 large onions, chopped
- 2 green peppers, chopped
- 1 red pepper, chopped
- 1½ to 2 tablespoons salt
- 3 pints vinegar
- 2 cups sugar
- 1 tablespoon celery seed
- 1 tablespoon dry mustard
- 1 teaspoon turmeric
- ¼ cup flour

Cut corn from cobs. Mix vegetables and salt. Add half of the vinegar; bring to a boil. Combine sugar, seasonings, and flour. Add remaining vinegar; stir until smooth. Cook until thickened. Add to vegetables and cook for 30 minutes or until vegetables are tender. Pour into hot sterilized jars and seal.

Sweet Relish

Makes 5 to 6 pints.

- 6 pounds (22 medium) green tomatoes, quartered, stem ends removed
- 3 onions, quartered
- 2 green peppers, quartered
- 1⅔ cups granulated sugar
- 1¾ cups white vinegar
- ½ teaspoon ground cinnamon
- ½ teaspoon ground allspice
- ½ teaspoon turmeric
- ¼ teaspoon cayenne pepper
- 1½ teaspoons celery seed
- 3 tablespoons salt

Put all vegetables through medium blade of food grinder. Drain excess liquid. Bring sugar, vinegar, and seasonings to a boil in a large kettle. Add vegetables. Simmer 10 minutes, stirring occasionally. Continue to simmer relish while quickly packing one hot sterilized jar at a time. Fill to within ½ inch from the top. Vinegar solution should be covering vegetables. Seal each jar immediately.

Tomato Relish

- 5 medium tomatoes, peeled, seeded and diced
- 1 medium green pepper, diced
- 1 medium onion, diced
- 1 rib celery, diced
- 1 small cucumber, diced
- 1 tablespoon horseradish
- 1 teaspoon salt
- ½ cup wine vinegar
- ¼ cup sugar
- 1 teaspoon mustard seed
- ⅛ teaspoon ground cloves
  Dash black pepper

Combine vegetables, horseradish, and salt. Cover; let stand at room temperature for 2 hours. Drain well. Pour vinegar, sugar, mustard seed, cloves, and pepper over vegetables, mixing well. Chill for 6 hours or overnight. Keeps 4 to 6 days.

Red Pepper Relish

- 1 peck red peppers, trimmed and seeds removed
- 2 ounces mustard seed
- 3 pounds sugar
- 3 pints white vinegar

Grind peppers with a fine cutter. Rinse mustard seed and soak in hot water 2 to 3 hours; drain. Combine all ingredients. Cook over low heat until mixture jells; stirring often to prevent scorching.

Three-Bean Salad

- 1 can green beans
- 1 can yellow beans
- 1 can kidney beans
- 1 medium onion, minced
  Salt and pepper to taste
- ¾ cup salad oil
- ½ cup wine vinegar
- 2 hard-cooked eggs, minced

Mix together all ingredients. Place in a covered bowl and marinate overnight in refrigerator. Salad will keep for a week, if refrigerated.

Bread-and-Butter Pickles

Makes 7 pints.

- 25 medium cucumbers, sliced
- 12 onions, sliced
- ½ cup salt
- 2 cups sugar
- 2 teaspoons turmeric
- 1 quart vinegar
- 2 teaspoons mustard seed
- 2 teaspoons celery seed

Soak cucumbers and onions in salted ice water for 3 hours. Combine remaining ingredients; heat to boiling. Drain cucumbers and onions and add to vinegar mixture. Heat for 2 minutes; do not boil. Fill clean jars; seal.

Pickled Beets

- 48 small red beets
- 2 cups cider vinegar
- 4 cups water
- 3 cups sugar
- 1 lemon, thinly sliced, optional
- 2 sticks cinnamon
- 1 teaspoon whole cloves
- 1 teaspoon whole allspice, optional

Cook beets; drain and peel. Make a syrup of vinegar, water, sugar, lemon, and spices. Simmer 15 minutes. Place beets in sterilized jars. Pour hot syrup over beets to within ½ inch of top of jar. Seal.

Icicle Pickles

Makes 6 pints.

- 3 pounds 4-inch cucumbers, cleaned and cut in spears
- 6 small onions, quartered
- 6 5-inch pieces celery
- 1 tablespoon mustard seed
- 1 quart vinegar
- ¼ cup salt
- 2½ cups sugar
- 1 cup water

Soak cucumber spears in ice water 3 to 5 hours. Drain and pack into pint jars. To each jar add 1 quartered onion, 1 piece of celery, ⅓ teaspoon

mustard seed. Combine vinegar, salt, sugar, and water in a saucepan; bring to a boil. Pour solution over cucumbers to within ½ inch of top of jars. Seal.

Refrigerator Pickles

- 12 to 15 6-inch cucumbers, sliced
- 3 onions, sliced

Wash and sterilize 3 large quart jars. Layer cucumbers and onions in the jars; pack well. Pour Syrup over cucumbers and onions; screw on lids. Refrigerate at least 5 days before using. Store pickles in refrigerator.

Syrup

- 4 cups sugar
- 4 cups vinegar
- ½ cup pickling salt
- 1⅓ teaspoons celery seed
- 1⅓ teaspoons turmeric
- 1⅓ teaspoons mustard seed

Mix sugar, vinegar, and spices together. Do not heat. Stir well.

Jerusalem Artichoke Pickles

- 1 gallon Jerusalem artichokes, washed, scraped and left whole
- 3 quarts vinegar
- 3 pounds sugar
- 2 tablespoons turmeric
- 1 tablespoon ground ginger
- 1 tablespoon mustard seed
- 1 tablespoon celery seed
- 2 to 3 sticks cinnamon

Pack artichokes into sterilized jars as tightly as possible. In a saucepan, combine remaining ingredients. Cook for ½ hour over low heat. Cool syrup until slightly warm. Pour over artichokes and seal jars.

Note: Be sure the syrup is only warm, as it will shrivel the artichokes if too hot.

Children's Party

Lime Party Salad

Makes 12 servings.

16 marshmallows
1 cup milk
1 package lime-flavored gelatin
2 3-ounce packages cream cheese, softened
2½ cups canned crushed pineapple and juice
1 cup whipping cream, whipped
⅔ cup mayonnaise

Melt marshmallows and milk in the top of a double boiler. Pour over the gelatin; stirring until the gelatin dissolves. Add the cream cheese and stir until the cheese melts. Fold in pineapple. Cool. Blend together whipped cream and mayonnaise; fold into mixture. Chill until firm.

Moist Chocolate Cake

Makes 2 9-inch cakes.

2 teaspoons baking soda
½ cup sour milk
2 cups sugar
½ cup vegetable shortening
2 eggs
¼ teaspoon salt
2 cups flour
1 teaspoon vanilla extract
4 tablespoons cocoa
1 cup boiling water

Dissolve baking soda in the sour milk. Mix all ingredients except boiling water in a mixing bowl. Add boiling water; mix. Grease 2 9-inch pans; dust with flour. Bake at 375° for 30 to 35 minutes.

Super Butterwhip Frosting

½ cup vegetable shortening
½ cup butter or margarine
1 cup granulated sugar
¾ cup milk
Dash salt
1 teaspoon vanilla extract

Cream shortening, butter, and sugar in a small bowl of an electric mixer; set aside. In a small saucepan heat the milk until very hot; do not let it boil. Add the milk to the creamed mixture slowly, 1 tablespoon at a time, beating well after each addition. Add the salt and vanilla. Continue beating until mixture is soft like whipped cream.

Slush

Makes 25 to 30 servings.

½ gallon fruit sherbet
2 quarts ginger ale or white soda
⅓ 46-ounce can unsweetened pineapple juice

Combine all ingredients.

Tasty Party Buns

Makes 12 servings.

1 pound bologna
¾ pound American cheese
¼ cup prepared mustard
⅓ cup salad dressing
1 tablespoon minced onion
2 tablespoons chopped sweet pickle
12 hot dog buns
Butter

Grind meat and cheese into a mixing bowl. Add mustard, salad dressing, onion, and chopped pickle; mix well. Cut buns in half, spread with butter and fill with meat mixture. Wrap each bun in foil. Heat at 325° for 25 minutes.

Burger Pizza

1 cup biscuit mix
Vegetable oil
1 pound ground chuck
Salt and pepper to taste
Garlic salt to taste
1 teaspoon dried oregano
1 8-ounce can tomato sauce
1 tablespoon parsley
¼ pound Swiss cheese, cut into 1-inch strips

Prepare biscuit dough according to package directions. Roll flat onto a pizza pan and brush with vegetable oil. In a skillet brown beef; mix in salt, pepper, garlic salt, oregano, and tomato sauce. Spoon over dough. Sprinkle with parsley. Arrange cheese strips on top like spokes of a wheel. Bake at 400° for 20 minutes or until cheese melts. Cut into wedges. Serve hot.

Teenager's Party

Cheese Dainties

½ pound grated sharp cheese
½ pound margarine
2 cups flour
1 teaspoon salt
Dash red pepper

Mix above ingredients well with hands and shape into balls a little smaller than a walnut. Press lightly onto ungreased baking sheets and bake at 375° for 8 to 10 minutes until light tan.

Barbecue Burgers

Makes 6 to 8 servings.

½ pound ground beef
2 tablespoons chopped onion
2 tablespoons chopped green pepper
1 rib celery, diced
½ cup catsup
½ cup water
1 tablespoon vinegar
1½ teaspoons Worcestershire sauce
½ teaspoon prepared mustard
1 tablespoon brown sugar
½ teaspoon salt
⅛ teaspoon allspice

Lightly brown beef; add onion, green pepper, and celery. Sauté. Combine remaining ingredients and pour over meat. Cover pan tightly; simmer for 30 minutes. Serve hot over toasted buns.

French-Fried Onion Rings

1½ cups flour
1 teaspoon baking powder
1½ teaspoons salt
2 eggs, beaten
1 cup milk
1 teaspoon shortening, melted
Bermuda onions, thinly sliced

Sift dry ingredients together. Stir eggs, milk, and shortening into flour mixture; beat until smooth. Separate onions into rings; dip into batter. Deep fry in hot oil about 2 minutes or until golden brown. Do not crowd.

Tossed Fruit Salad

2 cups shredded cabbage
1 cup diced oranges
1 cup sliced, unpeeled Delicious apples
2 teaspoons grated onion
1 tablespoon lemon juice
½ teaspoon sugar
⅓ cup mayonnaise

Combine all ingredients and toss lightly. Serve on crisp salad greens.

Party Dip

Makes 2½ cups.

1 envelope onion soup mix
1 pint sour cream
1 medium tomato, chopped
1 small green pepper, diced
¼ teaspoon dillweed

Blend soup with sour cream. Add remaining ingredients. Chill at least 1 hour. Serve with assorted chips and breadsticks.

Banana Split Dessert

Makes 25 servings.

Graham cracker crumbs
3 or 4 bananas, sliced
½ gallon Neapolitan ice cream
1 cup chopped walnuts
½ cup butter
1 cup chocolate chips
2 cups confectioners' sugar
1½ cups evaporated milk
1 pint whipping cream, whipped
¼ cup confectioners' sugar
1 teaspoon vanilla extract

Cover an 11 x 15-inch pan with graham cracker crumbs. Arrange bananas over crumbs. Slice ice cream ½ inch thick and place over bananas. Sprinkle with nuts. Place in freezer until firm. Melt butter and chocolate chips over low heat. Add sugar and milk; cook until thick, stirring constantly. Cool and pour over crumb mixture. Chill. Whip cream. Add the ¼ cup confectioners' sugar and vanilla; pour over all. Freeze. Serve in slices or squares.

Fondue Fun

Fondue Fun

A fondue party can create much fun. It is perfect for teens, small informal dinner parties, and cookouts. All you need is the ingredients and the guests. Allow the guests the fun of preparing their own meal at the table; each diner becomes his own chef. Be sure to warn guests that the fondue forks become very hot and advise them to transfer the cooked food to a dinner fork, dipping into sauces.

In planning a fondue party, give free rein to your imagination. Serve a tossed green salad, crunchy dinner rolls, and a simple dessert of fresh fruit and cheese.

Food to Fondue

Serve with assorted sauces.

> **Beef tenderloin cubes**
> **Fresh whole mushrooms**
> **Cooked shrimp**
> **Cherry tomatoes**
> **Green pepper wedges**
> **Ham pieces**
> **Small whole onions**
> **Potato cubes**
> **Pineapple chunks**
> **Broccoli**

Cheese Fondue

Makes 4 cups.

1¼ cups dry white wine
1 clove garlic, chopped
8 ounces natural Swiss cheese, cut into pieces
¼ cup flour
2 10¾-ounce cans condensed Cheddar cheese soup
French bread or whole wheat bread, cubed

Heat wine and garlic in a saucepan or fondue pot to simmering. Combine cheese and flour. Gradually blend into wine. Heat until cheese is melted, stirring occasionally. Blend in soup. Heat, stirring until smooth. Dip bread into fondue.

Chocolate Fondue

6 3-ounce bars of sweet baker's chocolate
¼ cup plus 2 tablespoons cream
¼ cup kirsch or brandy
1 tablespoon instant (not freeze-dried) coffee
⅛ teaspoon ground cinnamon

In a fondue pot or heavy saucepan over low heat, melt the chocolate in the cream. Add remaining ingredients and stir. To serve, provide small plates, long-handled forks and generous helpings of whole strawberries, pecan halves, banana slices, orange sections or a pound cake cut into cubes.

Beef Fondue

Cooking oil
1 teaspoon salt
2 pounds beef tenderloin, cut into 1-inch cubes

Place metal fondue pot in center of table. Heat oil to 425° or until a cube of bread browns quickly. Add salt. Pour into fondue pot over fondue burner. Use long-handled, two-prong fondue forks to spear meat cubes. Fry the cubes in the hot oil to desired doneness. Remove to a plate and dip in sauce with a dinner fork.

Dipping Sauce

1 beef bouillon cube
⅔ cup boiling water
2 tablespoons flour
2 tablespoons butter, melted
½ cup dairy sour cream
1 3-ounce can mushrooms, drained and minced
2 teaspoons Worcestershire sauce
Salt and pepper to taste

Dissolve bouillon in the water. Stir flour into the butter. Add bouillon and stir while cooking until thick and bubbly. Add sour cream, mushrooms, and Worcestershire sauce. Season to taste. Serve while hot.

Dainty Rolls

Makes 50 small rolls.

    2 cups warm water (110 to 115°)
    1 package dry yeast
    1 teaspoon salt
    ¾ cup sugar
    1 egg
    6 cups flour
    ¼ cup vegetable oil
       Butter

Combine warm water and yeast in a large bowl; let stand about 5 minutes. Add salt, sugar, and egg to the yeast mixture; mix. Sift in 3 cups of the flour, mixing well. Add oil. Mix in about 3 more cups flour. Oil top and let rise in a warm place until double in size. Knead until satiny; roll out ¼ inch thick, oil top and cut out as for biscuits. Place a pat of butter on top of each dough round; fold over. Place in a shallow, well-oiled pan. Let rise until double. Bake at 450° for 12 minutes.

Note: To freeze, reduce baking time to 8 minutes. When ready to serve, place rolls in oven and brown.

Beef Stroganoff

Makes 6 servings.

    ½ pound fresh mushrooms, sliced
    1 large onion, chopped
    ¼ cup butter
    2 pounds round steak, ¼- to ½-inch thick
       Flour
    1 teaspoon salt
       Dash pepper
    1 10½-ounce can consommé, diluted with water
       to make 2 cups
    1 cup sour cream

Sauté mushrooms and onion in 2 tablespoons butter and remove from pan. Remove fat from steak and cut steak into strips. Melt remaining 2 tablespoons butter in skillet; brown meat, adding flour to coat thoroughly. Add salt, pepper, consommé, and water. Combine and bake at 375° for 1½ to 2 hours. Fifteen minutes before serving, remove from oven and stir in sour cream. Heat well. Serve over noodles or rice.

Candy Apples

    10 medium apples
    10 wooden skewers
    2½ cups sugar
    ½ cup water
    1 teaspoon vanilla extract
    ½ cup light corn syrup
    1 teaspoon red food coloring

Wash and dry apples; insert skewers in the stem end. Combine sugar, water, vanilla, corn syrup, and food coloring and cook in a large, deep pan. During cooking the crystals which form on the pan should not be stirred into the candy. Continue cooking without stirring to hard crack stage (280°). Remove from heat, hold apples by skewers and dip into syrup. Place on buttered platter to cool.

Halloween Date Cake

    ½ cup shortening
    1 cup sugar
    ½ teaspoon salt
    1 teaspoon ground cinnamon
    ½ teaspoon ground cloves
    1 cup warm water
    1½ cups flour, sifted
    1 teaspoon baking soda
    1 cup chopped dates
    ½ cup chopped walnuts

Combine first 6 ingredients in a saucepan; mix well. Slowly bring to a boil and boil for 30 seconds. Cool. Sift together flour and baking soda. Add to cooled liquid, beating well. Fold in dates and nuts. Grease a 15½ x 10½-inch pan; line with waxed paper and grease paper. Distribute batter evenly in pan. Bake at 350° for 30 to 35 minutes or until top springs back when lightly touched. When cool, frost with Orange Butter Frosting.

Orange Butter Frosting

       Rind of ½ orange, grated
       Juice of ½ orange, strained
    2 tablespoons butter, melted
    1 tablespoon heavy cream
    4 cups confectioners' sugar, sifted

Combine first 4 ingredients. Gradually add sugar. Beat until creamy. Spread on cake.

Harvest Time

Apple Cider Punch

Makes 20 to 25 servings.

- 1 quart apple cider
- 2 cups cranberry juice
- 1 cup orange juice
- 1 12-ounce can apricot nectar
- 1 cup sugar
- 2 sticks cinnamon

Combine all ingredients in a large saucepan; simmer for 20 minutes. Garnish punch with floating orange slices, decorated with cloves.

Chocolate Intrigue

- 3 cups sifted all-purpose flour
- 2 teaspoons baking powder
- ½ teaspoon salt
- 1 cup butter
- 2 cups sugar
- 3 eggs
- 1 cup milk
- 1½ teaspoons vanilla extract
- ¾ cup chocolate syrup
- ¼ teaspoon baking soda
- ¼ teaspoon peppermint extract, optional

Sift together flour, baking powder, and salt. Cream butter, gradually adding sugar. Blend in one egg at a time, beating well after each addition. Combine milk and vanilla. Add alternately with the dry ingredients, beginning and ending with dry ingredients. Blend well after each addition. Pour ⅔ of the batter into a well greased and lightly floured tube pan. Add the syrup, soda, and peppermint to remaining batter; mix well. Spoon chocolate batter over white batter. Do not mix. Bake at 350° for 65 to 70 minutes. When cake is cool, frost with Chocolate Frosting.

Chocolate Frosting

- 4 ounces unsweetened chocolate, melted
- 3 tablespoons butter, softened
- 1 egg, lightly beaten
- 2½ cups sifted confectioners' sugar
- ⅓ cup milk

Combine all ingredients. Beat until of spreading consistency.

Pumpkin Bread

Makes 2 loaves.

- 4 cups flour
- 3 cups sugar
- 1 teaspoon baking powder
- 2 teaspoons baking soda
- 1 teaspoon ground cinnamon
- 1 teaspoon ground nutmeg
- 1 teaspoon ground allspice
- ½ teaspoon ground cloves
- 1 cup vegetable oil
- 1 14½-ounce can pumpkin
- ⅔ cup cold water
- 4 eggs

Sift dry ingredients into a large mixing bowl. Make a well in the flour and pour in vegetable oil. Add pumpkin and cold water; blend well. Add eggs, one at a time, beating well after each addition. Pour batter into 2 well greased and floured loaf pans. Bake at 350° for 1 hour.

Baked Zucchini Slices

- 2 cups sliced zucchini, cooked with 1 garlic clove
- 2 slices bread, cubed
- ½ cup grated yellow cheese
- 1 egg, beaten
- 2 tablespoons chopped parsley
- 2 tablespoons salad oil

Drain cooked squash. Combine all ingredients. Bake at 350° for 30 minutes.

Soft Molasses Cookies

Makes 5 to 6 dozen cookies.

- 1 cup molasses
- 1 cup sugar
- 5 cups flour
- 1 cup vegetable shortening, softened
- 1 egg, lightly beaten

Combine all ingredients and mix well. Roll out on floured board; cut with round cookie cutter. Bake at 400° for 8 to 10 minutes or until done.

Note: If dropped cookies are preferred, use less flour and drop from spoon.

Liver and Vegetable Sauté

½ pound sliced beef liver
2 tablespoons flour
3 tablespoons butter or margarine
1 cup sliced mushrooms
1 small green pepper, sliced
1 8-ounce can stewed tomatoes
¾ teaspoon salt
¼ teaspoon chili powder
  Dash cayenne pepper
  Lemon juice

Dust liver with flour. Heat liver in butter until brown on both sides, about 5 minutes. Stir in remaining ingredients, except lemon juice; heat to boiling. Reduce heat; simmer until liver is done, about 10 minutes. Sprinkle with lemon juice.

Orange Marmalade

5 oranges, chopped
2 grapefruit, chopped
12 cups cold water
8½ cups sugar
  Juice of 2 lemons

Combine oranges, grapefruit, and water in a large kettle; boil for 1 hour, or until fruit is soft. Add sugar and boil for 45 minutes. Add lemon juice; boil until thick. Pour into glasses and seal with paraffin.

Cranberry Squares

1 cup packed brown sugar
½ teaspoon salt
1 cup flour
1 cup quick-cooking rolled oats
¾ cup margarine, melted
1 can whole cranberry sauce

Mix sugar, salt, flour, and oats. Pour margarine over mixture and blend. Spread half of mixture in an 8- or 9-inch square pan. Spread cranberry sauce over bottom layer. Top with remaining half of mixture. Bake at 350° for 45 minutes. Serve with whipped cream or ice cream.

Zucchini Bread

Makes 2 loaves.

3 eggs
1 cup cooking oil
2 cups sugar
3 cups peeled, grated zucchini
2 teaspoons vanilla extract
3 cups flour
¼ teaspoon baking powder
1 teaspoon baking soda
1 teaspoon salt
3 teaspoons ground cinnamon
½ cup chopped nuts

Beat eggs until light and foamy. Add next 4 ingredients; mix lightly. In a separate bowl mix dry ingredients. Add to zucchini mixture and blend. Add nuts. Put in 2 greased and floured loaf pans and bake at 325° for 1 hour. Remove from pans immediately and cool on racks.

Note: This bread may be frozen for later use.

Harvest Casserole

3 pounds lean ground beef
1 large onion, chopped
2 cups chopped celery
1 8-ounce package egg noodles, cooked
1 13-ounce can evaporated milk
3 10¾-ounce cans cream of mushroom soup
¾ pound Velveeta cheese, grated

Sauté ground beef and onion; drain fat. Sauté celery in a small amount of margarine over low heat. Mix all ingredients and spoon into one large casserole or several small ones. Bake at 350° until bubbly.

Note: This casserole makes approximately 1 gallon. It freezes well either before or after baking.

Toasted Pumpkin Seeds

Spread 2 cups pumpkin seeds, washed and drained, on a baking sheet; sprinkle with salt. Toast at 350° for 15 minutes.

Thanksgiving

Corn and Peppers

    2 tablespoons chopped onion
    2 tablespoons chopped green pepper
    2 tablespoons butter or margarine
    2 tablespoons flour
    2 cups cooked corn
    1 cup milk
    ½ teaspoon salt
    ½ cup cracker crumbs
    2 tablespoons margarine, melted

Sauté onion and green pepper in the butter until soft. Add flour, corn, milk, and salt. Spoon into a baking dish. Stir cracker crumbs with melted butter; spread on top of corn mixture. Bake at 350° for 20 to 30 minutes or until brown.

Sweet Potato Bake

Makes 6 to 8 servings.

    1 9-ounce can pineapple chunks and juice
    5 cups mashed sweet potatoes or yams
    ½ teaspoon salt
    2 tablespoons butter or margarine
    1 small package miniature marshmallows
    ⅓ cup pecan halves

Cut pineapple chunks in half. Combine pineapple with juice, potatoes, salt, and butter. Place half of mixture in a buttered casserole. Top with half of the marshmallows. Add remaining half of potato mixture. Arrange pecans on top. Cover and bake at 350° for 30 minutes. Remove cover about 10 minutes before serving. Add remaining marshmallows.

Note: This can be made the night before and refrigerated. Add the nuts just before baking.

Turkey Stuffing

Makes enough for a 15- to 18-pound turkey.

    4 quarts day-old bread cubes
    3 cups boiled, peeled, and sliced potatoes
    3 or 4 ribs celery, diced
    ½ cup diced onion
    1½ teaspoons salt
    ½ teaspoon pepper

Combine all ingredients. Do not use fresh bread. Fill cavity lightly (do not pack) to prevent stuffing from becoming gummy.

Note: Potatoes cooked with skins give better flavor.

Cranberry Crunch

    1 cup rolled oats
    ¾ cup brown sugar
    ½ cup flour
    ½ cup coconut
    ⅓ cup butter
    1 16-ounce can whole cranberry sauce
    1 tablespoon lemon juice

Mix first 5 ingredients together, cutting in butter. Place half of the mixture in a greased 9-inch pan. Add whole cranberry sauce with lemon juice. Top with other half of crunch mixture. Bake at 350° for 45 minutes.

Miniature Pecan Pies

    1 3-ounce package cream cheese, softened
    ½ cup margarine, softened
    1 cup flour

Combine cream cheese and margarine; blend well. Add flour and mix thoroughly. Chill overnight. Divide pastry into 24 balls and press into miniature muffin tins, covering bottom and sides. Spoon Pecan Filling into pastry shells. Bake at 325° for 25 minutes. Cool in pans; turn out onto waxed paper.

Pecan Filling

    1 egg, lightly beaten
    ¾ cup firmly packed light brown sugar
    1 tablespoon margarine, melted
    1 teaspoon vanilla extract
      Dash salt
    ⅔ cup coarsely broken pecans

Combine all ingredients; mix well.

Note: For variety use coconut and dates in place of pecans. Pastry shells can be baked and then filled with jellies or marmalade.

Autumn Favorites

Autumn Pumpkin Cake

- 1 package yellow cake mix
- 4 eggs, lightly beaten
- ¾ cup sugar
- ½ cup salad oil
- 1 cup cooked or canned pumpkin
- ¼ cup water
- 1 teaspoon ground cinnamon
- Dash ground nutmeg

Combine all ingredients in a large mixing bowl. Beat 5 minutes with electric mixer. Pour into a greased and floured tube pan. Bake at 350° for 35 minutes or until done. Frost with Cream Cheese Icing.

Cream Cheese Icing

- 1 3-ounce package cream cheese, softened
- ½ cup margarine, melted
- 1 16-ounce box confectioners' sugar
- 1 teaspoon vanilla extract

Beat cream cheese and margarine until well blended. Add sugar and vanilla; beat until smooth.

Gingerbread

- ½ cup butter, softened
- ½ cup sugar
- 1 egg, beaten
- 1 cup molasses
- 2½ cups sifted flour
- 1½ teaspoons baking soda
- 1 teaspoon ground cinnamon
- 1 teaspoon ground ginger
- ½ teaspoon ground cloves
- ½ teaspoon salt
- 1 cup boiling water
- 4 ounces miniature marshmallows

Cream butter and sugar. Add egg and molasses; beat until blended. Combine dry ingredients; add to mixture alternately with boiling water, stirring after each addition. Place in 2 greased 8-inch pans and bake at 350° for 45 minutes. Remove from oven. Place 1 layer on oven proof dish. Arrange marshmallows on top. Cover with second layer. Return to oven and bake until marshmallows melt. Serve hot.

Apple Slices

- 2 cups flour
- 1 teaspoon salt
- ⅔ cup butter, softened
- 1 egg yolk, beaten
- ½ cup milk
- Sliced apples
- Ground cinnamon
- ⅔ cup sugar
- Butter
- 1 egg white, beaten

Combine flour, salt, and butter. Add egg yolk and milk; mix well. Divide dough in half; roll each half thin on a floured surface. Place one half on a buttered baking sheet. Add apples, cinnamon, sugar, and bits of butter. Top with remaining dough. Spread egg white over dough. Sprinkle with sugar. Bake at 350° until brown and apples are tender.

Carrot Marmalade

Scald several carrots and remove skins. Put carrots through a food chopper. To each pint of pulp, add juice and grated rind of 1 lemon and 1¾ cups sugar. Pour into a saucepan. Allow to stand overnight. Boil mixture until clear; spoon into jelly glasses.

Baked Apple Butter

- 10 pounds apples
- 1½ quarts cider
- 1 tablespoon ground cloves
- 1 tablespoon ground cinnamon
- 1 tablespoon ground nutmeg
- 5 pounds sugar

Peel, core and quarter apples; place in a large kettle. Add enough water to cover apples. Simmer until soft. Stir in the cider, cloves, cinnamon, nutmeg, and sugar. Pour the mixture into a roasting pan; cover. Bake at 350° until the mixture boils; stir occasionally. Lower heat to 250° and bake 5 hours, or overnight. Ladle the apple butter into sterilized jars and seal.

Crispy Corn Sticks

Makes 8 corn sticks.

- 1 cup cornmeal
- ¼ teaspoon salt
- ¼ teaspoon baking soda
- 3 tablespoons vegetable oil
- 1 cup buttermilk
- 1 or 2 tablespoons light corn syrup

Sift cornmeal, salt, and soda. Add oil; stir. Add buttermilk and syrup; mix well. Fill well-greased corn stick pans. Bake at 400° for 30 minutes.

Vermont Maple Custard

- 3 eggs
- ½ cup maple syrup
- Dash salt
- 2 cups milk

Beat eggs, syrup, and salt. Blend in milk. Pour into individual cups or molds and place molds in a pan of hot water. Bake at 350° for 40 to 50 minutes or until a knife inserted in center comes out clean.

Celery Supreme

- 6 cups sliced celery
- ½ cup water
- 1 teaspoon salt
- 1 can sliced water chestnuts, drained
- 1 2-ounce jar pimiento
- ½ cup chopped green pepper
- 1 10¾-ounce can cream of celery or cream of mushroom soup

Combine celery, water, and salt in a large kettle; simmer 10 minutes. Drain. Combine celery mixture, water chestnuts, pimiento, green pepper, and soup in a casserole, stirring gently. Spoon Topping over casserole. Bake at 350° for 20 minutes.

Topping

- ¼ cup butter, melted
- 1 cup coarse bread crumbs
- ½ cup sliced almonds

Combine all ingredients.

Red Cabbage with Raisins

Makes 6 servings.

- 1 head red cabbage, shredded
- ¼ cup raisins
- ½ cup water
- ½ cup apple juice
- 2 tablespoons light brown sugar
- 1½ teaspoons salt
- Juice of 1 lemon

Combine all ingredients in a large skillet; cover. Simmer until cabbage is tender and most of the liquid has evaporated.

Hot Percolator Punch

- 9 cups unsweetened pineapple juice
- 9 cups cranberry juice
- 4½ cups water
- 1 cup brown sugar
- 4½ teaspoons whole cloves
- 4 sticks cinnamon, broken
- ¼ teaspoon salt

Pour first 4 ingredients into a 25-cup coffee pot. In the percolator basket, place spices and salt; perk.

Turkey Casserole

- 5 or 6 cups diced cooked turkey
- ½ cup margarine
- ¾ cup chopped celery
- 1 onion, chopped
- 3 cups bread crumbs
- 1 teaspoon salt
- ¼ teaspoon baking powder
- ¼ teaspoon black pepper
- ¼ teaspoon poultry seasoning
- 1 egg
- 1 10¾-ounce can cream of mushroom soup
- ¾ cup broth or milk

Place turkey in a large casserole. Melt the margarine in a large skillet and sauté the celery, onion, and bread crumbs. Add salt, baking powder, pepper, and poultry seasoning. Beat the egg; combine egg, soup, broth or milk, and crumb mixture. Pour over turkey. Bake, uncovered, at 350° for 45 to 60 minutes.

Christmas Treats

Two-Tone Cookie Slices

Makes 7 dozen.

Dark Mixture

    3 cups sifted flour
    1 teaspoon baking soda
    ¼ teaspoon salt
    ½ teaspoon ground cinnamon
    ½ teaspoon ground cloves
    1 cup shortening, softened
    1½ cups dark brown sugar
    2 eggs
    1 cup finely chopped nuts
    1 cup raisins

Sift together flour, soda, salt, and spices; set aside. Cream shortening with brown sugar; add eggs. Beat well. Stir in dry ingredients, nuts and raisins.

Light Mixture

    2 cups sifted flour
    ½ teaspoon salt
    ¼ teaspoon baking soda
    ½ cup shortening, softened
    ¾ cup sugar
    1 egg
    1 teaspoon vanilla extract
    2 tablespoons water
    ¼ cup chopped candied cherries

Sift together flour, salt, and soda; set aside. Cream shortening and sugar. Add egg, vanilla, and water; mix well. Blend in dry ingredients. Stir in cherries.

Pack half of dark mixture into a waxed paper-lined, straight-sided 10½ x 3½-inch pan or loaf pan. Add all light dough to make a second layer; top with remaining dark dough. Pack firmly. Refrigerate 24 hours. Cut dough in half lengthwise; cut into ¼-inch slices. Bake on ungreased baking sheets at 400° for 8 to 10 minutes. Remove immediately.

Holly Cookies

    6 tablespoons margarine
    24 large marshmallows
    ½ teaspoon vanilla extract
       Green food coloring
    2½ cups cornflakes

Melt all ingredients except cornflakes in the top of a double boiler or over low heat. Pour mixture over cornflakes; fold until entire mixture is colored green. Drop by teaspoonfuls onto waxed paper. Decorate with small cinnamon candies, if desired.

Christmas Trees

    2 9½-ounce packages refrigerated cinnamon rolls
      with icing, prepared according to
      package directions
    6 tablespoons chopped candied mixed fruit

Arrange rolls on a greased baking sheet in rows to simulate a Christmas tree. Bake in a preheated 375° oven for 18 to 20 minutes. Remove from baking sheet onto a large platter or breadboard or cut cardboard which has been covered with foil. While rolls are hot, spread with icing and sprinkle with fruit to decorate.

Poinsettia Cookies

Makes about 5 dozen.

    2 cups confectioners' sugar
    1 cup butter or margarine, softened
    2 eggs
    1 teaspoon vanilla extract
    ½ teaspoon rum extract
    3 cups flour
    1 teaspoon salt
    1 cup shredded coconut
    1 cup butterscotch chips
      Granulated sugar
    ½ cup candied red cherries, cut in wedges

Cream confectioners' sugar and butter; add eggs and extracts. Sift together flour and salt; stir into butter mixture. Stir in coconut and ¾ cup of the butterscotch chips. Chill dough until firm. Roll into 1-inch balls. Place on ungreased baking sheets. Flatten cookie with the bottom of a glass dipped in granulated sugar. Place a butterscotch chip in the center of each cookie. Place cherry wedges in a circle to resemble a poinsettia. Bake at 375° for about 12 minutes.

Kris Kringles

Makes 40 slices.

- 1 6-ounce package semisweet chocolate chips
- 2 tablespoons butter or margarine
- 1 egg
- 1 cup sifted confectioners' sugar
    Dash salt
- ½ teaspoon vanilla extract
- ½ cup flaked coconut
- ½ cup chopped dry roasted peanuts

In a medium saucepan, melt chocolate and butter over low heat, stirring constantly. Remove from heat; cool to lukewarm. Beat in egg until smooth and glossy. Add confectioners' sugar, salt, and vanilla; mix well. Stir in coconut and nuts. Chill. Form into a 10-inch-long roll. Wrap and chill until firm, several hours or overnight. Slice ¼ inch thick.

Holiday Divinity

- 2 egg whites
- 1 3-ounce package fruit-flavored gelatin
- 3 cups sugar
- ¾ cup light corn syrup
- ¾ cup water

Beat egg whites until light. Add gelatin and beat until stiff. Cook remaining ingredients. Stir until mixture reaches hard ball stage (250° on a candy thermometer). Beat in the egg whites and pour into a buttered 8-inch square pan. Cool. Cut into squares.

Pecan Pralines

- 2 cups white sugar
- 1 cup brown sugar
- 1 tablespoon butter
- ½ cup milk
- 3 cups pecans

Combine first 4 ingredients and bring to a boil. Add pecans and cook 4 minutes. Remove from heat and drop by spoonfuls onto waxed paper.

Date-Walnut Pinwheel Cookies

Makes 4 dozen.

- 1 cup chopped dates
- ½ teaspoon grated lemon rind
- ½ teaspoon lemon juice
- ½ cup water
- ½ cup sugar
- 1 cup chopped walnuts
- 1 13-ounce package plain cookie mix
- 1 egg, beaten
- 1 tablespoon water

Combine dates, lemon rind, lemon juice, ½ cup water, and sugar in a saucepan. Cook about 10 minutes, stirring until thick. Add walnuts. Cool. Blend cookie mix with egg and the 1 tablespoon water. Roll in 2 10 x 7-inch rectangles. Spread with walnut and date mixture. Roll up jelly-roll fashion. Wrap in waxed paper; chill until firm. Slice ¼-inch thick. Bake on a greased baking sheet at 375° for 8 to 9 minutes.

Note: These rolls can be frozen. Slice frozen and bake.

Two-Flavored Fudge

Makes about 2½ pounds.

- 2 cups firmly packed brown sugar
- 1 cup sugar
- 1 cup evaporated milk
- ½ cup butter
- 1 7-ounce jar marshmallow creme
- 1 6-ounce package butterscotch chips
- 1 6-ounce package semisweet chocolate chips
- 1 cup chopped walnuts
- 1 teaspoon vanilla extract

In a saucepan combine first 4 ingredients. Bring to a full boil over moderate heat, stirring frequently. Boil 15 minutes over moderate heat, stirring occasionally. Remove from heat. Add marshmallow creme, butterscotch chips, and chocolate chips. Stir until chips are melted and mixture is smooth. Blend in walnuts and vanilla. Pour into a greased 9-inch square pan. Chill until firm.

Peanut Butter Candy

3 cups sugar
⅛ teaspoon salt
1 cup milk
2 tablespoons butter
1 cup peanut butter
1 teaspoon vanilla extract

Combine sugar, salt, and milk in a 2-quart saucepan. Quickly bring to a boil, stirring only until sugar is dissolved. Boil, without stirring, until mixture reaches soft ball stage (234° on a candy thermometer). Remove from heat and add butter, peanut butter, and vanilla. Mix thoroughly. Pour into buttered 8-inch square pan. When cool, cut into pieces.

Oatmeal Fruit Cookies

¾ cup butter or margarine, softened
1 cup packed brown sugar
2 eggs
2 cups whole wheat flour
1 cup rolled oats
½ teaspoon baking soda
1 teaspoon baking powder
1 teaspoon ground cinnamon
¼ cup milk
1 cup chopped candied cherries or mixed fruit
1 cup chopped pecans or walnuts

Cream butter, sugar, and eggs until well blended. Combine dry ingredients; add to butter and egg mixture. Mix well. Add enough milk to make the dough easy to handle. Mix in fruits and nuts. Drop by teaspoonfuls onto a greased baking sheet. Bake at 350° for 8 to 12 minutes or until browned.

Cinnamon Crisps

½ pound butter, softened
1 cup sugar
1 egg
3 cups flour
½ teaspoon salt
1½ teaspoons ground cinnamon
1 teaspoon baking powder

Cream butter and sugar until light and fluffy. Add egg; beat well. Sift together flour, salt, cinnamon, and baking powder. Add to creamed mixture. Chill about 1 hour for easy handling. Roll out on a floured board to ⅛-inch thickness; cut into desired shapes. Place on ungreased baking sheets. Bake at 350° for 11 to 12 minutes or until light brown. Remove cookies from baking sheet immediately. Cool on wire racks. Store in an airtight container.

Mock Fondant Balls

½ cup butter, softened
1 pound confectioners' sugar
¼ cup heavy cream
1 teaspoon vanilla extract
    Hazelnuts, pecans or walnuts
    Candied fruit, chopped

Cream butter until light; gradually add sugar. When very thick add cream and vanilla a little at a time. Turn out on a board sprinkled with confectioners' sugar; knead. Break off about 2 teaspoons of the mixture and place around a nutmeat or piece of candied fruit to form a ball. Roll in confectioners' sugar. Repeat with remaining dough. Store in an airtight container in refrigerator.

Melt-in-the-Mouth Caramels

Makes about 2½ pounds.

1 cup butter or margarine
1 pound brown sugar
    Dash salt
1 cup light corn syrup
1 15-ounce can sweetened condensed milk
1 teaspoon vanilla extract

Melt butter in a heavy 3-quart saucepan. Add brown sugar and salt. Stir until thoroughly combined. Stir in corn syrup; mix well. Gradually add milk, stirring constantly. Cook and stir over medium heat until candy reaches firm ball stage (245° on candy thermometer), about 12 to 15 minutes. Remove from heat. Stir in vanilla. Pour into buttered 9-inch square pan. Cool and cut into squares.

Holiday Get-together

Yuletide Casserole

    2 3-ounce cans whole mushrooms, drained,
      reserve liquid
    2 tablespoons butter
    ½ teaspoon paprika
    2½ cups diced cooked ham
      Chicken broth
    2 10¾-ounce cans cream of chicken soup, undiluted
    6 hard-cooked eggs
      Pimiento
      Parsley

Sauté mushrooms in butter and paprika a few minutes. Add ham and sauté 2 minutes. Add enough chicken broth to mushroom liquid to make ¾ cup. Stir in mushroom liquid and soup; simmer over low heat, stirring, until smooth and hot. Separate 1 hard-cooked egg yolk from the white; set aside. Quarter egg white and remaining eggs and fold into ham mixture. Garnish with crumbled reserved egg yolk, pimiento, and parsley. Serve immediately with Saffron Rice with Peas.

Note: Casserole may be cooled, covered and refrigerated overnight if desired. Reheat at low temperature before serving.

Saffron Rice with Peas

Cook 6 servings of rice in water seasoned with powdered saffron to taste. Cook 1 10-ounce package frozen peas; drain. Fold into rice.

Dinner Rolls

    1 package dry yeast
    ½ cup warm water (110 to 115°)
    ½ cup scalded milk
    ¼ cup butter
    2 tablespoons sugar
    1½ teaspoons salt
    1 egg
    3 cups sifted flour

Dissolve yeast in water; set aside. Combine milk, butter, sugar, and salt. Add yeast mixture; mix well. Blend in the egg. Gradually add flour. Mix until dough is well blended and soft. Shape dough into rolls on a well-floured board. Let rise in a warm place until double in bulk. Bake at 350° for 15 to 20 minutes or until done.

Note: If dough is to be chilled, place in a greased bowl, cover, and refrigerate at least 2 hours. Remove and let rise in a warm place until double in bulk, about 1½ to 2 hours. Bake as above.

German Christmas Stollen

Makes 1 stollen.

    ¾ cup milk, scalded
    ¼ cup sugar
    ½ teaspoon salt
    ¼ cup butter or margarine
    ¼ cup warm water (110 to 115°)
    1 package dry yeast
    2¾ cups unsifted flour
    ⅛ teaspoon ground cardamom
    ½ cup seedless raisins
    ¼ cup chopped citron
    ½ cup chopped pecans
    1 tablespoon butter or margarine, melted

To the scalded milk, add sugar, salt, and butter. Cool to lukewarm. Measure warm water into a large, warm bowl. Add yeast; stir until dissolved. Add lukewarm milk mixture, 2 cups of the flour and cardamom. Beat until smooth. Stir in remaining flour, raisins, citron, and pecans. Turn out on a lightly floured board and knead until smooth and elastic, about 5 minutes. Place in a greased bowl, turning to grease top. Cover. Let rise in a warm place until double in bulk, about 1 hour. Roll dough into an oblong shape about ½ inch thick. Brush with melted butter. Fold in half lengthwise. Place on a greased baking sheet; cover. Let rise in a warm place until double in bulk, about 45 minutes. Bake at 350° about 40 minutes. Ice with Confectioners' Sugar Frosting.

Confectioners' Sugar Frosting

    1 cup confectioners' sugar
    1 to 2 tablespoons hot milk or water

In a small bowl, add milk or water gradually to sugar. Blend until mixture is smooth; spread over stollen. Decorate stollen with candied cherries and nuts if desired.

Fruitcake

  1 pound candied citron
  8 ounces raisins
12 ounces green and red candied cherries, chopped
  1 pound pecans, chopped
  1 pound dates, chopped
  4 ounces almond halves
  ¼ cup flour

Toss all ingredients together until well blended. Set aside and mix Batter.

Batter

  1 cup shortening, softened
  ½ cup sugar
  ½ cup brown sugar
  ½ cup honey
  5 eggs, beaten
1½ cups flour
  1 teaspoon salt
  3 teaspoons baking powder
  1 teaspoon ground cinnamon
  ½ teaspoon ground allspice
  ½ teaspoon ground cloves
  ½ teaspoon ground nutmeg

Cream shortening and sugars well. Add honey and eggs, mixing after each addition. Sift dry ingredients together; add to creamed mixture. Pour Batter over fruit mixture and mix thoroughly. Line greased tube pan with brown paper; grease paper. Bake at 250° over a pan of water for 4 hours. Cool in pan; remove. Pour about 1 cup fruit juice or brandy over top as desired. Wrap in foil and store in the refrigerator.

Note: If desired, decorate with cherries and almonds, using almonds for flower petals and cherries for centers.

Holly Wreath Pie

  2 envelopes unflavored gelatin
  ¼ cup sugar
  4 cups eggnog
  1 cup whipping cream, whipped
  ½ cup chopped maraschino cherries
  ½ cup chopped nuts
  1 baked pastry shell
    Green citron
    Red maraschino cherries

Combine gelatin and sugar in the top of a double boiler. Stir in 1 cup of the eggnog. Place over boiling water; stir until gelatin and sugar are dissolved. Remove from heat. Add remaining eggnog. Chill to consistency of unbeaten egg white. Whip until light and fluffy. Fold in the whipped cream, chopped cherries, and nuts. Turn into baked pie shell. Chill until firm. To decorate, make small holly wreaths of citron, cut into quarter-moon shapes and placed on top of filling to form rings. Place a tiny piece of red maraschino cherry in the centers.

English Mincemeat

1 pound dried currants, rinsed
1 pound seedless raisins, rinsed
3 large apples, chopped with skins
1 pound mixed fruit peel
2 teaspoons salt
1 pound suet, chopped
  Juice and grated peel of 1 lemon
1 pound brown sugar
  Ground nutmeg, allspice and cinnamon to taste

Combine all ingredients; mix thoroughly. Pour into a large covered jar. Store in refrigerator.

Mincemeat Cookies

Makes 5½ dozen.

3¼ cups flour
  ½ teaspoon salt
  1 teaspoon baking soda
  1 cup shortening, softened
1½ cups sugar
  3 eggs, well beaten
1⅓ cups prepared mincemeat

Sift flour, salt, and baking soda; set aside. Cream shortening and sugar until smooth. Beat in the eggs. Stir in mincemeat. Add flour mixture, mixing well. Drop by teaspoonfuls, 2 inches apart, onto a greased baking sheet. Bake at 400° for 12 minutes.

Festive Eggnog Cake

Makes 1 9-inch layer cake.

  2 cups flour
1½ cups sugar
  1 tablespoon baking powder
  1 teaspoon salt
 ¼ teaspoon ground nutmeg
  3 eggs
  1 teaspoon vanilla extract
  1 cup eggnog
 ½ cup butter, softened

Combine all ingredients in a large mixing bowl. Blend well at low speed of electric mixer. Grease and flour the bottoms of 2 9-inch pans; pour batter into pans. Bake at 350° for 25 to 30 minutes or until cake springs back when lightly touched in center. Cool. Fill and frost with Eggnog Frosting.

Eggnog Frosting

 ¼ cup flour
 ¼ teaspoon salt
  1 cup eggnog
⅔ cup butter, softened
  1 cup sugar
  1 teaspoon vanilla extract

Combine flour, salt, and eggnog in a small saucepan. Cook over low heat, stirring constantly, until very thick. Cool. Gradually cream butter and sugar. Add flour mixture; beat until light and fluffy. Blend in vanilla.

Marmalade Noel

Makes 7 to 8 jars.

  3 oranges
  1 lemon
  2 cups crushed pineapple, drained
  3 pounds sugar
 ½ cup hot water
  1 bottle maraschino cherries, drained

Wash oranges and lemon; peel very thin. Scrape white from peel and remove all membrane. Chop fruit and peels or grind in food chopper. Add pineapple, sugar, and water. Boil slowly for ½ hour. Add cherries. Pour into jars and seal with paraffin.

Traditional Suet Cake

  2 teaspoons baking soda
1⅓ cups sour milk or buttermilk
  1 cup molasses
⅔ cup sugar
  2 eggs, lightly beaten
  3 cups flour
  1 teaspoon baking powder
  2 teaspoons ground cinnamon
  2 teaspoons ground ginger
  2 cups chopped suet
  2 cups chopped nuts
  2 cups chopped dates or raisins, dusted with flour

Dissolve soda in sour milk; set aside. Mix molasses, sugar, and eggs in a large mixing bowl. In a separate bowl sift together dry ingredients. Alternately add with sour milk and soda mixture. Add suet, nuts, and floured dates or raisins. Pour into a 9 x 13-inch greased and floured pan. Bake at 275° for 30 to 40 minutes. Serve warm with whipped cream or a lemon sauce.

Charlotte Russe

Makes 10 to 12 servings.

  2 envelopes unflavored gelatin
 ¼ cup water
  4 eggs, separated
  1 cup sugar
  1 pint milk
 ½ teaspoon cream of tartar
  1 pint whipping cream
  1 teaspoon vanilla extract
    Confectioners' sugar to taste
  1 sponge cake

Dissolve gelatin in the water over low heat. Cool. Beat egg yolks. Gradually beat in ¾ cup of the sugar. Add milk. Cook in the top of a double boiler over low heat until mixture thickens slightly. Stir in gelatin. Cool. Stir until smooth. Beat egg whites and cream of tartar until mixture forms soft peaks. Gradually add the remaining ¼ cup sugar, beating until stiff. Fold into custard. Whip cream with vanilla; add confectioners' sugar. Fold into custard. Break cake into pieces in dessert dishes. Pour custard over. Refrigerate overnight.

Black Forest Cherry Cake

Makes 8 servings.

- 4 eggs
- ¾ teaspoon vanilla extract
- ⅔ cup sugar
- ⅓ cup cocoa
- ⅓ cup sifted flour
- 6 tablespoons butter, melted
- ½ cup sugar
- ¾ cup water
- ¼ cup kirsch
- ⅓ cup confectioners' sugar
- 2 cups whipping cream, whipped
- 1 cup pitted dark cherries, drained
  Maraschino cherries
- 1 4-ounce bar semisweet chocolate, shaved
  into curls

Combine eggs, vanilla, and the ⅔ cup sugar; beat with electric mixer 10 minutes at high speed. Sift together flour and cocoa; fold into egg mixture. Add melted butter, stirring just until mixed. Do not overmix. Pour into 3 greased and floured 8-inch round pans. Bake at 350° for 10 to 15 minutes. Cool 5 minutes. Remove from pans and cool on racks. In a saucepan, combine the ½ cup sugar and water; boil 5 minutes. Cool to luke-warm and add kirsch. Sprinkle over cake layers. Fold confectioners' sugar into whipped cream. Spread on one cake layer; top with half of the cherries. Repeat with second layer; then add top layer. Frost top and sides of cake with remaining whipped cream and garnish with maraschino cherries and shaved chocolate.

Pretzel Torte

- 2½ cups crushed pretzel sticks with
  some salt removed
- ½ cup butter, melted
- ¾ cup sugar
- 2 3-ounce packages cream cheese, softened
- ½ cup confectioners' sugar
- 2 packages nondairy whipped topping, prepared
- 1 21-ounce can cherry pie filling

Mix 2 cups of the crushed pretzels, butter, and sugar together; press into a 9 x 13-inch pan. Bake at 350° for 5 to 10 minutes. Remove from oven and cool. Mix cream cheese with confec-tioners' sugar. Fold whipped topping into cheese mixture and spread on baked crust. Pour cherry pie filling over mixture. Sprinkle the remaining ½ cup pretzel crumbs on top. Refrigerate overnight.

Cherry Squares

- 1 cup sugar
- 1 cup flour
- 1 teaspoon ground cinnamon
- 1 teaspoon baking soda
- 1 egg
- 1 cup chopped nuts
- 3½ cups canned bing cherries, drained, reserve juice
- 2 tablespoons butter, melted

Mix ingredients in order given. Bake in a 9-inch square pan at 325° for 45 minutes. Serve topped with Sauce and a dollop of whipped cream.

Cherry Sauce

- Cherry juice
- ⅓ cup sugar
- 1 tablespoon cornstarch mixed with cold water
- 1 tablespoon butter

Heat cherry juice in a saucepan. Add sugar and cornstarch mixture. Add butter; stir to blend. Cool until thickened.

Carrot Cake with Pineapple

- 3 eggs, lightly beaten
- 2 cups sugar
- 1⅓ cups vegetable oil
- 3 cups flour
- 1 teaspoon salt
- 2 teaspoons baking soda
- 2 teaspoons ground cinnamon
- 2 cups grated carrots
- 1 cup chopped walnuts or pecans
- 1 cup drained, crushed pineapple
- 2 teaspoons vanilla extract

Blend eggs, sugar, and oil. Sift together flour, salt, soda, and cinnamon. Stir in egg mixture, carrots, nuts, pineapple, and vanilla. Pour batter into an ungreased 10-inch tube pan. Bake at 350° for 1 hour and 15 minutes. Cool cake right-side up for 25 minutes; then loosen around sides. Ice with a lemon glaze.

Index

Book III

Christmas Around the World
COOKBOOK

Throughout the world, Christmas is a time of religious observance and traditional feasting. The common denominator of the season everywhere is the lavish preparation of meals to be enjoyed with family and friends.

Quite often the mode of feasting and the dishes served reflect the religious and secular celebrations of a particular people. For instance, the people of Italy, Hungary, Poland, Spain, and Russia observe a religiously inspired meatless Christmas Eve dinner. The next day brings an elaborate Christmas Day feast. The French, after Midnight Mass on Christmas Eve, enjoy a festive supper which includes the log-shaped *Buche de Noel,* or Yule Log. This light cake, filled with custard cream and coated with a chocolate frosting, symbolizes the ancient and secular custom of the lighting of the Yule log.

On Christmas Eve in Poland, the table is covered with a white cloth for good luck and set with extra places for absent family members and a special place for the Christ Child. In a special religious observance, the family partakes of *Oplatki,* small white wafers, which symbolize the Sacred Host.

Because the food and the traditions at Christmastime are as numerous as people on the earth, this cookbook contains only a few of the special dishes of the season. Each chapter presents only one of a country's traditional Christmas or holiday menus. Many of the dishes, because of their popularity, can be prepared in a variety of ways; but the recipes chosen represent what we believe is the most traditional method of preparation.

We wish you pleasure in your holiday preparations and trust that the menus in this book will lend an international flavor to your holidays.

Christmas Day Menu for Six

Oyster Bisque
Roast Prime Rib of Beef
Roast Onions
Yorkshire Pudding
Creamed Spinach with Croutons
Christmas Trifle
Plum Pudding

Oyster Bisque

½ cup butter
1 cup minced celery
¼ cup minced shallots
liquid from 1 quart oysters
5 cups milk
1 cup heavy cream

Melt the butter in a heavy kettle. Add the celery and shallots. Cook, stirring, for 10 minutes over moderately low heat until vegetables are soft. Pour in the strained liquid, milk and cream. Bring the mixture to a simmer.

4 egg yolks
1 cup simmering milk mixture
1 quart shucked oysters
salt and pepper to taste
paprika to taste

Beat the egg yolks lightly in a small bowl. Whisk the hot milk mixture into the egg yolks; stir the milk-egg mixture into the kettle. Add the oysters, salt and pepper. Simmer, stirring, until bisque is lightly thickened, and the edges of the oysters have curled. Do not let the bisque come to a boil. Transfer to a heated tureen and sprinkle with the paprika.

Roast Prime Rib of Beef

1 10-pound beef roast
salt and pepper

Have your butcher trim the short ribs from the roast. Place the meat in a dish and let it come to room temperature. Rub on all sides with salt and pepper. Place the meat on a rack in a shallow roasting pan. Roast in a preheated 450° oven for 25 minutes. Reduce the heat to 325° and roast 2 hours longer for medium-rare. Transfer the roast to a heated platter. Cover loosely and let stand for 15 minutes before carving.

1 cup beef broth
salt and pepper to taste

For the au Jus:
Spoon off any excess fat from the roasting pan. Measure out ½ cup of the beef juices and reserve for the Yorkshire pudding. Pour the beef broth into the roasting pan. Bring to a simmer over moderately high heat, scraping up any brown bits clinging to the bottom and sides of the pan. Season with salt and pepper. Strain the roasting juices into a heated sauceboat and serve with the roast.

Roast Onions

3 tablespoons butter
10 yellow onions, quartered
salt and pepper to taste

Heat the butter in a large, heavy skillet until it is foaming. Add the onion quarters in quantities that fit easily in the pan. Toss the onions over moderate heat until well coated on all sides. Transfer to a shallow baking dish. Sprinkle the onions with salt and pepper. Bake in a preheated 350° oven for 1 hour and 15 minutes, turning the onion every 20 minutes during roasting.

Yorkshire Pudding

Sift together the flour and salt in a large mixing bowl. Add the milk, water and eggs. Beat the mixture until smooth. Cover the bowl and let stand at room temperature for 2 hours.

Pour the beef drippings into a shallow 10 x 15-inch baking dish. Place in a preheated 450° oven 10 minutes. Stir the batter again and pour into the baking dish. Bake 15 minutes. Reduce the heat to 350° and bake 20 to 30 minutes, until the pudding is puffed and golden.

3¾ cups all-purpose flour
1 teaspoon salt
1¼ cups milk
¾ cup water
4 eggs

the ½ cup reserved drippings from the roasting pan

Creamed Spinach with Croutons

Wash the spinach in cold water; drain. Drop into a kettle of boiling, salted water. Return the water to a boil. Cook slowly, uncovered, for 5 minutes. Drain the spinach in a colander. Immediately rinse under cold running water for 1 minute. Squeeze the spinach, a handful at a time, to extract as much water as possible. Chop very fine.

3 pounds fresh spinach
boiling, salted water

Heat the butter until bubbling in a saucepan over moderately high heat. Stir in the spinach. Continue stirring for 2 to 3 minutes until all the moisture has evaporated. Season with salt, pepper and nutmeg. Lower the heat to moderate. Sprinkle on the flour and cook, stirring, for 2 minutes.

2 tablespoons butter
the chopped spinach
salt and pepper to taste
pinch nutmeg
1½ tablespoons flour

Remove the pan from the heat. Add the cream by spoonfuls while stirring until ⅔ cup has been added. Return to the heat and bring to a simmer. Cover and cook very slowly for 15 minutes, stirring occasionally and adding the remaining ⅓ cup cream by spoonfuls.

1 cup heavy cream

Remove the spinach from the heat. Stir in the butter. Transfer the creamed spinach to a deep serving dish and mound it decoratively with a spatula. Garnish the spinach with sieved egg yolks and croutons.

1 tablespoon butter
the sieved yolks from 2 hard-boiled eggs

For the croutons:
Cut decorative shapes out of the bread using a Christmas cookie cutter. Toast the bread shapes under the preheated broiler. Place around the spinach for garnish.

1 or 2 slices of bread

Christmas Trifle

Butter the bottom and sides of the pans. Line with waxed paper. Butter the paper and dust lightly with the flour. Set the pans aside.

softened butter
11 x 16-inch jelly roll pan
8-inch square cake pan
2 tablespoons flour

Beat the egg yolks, sugar and vanilla with an electric mixer until the mixture is light and ribbons when the beater is lifted.

6 egg yolks
½ cup sugar
1 teaspoon vanilla

Beat the egg whites with the salt until they hold stiff peaks. Fold one-fourth of the egg whites into the yolk mixture. Pour the yolk mixture on top of the remaining egg whites and sprinkle on the flour. Fold the mixture together. Pour into the prepared jelly roll pan and 1-inch

6 egg whites
pinch salt
½ cup flour

5

deep into the prepared cake pan. Bake in a preheated 350° oven for 15 minutes or until lightly browned. Invert the cake onto a rack or baking sheet to cool. Peel off the waxed paper.

the cooled cakes
8 ounces raspberry jelly

Split the 11 x 16-inch cake in half crosswise. Spread one half with some of the raspberry jelly. Top with the other half of the cake. Cut the layered cake into triangles.

1½ quart glass serving bowl
12 almond macaroons, crumbled
½ cup brandy

Line the bottom of the bowl with the sandwiched triangles. Line the sides of the bowl with the triangles alternately pointing up, then down, leaving about ⅓ inch between each triangle. Fill the spaces between triangles with the remaining raspberry jelly. Cut the 8-inch square cake into small pieces and sprinkle inside the bowl along with the macaroons. Sprinkle with the brandy.

12 egg yolks
⅓ cup sugar
2 cups scalded milk
2 cups scalded cream
1 tablespoon vanilla

For the custard:
Beat the egg yolks and sugar in a large bowl until the mixture is light and ribbons when the beater is lifted. Pour on the milk and cream in a stream while beating. Transfer the mixture to a heavy saucepan. Cook over low heat, stirring, until thickened. Do not let it boil. Remove from the heat and stir in the vanilla. Pour the hot custard into a metal bowl. Place the bowl in a larger bowl filled with cracked ice. Stir the custard until cool. Pour the cooled custard on top of the crumbled cake and macaroons, filling the bowl to within ¾ inch of the top. Chill, covered, for at least 6 hours.

1 cup whipping cream
2 tablespoons sugar
1 tablespoon brandy
red maraschino cherries, split
angelica leaves
blanched sliced almonds

Beat the cream with the sugar and brandy until it holds stiff peaks. Place in a pastry bag fitted with a fluted tip and pipe the whipped cream over the edges of the cake sandwiches. Pipe a large rosette in the center of the custard. Decorate the trifle with the cherries and angelica leaves. Sprinkle with the almonds and serve.

Plum Pudding

1 cup seedless raisins
1 cup dried currants
¼ pound mixed candied fruit peel, diced
2½ cups beef suet, diced
2 cups flour
1 cup brown sugar
1 teaspoon each ground cloves, cinnamon and nutmeg
¼ teaspoon salt
grated rind from 1 lemon
2 large eggs
1 cup light cream
¼ cup brandy

In a deep mixing bowl combine the raisins, currants, candied fruit peel, beef suet, flour, brown sugar, spices, salt and lemon rind. Blend the ingredients thoroughly.

In another bowl beat the eggs with the cream and brandy. Pour over the dried fruit mixture and blend well. Cover the bowl and let stand in a cool place for 12 hours.

Transfer to a large pudding mold. Cover tightly with waxed paper and foil. Place in a deep pan. Add enough boiling water to reach ⅓ the way up the side of the mold. Cover the pan and steam for 4½ hours, adding more water as necessary. When cooked, remove from the water and let stand until cooled. Cover with fresh waxed paper and foil. Refrigerate for 2 weeks for best flavor.

2 tablespoons heated brandy
whipped cream

To serve the pudding, steam a second time for 2 hours. Turn the pudding onto a heated serving plate. Pour on the hot brandy and light. Serve with whipped cream.

*Irish Soda Bread
Consommé with Celery
Roast Turkey
    with Chestnut and Sausage Stuffing
Creamed Brussels Sprouts
Mincemeat Pie*

Irish Soda Bread

3 cups whole wheat flour
1 cup all-purpose flour
2 teaspoons salt
1 teaspoon baking soda
¾ teaspoon baking powder
1½ cups, or more, buttermilk

Combine the flours, salt, baking soda and baking powder in a bowl. Mix thoroughly. Add the buttermilk, working with your hands to make a dough firm enough to hold its shape. Add more buttermilk if necessary. Knead the dough on a lightly floured board for 2 to 3 minutes. The texture should be smooth and velvety. Form into a round loaf. Place on a well-buttered baking sheet. Cut a cross into the top of the loaf with a knife. Bake in a preheated 375° oven for 35 to 40 minutes. The loaf is done when it is browned and has a hollow sound when tapped. Cool on a wire rack.

Consommé with Celery

4 pounds meaty beef shanks
2 onions, quartered
1 carrot, quartered
3½ quarts water
2 cups water
2 celery ribs
1½ teaspoons salt
4 sprigs parsley
1 bay leaf
⅛ teaspoon thyme

Have your butcher saw the beef shanks into 1-inch pieces. Spread the shanks, onion and carrot in a large baking pan. Brown in a preheated 450° oven for 20 minutes, turning once. Transfer the meat and vegetables to a kettle, adding the 3½ quarts water. Pour the 2 cups water into the baking pan; bring to a boil, scraping up any bits of meat or vegetables clinging to the bottom. Pour the liquid into the kettle. Add the celery, salt, parsley, bay leaf and thyme. Bring to a boil, skimming away any froth that rises to the surface. Simmer gently, uncovered, for 3 hours. Add boiling water, if necessary, to keep the ingredients covered.

1 5- to 7-pound stewing hen, halved
neck, heart and gizzard of hen, chopped

Add the hen, neck, heart and gizzard to the beef stock. Add boiling water to cover. Skim away any froth that rises to the surface. Simmer, uncovered, for 2 to 3 hours or until liquid is reduced to 2 quarts. Remove the hen. Strain the stock and let cool. Chill until the fat solidifies on the surface. Scrape away the fat. Bring the stock to a simmer.

3 tablespoons butter
1½ cups chopped celery ribs and leaves
½ cup chopped leek
½ cup minced celery leaves
salt and pepper to taste

Melt the butter in a kettle. Add the chopped celery and leek. Cover and let the vegetables steam for 20 minutes. Add the beef stock and simmer, uncovered, for 30 minutes. Strain. Salt and pepper to taste. Garnish the consommé with the minced celery leaves.

Roast Turkey with Chestnut and Sausage Stuffing

1 10- to 12-pound turkey
salt and pepper

Wash the turkey under cold water. Pat dry. Lightly salt and pepper inside and outside of the bird. Set aside.

Ireland

8

For the stuffing:

Set the chestnuts in a pan and cover with cold water. Boil for 1 minute. Remove from heat. Remove 3 chestnuts at a time from the hot water. Peel and remove inner skins. Place the chestnuts in a saucepan. Add the bouillon and water to cover the nuts by 1½ inches. Add the celery, parsley and bay leaf. Simmer, uncovered, for 45 to 60 minutes or until the chestnuts are cooked through. Drain.

1½ pounds fresh chestnuts
1 cup beef bouillon
1 celery rib
2 sprigs parsley
½ bay leaf

Heat the butter in a skillet. Add the onion. Cook for 8 to 10 minutes until soft. Transfer the onion to a mixing bowl. Put the turkey liver in the skillet. Sauté until just browned. Add to the onion. Pour the wine into the skillet. Boil until the wine is reduced to ¼ cup. Add to the onion. Add the pork, veal, pork fat, eggs, salt, thyme, pepper and allspice to the onion. Stir with a wooden spoon until thoroughly blended.

2 tablespoons butter
½ cup chopped onion
the turkey liver, minced
½ cup port or Madeira wine
¾ pound ground pork
¾ pound ground veal
½ pound ground pork fat
2 eggs, beaten
1½ teaspoons salt
½ teaspoon thyme
pinch each pepper and allspice

Stuff the turkey neck and body cavities loosely with alternate layers of the meat mixture and chestnuts. Close the cavities with skewers and lace with kitchen string. Truss the bird securely with kitchen string.

Brush the turkey generously with the butter. Fold the cheesecloth in half crosswise forming a square. Dip the cheesecloth into the remaining melted butter and lay over the turkey breast. Set the turkey on a rack in a shallow roasting pan. Roast in a preheated 325° oven, basting occasionally. A 10- to 12-pound stuffed turkey will take about 4 to 4½ hours to roast. To test for doneness, pierce a thigh with a fork. Juices should run clear yellow.

1 cup butter, melted
8 x 16-inch piece of
   cheesecloth
wire rack
shallow roasting pan

For the gravy:

Prepare the gravy while the turkey is roasting. Heat the oil in a large saucepan. Stir in the giblets. Brown on all sides and transfer to a side dish. Put the onion and carrots in the pan. Cover and cook slowly for 5 minutes. Uncover and brown lightly for 5 minutes. Add the browned giblets, wine, chicken stock, bay leaf and thyme. Add water to cover the ingredients by 1 inch. Simmer, partially covered, for 2½ to 3 hours. Strain the stock. Skim the fat from the surface. Blend the cornstarch and wine in a bowl. Stir into the stock. Simmer for 2 to 3 minutes until just thickened. Set aside.

3 tablespoons vegetable oil
the turkey giblets, chopped
1 onion, chopped
2 carrots, chopped
1 cup dry white wine
2 cups chicken stock
1 bay leaf
½ teaspoon thyme
3 tablespoons cornstarch
¼ cup port wine

Transfer the turkey to a heated platter when it is done. Remove the strings and skewers, cover loosely and let stand for 20 to 30 minutes. Scoop the stuffing into a warm dish when ready to serve. Spoon excess fat from the roasting pan. Pour the turkey stock into the roasting pan. Stir over moderately high heat, scraping up the turkey bits from the bottom. Skim any fat from the surface of the gravy. Pour into a warm sauceboat and serve with the turkey and stuffing.

the turkey stock

Creamed Brussels Sprouts

Cut a cross in the base of each sprout. Drop into boiling salted water. Boil slowly, uncovered, for 6 to 8 minutes. Drain. Lay the sprouts in one layer on a towel to cool.

1½ quarts Brussels sprouts

Butter a shallow baking dish. Arrange the sprouts in two layers in the dish. Sprinkle lightly with salt, pepper and melted butter. Set over moderate heat, cover and cook until the sprouts begin to sizzle. Transfer to a preheated 350° oven for 10 minutes.

the blanched sprouts
salt and pepper
2 tablespoons butter, melted

Bring the cream to a boil. Pour boiling cream into the dish and continue to bake for 10 minutes more. Dot the sprouts with butter and serve.

¾ cup heavy cream
2 tablespoons butter

Mincemeat Pie

For the filling:
Core the apple but do not peel. Mince the apple, raisins, currants, sultana raisins, candied fruit peel and almonds. Combine in a large mixing bowl.

1 large apple
2 cups raisins
2 cups currants
1 cup sultana raisins
½ cup candied fruit peel
½ cup almonds

Combine the orange and lemon rind, sugar, salt, cinnamon, allspice and cloves in a small bowl. Stir with a fork to blend thoroughly. Sprinkle in the minced fruit and almonds. Blend with a fork.

grated rind from 1 orange
grated rind from 1 lemon
1 cup sugar
¼ teaspoon each salt, ground
    cloves, cinnamon and allspice

Combine the orange juice, lemon juice and whiskey in a cup. Pour over the minced fruit mixture. Pour the butter over the ingredients and blend. Pour the filling into a glass jar, cover tightly and refrigerate overnight.

juice of 1 orange
juice of 1 lemon
¼ cup Irish whiskey
½ cup butter, melted

For the pastry crust:
Combine the flour, salt, and sugar in a bowl. Cut in the butter and shortening. Mix with a pastry blender until the mixture resembles coarse meal. Add the water to the dough, a little at a time, while gathering the dough into a ball. Wrap with waxed paper and refrigerate for 2 hours.

2 cups all-purpose flour
½ teaspoon salt
¼ teaspoon sugar
¼ pound chilled butter, cut
    into ½-inch pieces
3 tablespoons chilled
    shortening
3 tablespoons, or more, cold
    water

Assembling the pie:
Roll out the dough ⅛ inch thick on a lightly floured surface and line a 9-inch pie pan allowing a 1-inch overhang. Cover and chill.

Roll the remaining dough into a rectangle ¼ inch thick and 12 inches long. Cut the dough into ½-inch wide strips. Fill the shell with the mincemeat. Lay the strips of dough over the pie in a lattice pattern. Turn up the edges and crimp decoratively. Bake in a preheated 425° oven for 20 minutes. Reduce heat to 350° and bake for 30 minutes until golden.

Christmas Day Menu for Six

Christmas Punch
Cheese Pastries
Pea Soup with Champagne
Roast Goose
Apple Halves Stuffed with Prunes
Sugar-Browned Potatoes
Rice and Almond Pudding
Vanilla Wreaths

Christmas Punch

rind of ½ lemon
2¼ pints dry red wine
1 cinnamon stick
3 cloves
8 cardamom seeds
½ cup sugar
½ cup chopped almonds
½ cup seedless raisins
1 cup Cognac

Shave the outermost yellow peel from the lemon with a vegetable peeler. Cut the peel into ⅛-inch strips. Combine the sliced lemon rind, red wine, cinnamon stick, cloves, cardamom seeds, sugar, almonds and raisins in a large saucepan. Stir over low heat until the sugar is dissolved. Just before it reaches a boil, transfer to a serving bowl. Add the Cognac just before serving. Light it with a match and ladle into punch cups.

Cheese Pastries

⅔ cup softened butter
1⅔ cups grated Gruyére cheese
2 cups all-purpose flour
1½ teaspoons salt
1 teaspoon paprika
½ teaspoon baking powder
½ cup heavy cream

Blend the butter and cheese in a bowl. Combine the flour, salt, paprika and baking powder in another bowl. Blend well with a fork. Add the flour mixture and heavy cream alternately to the butter and cheese mixture. Blend until a soft dough forms. Form into a ball. Wrap in waxed paper; chill for 1 hour.

1 egg yolk
2 tablespoons water
sliced blanched almonds
poppy seed

Roll out the dough ⅛-inch thick on a lightly floured work surface. Cut with decorative Christmas cookie cutters. Put the cut-out shapes on a lightly buttered baking sheet. Combine the egg yolk and water in a small bowl; brush on the pastries. Sprinkle half the pastries with the almonds. Sprinkle the other half with the poppy seed. Bake the pastries in a preheated 375° oven for 12 minutes until puffed and golden. Serve warm with the soup course.

Pea Soup with Champagne

3 cups shelled fresh peas or
20 ounces frozen peas
1 carrot
1 medium onion, quartered
¾-ounce slab bacon rind
1 small bay leaf
pinch each sage, chervil and thyme

Combine the peas, carrot, onion, bacon rind, bay leaf, sage, chervil and thyme in a saucepan. Cover with cold water. Bring to a boil. Reduce heat and simmer, covered, for 15 minutes, until the peas are soft. Remove from heat. Discard the carrot, onion, bacon rind and bay leaf. Press the peas and their liquid through a sieve into a bowl.

Return the puree to the pan. Stir in the chicken stock, sherry, lemon juice, salt and pepper to taste. Bring to a boil, stirring.

3 cups chicken bouillon
⅓ cup dry sherry
lemon juice
salt and pepper

Beat the cream until it forms stiff peaks. Fold into the pea mixture. Pour in the champagne. Ladle the soup into heated bowls and serve.

¾ cup heavy cream
1 split bottle of champagne, at room temperature

Roast Goose Stuffed with Apples and Prunes

In a small bowl, soak the prunes in hot water to cover for 5 minutes. Pit and chop the prunes.

2 cups dried prunes
hot water

Wash the goose under cold running water; pat dry with a towel. Rub the bird inside and out with the lemon. Lightly salt and pepper the inside and stuff the cavity with the apples, prunes and onion quarters. Close the opening of the bird with skewers and lace with kitchen string. With a skewer, close the neck opening. Truss the bird securely with kitchen string. With a fork, prick the skin around the thighs, back and lower breast so the fat will drain during roasting. Place the goose, breast side up, in the roasting pan and set in the middle of a preheated 425° oven for 15 minutes, to brown lightly. Reduce oven to 350° and turn the goose on one side. Remove fat occasionally with a bulb baster during roasting. Baste every 15 to 20 minutes with boiling water to help dissolve the fat. After 1 hour, turn the goose on the other side. An 8-pound stuffed goose will take about 2 hours and 20 minutes; a 10-pound stuffed bird will take about 25 minutes longer. Fifteen minutes before the end of the estimated roasting time, salt the goose and turn breast side up. To test whether the bird is done, pierce the thigh with a small knife. If the juice is rosy-colored, roast another 5 to 10 minutes, or until the juice runs clear yellow. When done, discard trussing string and skewers. Scoop out the apples, prunes and onions; discard. (They will have accumulated fat from the goose, but they will have imparted their flavor to the meat.) Set bird on a heated platter, covered, for 15 minutes before carving.

1 8- to 10-pound young goose
½ lemon
salt and pepper
2 cups peeled, cored and chopped apples
the chopped prunes
1 large onion, peeled and quartered
skewers
kitchen string

Apple Halves Stuffed with Prunes

Combine the wine and sugar in a small saucepan. Bring to a simmer; stir to dissolve the sugar. Add the prunes and simmer, very gently, for 20 minutes or until prunes are just tender. Remove from heat and cool. Cover and refrigerate for 6 hours.

⅔ cup port wine
2 teaspoons sugar
12 medium prunes

Core and peel the apples; cut them in half, lengthwise. In a 2- to 3-quart saucepan, combine the sugar and water and boil for 2 to 3 minutes. Lower the heat and add 6 apple halves. Simmer for 10 minutes until just tender. Remove the apples from the saucepan and keep warm. Poach the remaining 6 apple halves.

6 large baking apples
1 cup sugar
1 quart cold water

13

Drain the prunes and place 1 prune in each apple half. These may be prepared in advance and covered with plastic wrap. Refrigerate until 10 minutes before serving time. Preheat oven to 400°. Uncover prune-filled apples and place on a lightly buttered cookie sheet. Bake 10 minutes. Surround the goose with the stuffed apples.

Sugar-Browned Potatoes

Drop the potatoes into the boiling water and cook 15 to 20 minutes or until tender. Drain off the hot water. Cover the potatoes with cold water and let them set until cool enough to handle, but still warm. Peel the potatoes.

24 small new potatoes
2½ quarts boiling water

Melt the sugar in a heavy skillet over low heat for 3 to 5 minutes. Stir constantly with a wooden spoon. The sugar will turn color very rapidly and will burn easily. The sugar should turn a light brown. Stir in the melted butter and blend until smooth. Add as many potatoes as can easily fit into one layer. Shake the pan constantly to coat the potatoes. Remove the potatoes as they are coated and repeat the same process until all the potatoes are coated.

½ cup sugar
½ cup butter, melted

Rice and Almond Pudding

Bring the milk to a boil in a heavy saucepan. Add the rice and sugar. Stir to blend. Lower the heat and simmer gently, uncovered, for 25 minutes or until the rice is tender. To test the rice, rub a grain between your thumb and forefinger. If there is no hard kernel in the center, the rice is done. Remove from the heat and cool.

3¾ cups milk
1 cup long grain white rice
⅓ cup sugar
½ cup blanched almonds, chopped
½ cup sweet sherry
1 teaspoon vanilla
¼ teaspoon grated orange rind
pinch nutmeg

When the rice is cool stir in the chopped almonds, sherry, vanilla, grated orange rind and nutmeg.

Vanilla Wreaths

Beat the cream until it holds a peak in a chilled bowl. Fold into the rice mixture. Pour the pudding into a large serving bowl or divide among serving glasses. Chill well before serving.

1 cup heavy cream

Vanilla Wreaths

Sift together the flour, sugar, baking powder and salt in a large mixing bowl. Cut the butter into ½-inch pieces and distribute over the flour mixture. Blend the mixture with a pastry blender until it resembles coarse meal. Sprinkle the ground almonds and vanilla over the mixture. Continue to blend until a dough forms. Wrap in waxed paper and chill for 30 minutes.

1¼ cups all-purpose flour
¾ cup sugar
⅛ teaspoon baking powder
pinch salt
½ cup plus 2 tablespoons chilled butter
⅓ cup blanched almonds, ground
½ teaspoon vanilla

Fill a metal cookie press fitted with a ½-inch star plate with the dough. Press 2-inch strips ½ inch apart onto a lightly greased baking sheet. Form each strip into a round, pressing the ends together. Chill the unbaked cookies 15 minutes. Bake in a preheated 375° oven for 8 minutes or until golden. Transfer the cookies to racks and let them cool. Makes about 60 cookies.

Roast Goose, Apple Halves
Stuffed with Prunes, Christmas Punch

Oysters on the Half Shell
Paté with Pistachios
Shrimp Soup with Curry
Chicken Bonne Femme
Buche de Noel

Oysters on the Half Shell

36 fresh oysters
rock salt
lemon wedges

Scrub the shells under cold water. Force a shucking knife between the shell at the thin end and cut the abductor muscle. Remove the top shell with a twisting motion. Cover 6 serving plates with the rock salt. Arrange 6 oysters on each. Garnish with lemon.

Paté with Pistachios

1 pound diced pork
1 pound diced veal
1 cup diced pork fat
1 small chicken breast, diced
3 chicken livers

Place the uncooked pork, veal, pork fat, chicken breast and chicken livers in a food processor and grind together. Or put each ingredient through a meat grinder and blend together in a large bowl.

3 tablespoons butter
¾ cup chopped onion
4 cloves garlic, minced

Heat the butter until foaming in a heavy skillet. Add the onion and garlic. Sauté 3 minutes until soft. Add to the meat mixture.

½ cup Madeira or dry sherry
¼ cup Cognac

Pour the Madeira and Cognac into the skillet. Boil until reduced to ⅓ cup. Add to the meat mixture.

3 eggs, lightly beaten
½ cup pistachio nuts
1½ teaspoons salt
½ teaspoon ground pepper
½ bay leaf, crumbled
pinch each ground cloves,
sage, ginger, nutmeg, mace,
cinnamon, paprika, thyme,
basil, marjoram, oregano
an 8-cup terrine
4 or 5 sheets fresh pork fat,
cut ⅛ inch thick

Add the eggs, pistachio nuts, salt and pepper to the meat mixture. Add a pinch each of herbs and spices. Stir to blend ingredients thoroughly.

Line an 8-cup terrine with the fat; allow the fat to hang over the sides. Fill with the meat mixture, pressing firmly. Fold fat over the meat to enclose. Wrap the terrine in foil. Place in a baking pan filled with boiling water. Bake 1½ hours in a preheated 350° oven. Remove the terrine from the water. Set on a wire rack. Place a weight on top and let stand 2 hours. Refrigerate overnight.

Shrimp Soup with Curry

1 pound fish trimmings
2 cups cold water
1½ cups clam juice
1 cup dry white wine
1 onion, sliced
1 teaspoon lemon juice
5 parsley stems

Place the fish trimmings in a large kettle. Add the water, clam juice, white wine, sliced onion, lemon juice and parsley stems. Bring slowly to a simmer. Skim off any fat that rises to the surface. Simmer gently, uncovered, for 30 minutes. Strain through a sieve. Return the fish stock to the saucepan and simmer slowly until ready to use.

3 tablespoons butter
½ cup chopped onion
2 garlic cloves, minced
3 tablespoons flour
1 tablespoon curry powder

Heat the butter in a heavy skillet. Sauté the onion and garlic 5 minutes. Add the flour and curry powder. Cook, stirring constantly, 2 minutes. Remove from the heat. Whisk in the simmering fish stock. Beat until smooth. Return to the heat. Simmer for 5 minutes.

France

Drain the tomatoes, reserving liquid. Chop and add to the soup. Add tomato liquid, carrots, potato and allspice. Bring to a boil. Reduce heat and simmer, uncovered, for 12 to 15 minutes. Potatoes should be just tender.

Cut the fish into 2 x ½-inch strips. Add to the soup along with the shrimp. Simmer 3 minutes. Stir in the cream. Add salt and pepper to taste. Stir until heated through. Do not allow to boil. Garnish the soup with lemon slices and fresh minced parsley.

8-ounces pear-shaped tomatoes
2 carrots, chopped
1 potato, peeled and diced
pinch allspice

1 pound fish fillets
12 large shrimp, halved
½ cup heavy cream
salt and pepper to taste
lemon slices
fresh parsley, minced

Chicken Bonne Femme

Rinse the chickens under cold running water. Pat dry inside and out with a towel. Salt the outside and inside of the birds lightly. Set aside.

2 2½- to 3-pound frying
  chickens
salt

Heat the butter until foaming in a large, heavy-bottomed skillet. Add the onion and garlic. Sauté for 2 minutes.

Cut the potatoes, carrots and zucchini into ¼-inch cubes and add to the skillet. Sauté 2 minutes. Stir in the parsley, salt and pepper.

Spoon the stuffing into the neck and body cavities of the birds. Close the cavities with skewers. With kitchen string, truss the birds so they hold their shape while roasting. Place breast side up in a shallow roasting pan. Spread 1 tablespoon of the butter over each chicken. Set in a preheated 425° oven 15 minutes to brown.

4 tablespoons butter
1 large onion, finely chopped
2 cloves garlic, minced
2 medium potatoes, peeled
3 carrots, peeled
2 medium zucchini
½ cup minced fresh parsley
salt and pepper to taste
2 tablespoons softened butter
4 strips of bacon
1 cup dry white wine

Remove chickens from the oven and lay 2 strips of bacon over each. Pour the wine into the pan. Reduce heat to 350° and roast, uncovered, 1¼ hours, basting every 20 minutes. The chickens are done when juices are clear yellow when the thigh is pierced with a fork. Remove to a heated platter. Skim the fat from the pan. Reserve the pan juices.

For the sauce:
Melt the butter in a saucepan. Stir in the flour. Cook, stirring constantly, 3 minutes. Stir in the pan juices with a wire whisk. Heat to a simmer. Whisk in cream. Cook, stirring, until the mixture thickens. Simmer for 1 minute.

2 tablespoons butter
1½ tablespoons flour
the pan juices
1 cup heavy cream

Whisk a small amount of the sauce at a time into egg yolks until ¼ cup has been added. Whisk the egg yolks back into the sauce. Stir over low heat 2 to 3 minutes. Remove from heat. Add salt and white pepper to taste.

2 egg yolks
salt and white pepper

To serve the chicken:
Remove the stuffing from the birds. Mound around the chickens on the platter. Pour some sauce over the birds. Serve the remaining sauce in a sauceboat.

Buche de Noel (Yule Log Cake)

Place the eggs, egg yolk, sugar and vanilla in a mixing bowl. Place the bowl over a pan of simmering water for a few seconds. Remove from the heat and beat on high speed for 5 to 6 minutes. Sift on the flour and fold in with a rubber spatula. Then pour on the butter in a stream and fold into the batter.

5 large eggs
1 egg yolk
¾ cup sugar
½ teaspoon vanilla
¾ cup all-purpose flour
3 tablespoons melted butter

17

12 by 16-inch jelly roll pan **waxed paper** **butter** **flour**	Lightly butter the pan and line with a sheet of waxed paper. Butter the waxed paper and dust lightly with the flour. Pour the batter into the pan, spreading it evenly out to the sides. Bake in a preheated 325° oven for 12 minutes. Let the cake set for 5 minutes before unmolding. Lay a piece of waxed paper on the table; turn the cake out on the paper. Remove the waxed paper which covered the bottom of the cake, then cover the cake loosely with it. Let the cake cool to lukewarm. Starting at one of the long sides, roll the cake between the two sheets of waxed paper. Refrigerate until ready to use.
3 egg yolks **⅓ cup sugar** **½ teaspoon vanilla extract** **¼ cup flour** **1 cup boiling milk** **½ cup heavy cream**	Place the egg yolks, sugar and vanilla in a bowl. Beat until light and mixture ribbons when the beater is lifted. Add the flour and blend together. Add the milk in a stream, stirring with a wire whisk. Transfer the mixture to a saucepan set over moderate heat; stir constantly until the sauce reaches a boil. Reduce heat and cook, stirring, for 2 to 3 minutes longer. Remove from the heat. Cover and cool to room temperature. Whip the cream until it holds stiff peaks. Fold the whipped cream into the custard. Set aside.
3 ounces semisweet chocolate **2 ounces bittersweet chocolate**	Place the chocolate in a small bowl. Cover and set in a pan of barely simmering water until melted.
⅓ cup sugar **¼ cup water**	Combine the sugar and water in a saucepan. Boil until the syrup reaches the softball stage (236° to 238° on a candy thermometer).
3 egg yolks **the sugar syrup** **½ pound unsalted butter,** **softened** **the melted chocolate**	Place the egg yolks in a mixing bowl and begin beating with an electric mixer. Pour the hot sugar syrup over the yolks a few drops at a time while beating at medium speed. Increase speed to high and beat for 5 minutes, until mixture is thick and pale yellow. Reduce speed to low and add the butter, a little at a time. Beat until the mixture is smooth. Place ¼ cup of the buttercream in a small bowl; set aside. Add the melted chocolate to the remaining buttercream and beat until smooth. Set aside.
the cake roll **the custard-cream**	Unroll the cake. Remove the waxed paper on top. Spread the custard-cream over the cake. Roll the cake up to form a log, removing the waxed paper. Cut a 2-inch diagonal piece from both ends of the cake. Transfer the cake to a platter. Arrange the pieces against the sides of the cake to form branch stumps.
the chocolate buttercream **the ¼ cup reserved buttercream** **glacéed cherries** **candied angelica or holly**	Using a spatula, spread the chocolate buttercream on the log, reserving ¼ cup for piping. Spread the reserved buttercream over both ends and on tops of the stumps. Pull the tines of a fork down the full length of the cake roll to simulate bark. Fill a pastry bag with the ¼ cup chocolate buttercream. Pipe rings around both ends of the cake and on the ends of the stumps to simulate wood. Decorate the cake with glacéed cherries and candied angelica, cut to look like holly leaves.

18

Buche de Noel (Yule Log Cake)

Potato and Cucumber Soup
Knockwurst Salad
Red Cabbage
Spaetzle   Carrots in Beer
Sauerbraten with Gingersnap Gravy
Pumpernickel Pudding   Filbert Balls

Potato and Cucumber Soup

2 medium cucumbers, peeled

6 boiling potatoes, peeled and quartered
5 cups chicken bouillon

2 tablespoons butter
1 small onion, minced
the chicken and potato stock
2 cups heavy cream
salt and pepper to taste
2 teaspoons dried dillweed

Slice the cucumbers lengthwise. Scoop out the seeds with a small spoon. Dice and set aside.

Combine the potatoes and bouillon in a kettle. Simmer, partially covered, and cook until the potatoes are tender. Press the stock and potatoes through a sieve into a bowl.

Melt the butter in a kettle. Add the onion and sauté for 5 minutes. Add the chicken and potato stock. Stir in the cream, salt, pepper and cucumbers.

Simmer 6 to 8 minutes until the cucumber is tender. Stir in the dillweed and serve.

Knockwurst Salad

¾ pound knockwurst, cooked
6 tablespoons chopped pickles
½ cup chopped onion

3 tablespoons vegetable oil
3 tablespoons vinegar
1 tablespoon lemon juice
2 tablespoons capers
1½ teaspoons Dijon mustard
½ teaspoon sugar
½ teaspoon salt
pinch paprika
pinch pepper
2 tablespoons chopped parsley

Cool the knockwurst and cut into ½-inch cubes. Combine the knockwurst, pickles and onion in a mixing bowl. Cover and refrigerate for 1 hour.

Combine the vegetable oil, vinegar, lemon juice, capers, mustard, sugar, salt, paprika and pepper in a glass jar. Cover the jar and shake well. Refrigerate for an hour and let set at room temperature for 15 minutes before serving.

Arrange the knockwurst mixture in a shallow salad bowl. Shake the dressing again before pouring onto salad. Garnish with chopped fresh parsley.

Red Cabbage

1 medium head red cabbage
2 tablespoons vegetable oil
1 cup sliced onion
2 tablespoons vinegar
salt to taste
2 teaspoons sugar
2 tart red cooking apples, peeled, cored and sliced
3 slices bacon
½ cup red wine
½ cup beef broth

Remove the outer leaves from the cabbage and discard. Cut cabbage into quarters and cut out core. Shred cabbage. Heat oil in a large skillet and sauté onion for 3 minutes. Add cabbage and immediately pour vinegar over cabbage to prevent it from losing color. Sprinkle with salt and sugar, tossing to coat cabbage.

Cut the bacon into ½-inch pieces. Add apples and bacon. Pour in red wine and beef broth. Cover and simmer slowly for 45 to 60 minutes until cabbage is just tender but not soft.

Germany

Spaetzle

Combine flour, salt and nutmeg in mixing bowl. Make a well in the center and add the eggs and ¼ cup of the water. Beat until a stiff dough forms. Add water, a little at a time, until dough is firm and comes away from the sides of the bowl easily. Knead until smooth. Let stand in the bowl 30 minutes.

Place the dough in the colander, set over a kettle holding the boiling water. Press dough through the colander. Cook about 5 minutes or until noodles rise to the surface. Remove promptly with a slotted spoon and drain on a towel. Brown noodles in melted butter over low heat. Serve immediately.

3 cups sifted all-purpose flour
1 teaspoon salt
pinch nutmeg
4 eggs, beaten
½ cup, or more, water

colander with ¼-inch holes
2½ quarts boiling salted water
3 tablespoons butter

Carrots in Beer

Peel the carrots. Cut into long diagonal slices. Heat the butter in a heavy saucepan. Add the carrots, stirring until they are coated with butter. Sprinkle in the sugar and salt. Pour in the beer. Lower the heat and simmer, uncovered, until the carrots are tender. Serve immediately.

8 large carrots
2 tablespoons butter
2 teaspoons sugar
½ teaspoon salt
1½ cups dark beer or lager

Sauerbraten

Place meat in a large glass bowl. Rub the meat with the salt and pepper. Cover and let come to room temperature. Bring water, vinegar, wine, onion, cloves and bay leaves to a boil in a saucepan. Simmer for 10 minutes. Cool marinade to room temperature. Pour over beef and refrigerate for 2 to 3 days turning meat several times a day.

1 4-pound beef rump roast
1 teaspoon each salt and pepper
2 cups water
1 cup red wine vinegar
1 cup dry red wine
2 cups sliced onion
8 cloves
2 bay leaves

Heat the vegetable oil in a Dutch oven or ovenproof casserole. Add the meat and brown on all sides. Add the tomato, carrots, celery and marinade liquid. Cover and simmer gently for 1½ to 2 hours. Or bring to a simmer on top of the stove, cover and bake in a preheated 325° oven for 1½ to 2 hours.

2 tablespoons vegetable oil
1 medium tomato, peeled, seeded and chopped
1 cup diced carrots
1 cup diced celery

When the meat has finished cooking, remove it from the marinade. Cover the meat and keep warm while preparing the gravy. Remove cloves and bay leaves from marinade. Blend together flour, crushed gingersnaps, sugar and the ¼ cup marinade in a small bowl to make a thick paste. Add to the remaining marinade in the Dutch oven and cook, stirring, until thickened. Spoon some of the gravy over meat. Serve remaining gravy in a sauceboat.

2 tablespoons flour
¼ cup crushed gingersnaps
2 teaspoons sugar
¼ cup marinade

Pumpernickel Pudding

Butter the mold and coat it well with the bread crumbs. Set aside.

Soak the raisins in the orange liqueur for 30 minutes in a small bowl.

8-cup pudding mold
softened butter
dry bread crumbs

⅓ cup golden raisins
⅓ cup orange liqueur

3 cups fine, pumpernickel
bread crumbs
1 cup brown sugar
⅔ cup ground almonds
⅔ cup ground vanilla wafers
½ cup plus 3 tablespoons
melted butter
1 teaspoon grated orange rind
1 teaspoon grated lemon rind

Combine the pumpernickel crumbs, brown sugar, ground almonds and vanilla wafer crumbs in a large mixing bowl. Stir with a fork to press any lumps out of the sugar; blend thoroughly. Add the raisin mixture, grated orange rind and grated lemon rind. Blend with a fork. Stir in the melted butter. Cover the mixture and let stand for 3 hours.

3 eggs
2 egg yolks

Beat the eggs and egg yolks until they are thick and lemon-colored. Stir into the pumpernickel mixture.

4 egg whites
pinch cream of tartar
pinch salt

Beat the egg whites with the cream of tartar and salt until they hold stiff peaks. Stir one-fourth of the whites into the pumpernickel mixture, and fold in the remaining whites.

1 cup heavy cream

Beat the cream in a chilled bowl until it holds stiff peaks. Fold the whipped cream into the pumpernickel mixture. Spoon the batter into the mold and cover with foil or a lid. Place on a rack in a deep kettle. Add enough boiling water to reach three-fourths of the way up the mold. Cover the kettle and steam the pudding, keeping the water at a boil, for 1½ hours. Add water as necessary to keep it at the same level.

sweetened whipped cream

Remove the mold from the kettle and let stand for 5 minutes. Place a heated platter over the mold and turn the pudding right side up onto the platter. Serve with sweetened whipped cream.

Filbert Balls

1¾-ounces semisweet chocolate

Melt the chocolate in the top of a double boiler. Remove from heat and stir to cool.

¼ cup plus 2 tablespoons
butter, softened
½ cup confectioners' sugar
the melted chocolate
½ cup plus 2 tablespoons
filberts, ground

Beat the butter and sugar in a mixing bowl until the mixture is fluffy. Stir in the chocolate and beat until creamy and smooth. Stir in the ground filberts. Form the mixture into a ball. Wrap in waxed paper and chill for 30 minutes.

Pinch off a teaspoonful of dough at a time, rolling it into a ball. Arrange the balls on a lightly greased and floured baking sheet. Bake in a preheated 300° oven for 8 minutes or until the balls have lost their gloss. Let cool on a baking sheet before serving. Makes about 30 balls.

Christmas Eve Menu for Six

Almond Soup
Avocado and Tomato Salad
Seafood Canalones with Parmesan Sauce
Baked Sea Bream
Turrón

Almond Soup

1 3-pound stewing hen or parts
1 medium onion, quartered
2 celery ribs, sliced
2 carrots, sliced
1 clove garlic, crushed
2 tomatoes, quartered
½ green pepper, sliced
2 bay leaves
1 tablespoon salt
pinch saffron

For the chicken broth:
Place the whole hen or parts in a large kettle. Cover with 3 quarts cold water. Add the remaining ingredients. Be sure water covers the ingredients by a full inch. Bring to a simmer. Skim the surface as necessary. Lower the heat and simmer gently, partially covered, for 3 to 4 hours, adding more water if necessary. Remove stewing hen and reserve for another use. Strain the broth through a colander, pressing the vegetables with a wooden spoon to extract juices. Allow the broth to cool. Skim the fat from the surface. Pour 1½ quarts broth into a clean, 2½-quart kettle and bring to a simmer.

¼ cup butter
¼ cup chopped almonds
¼ cup flour
2 cups hot chicken broth

Melt the butter in a heavy skillet. Add the almonds, stirring frequently. Allow the almonds to brown lightly. Add the flour. Stir constantly for 2 minutes. Remove from the heat and add the hot broth. Beat with a wire whisk until smooth. Add the mixture to the remaining chicken broth. Cook, stirring, over moderate heat until the broth thickens. Simmer for 10 minutes more.

½ cup heavy cream
½ cup milk
the stewing hen breast meat
¼ cup chopped pimientos
2 tablespoons chopped chives
2 tablespoons dry sherry

Stir the cream and milk into the broth mixture. Finely dice the breast meat and add to the broth. Add the pimientos and chives. Simmer ten minutes longer, stirring occasionally. Before serving, add the sherry and stir. Remove from heat immediately and serve.

Avocado and Tomato Salad

2 firm, ripe avocados
lime juice
3 tomatoes

Cut the avocados in half and remove the pits. Peel and cut into slices. Place the slices in a deep plate; sprinkle with the lime juice. Wash and slice the tomatoes into wedges.

3 tablespoons olive oil
2 tablespoons wine vinegar
1 tablespoon lime juice
1 tablespoon chopped parsley
½ teaspoon sugar
salt and pepper to taste

For the dressing:
Combine the olive oil, wine vinegar, lime juice, parsley, sugar, salt and pepper in a small glass jar. Cover and shake well to blend. Refrigerate for 1 hour and let stand at room temperature 15 minutes before pouring.

lettuce leaves
optional garnish:
3 hard-boiled eggs, chopped
Bermuda onion rings

Place a lettuce leaf on each of 6 salad plates. Arrange the tomato and avocado slices alternately in a pinwheel across the lettuce. Shake the salad dressing before pouring and coat each salad lightly. You may garnish with chopped hard-boiled eggs and a slice of onion if you wish.

Seafood Canalones with Parmesan Sauce

For the canalones:
Combine the flour, milk, water, eggs, butter, salt, pepper and nutmeg in a large bowl. Beat until smooth with an electric or hand mixer. You can also mix in a blender until smooth. Let stand for 30 minutes.

½ cup flour
½ cup milk
¼ cup water
4 eggs
1 tablespoon butter, melted
½ teaspoon salt
pinch each pepper and nutmeg
3 tablespoons butter, softened
2 tablespoons olive oil

Mix the butter and oil in a small cup. Place a 7-inch omelet or crepe pan over moderate heat. Use a basting brush to spread the butter and oil mixture onto the skillet. Spoon out enough batter to coat the bottom of the skillet (about 2 to 3 tablespoons); tilt the skillet to spread batter. Cook until a light, golden crust forms on the bottom and the batter is dry on the top. Flip the canalone over and cook a few seconds longer. Remove to a platter and continue cooking canalones until all batter has been used.

For the filling:
Place the fish in a shallow baking dish. Add the cold water, wine and salt and bring to a simmer. Cover with a sheet of waxed paper. Set in a preheated 350° oven for 8 to 12 minutes or until the fish flakes easily when pierced with a fork. Allow the fish to cool completely in the dish. Remove the fish from the liquid and flake it into a bowl. Set the baking dish with the poaching liquid over moderate heat. Boil the liquid, reducing it to ¼ cup.

1 pound fillet red snapper, flounder, sole or crab meat
1½ cups cold water
¼ cup dry white wine
1 teaspoon salt

Heat the oil in a heavy skillet. Sauté the parsley and onion, stirring constantly for 8 minutes until the onion is soft. Add the chopped tomato and cook 5 minutes longer. Sprinkle in the flour and cook, stirring constantly, for 3 minutes. Remove from the heat and pour in the fish poaching liquid and the wine. Stir with a wire whisk until smooth. Add salt, pepper and nutmeg. Return to heat and stir until thickened. Add the flaked fish and blend thoroughly. Cool completely before using.

2 tablespoons olive oil
1 tablespoon chopped parsley
1 small onion, minced
1 tomato, seeded and chopped
2 tablespoons flour
the ¼ cup poaching liquid
2 tablespoons dry white wine
salt and pepper to taste
⅛ teaspoon nutmeg

Parmesan Sauce:

Melt the butter in a heavy saucepan over low heat. Add the flour and cook, stirring constantly, until mixture just begins to turn golden. Remove from heat and pour in the milk. Beat with a wire whip until sauce is smooth. Return to heat and cook, stirring, until thick. Beat the egg yolk in a small bowl. Stir in a few drops of the hot white sauce. Continue to blend in gradually. When all the sauce has been added, return the mixture to the saucepan. Stir over low heat for 1 minute.

3 tablespoons butter
2 tablespoons flour
2 cups milk
1 egg yolk

Add the Parmesan cheese, nutmeg, salt, pepper and sherry to the white sauce. Simmer 2 minutes, stirring constantly. Remove from heat.

¼ cup grated Parmesan cheese
⅛ teaspoon nutmeg
salt and pepper to taste
2 tablespoons dry sherry

To prepare canalones:
Place 2 tablespoons of the filling along the center of each canalone. Roll up and place in a single layer in a buttered baking dish. Pour the Parmesan Sauce over the canalones and broil for 10 to 15 minutes until golden and bubbly.

Baked Sea Bream

Have the fish cleaned and scaled at the market. Leave the fish whole. Make diagonal cuts at 1-inch intervals on one side of the fish. Place a lemon slice in each cut.

Combine the olive oil, sherry, onion, garlic, parsley, bay leaf, salt and pepper in a small glass jar. Cover and shake well to blend. Pour ¼ of the mixture into a shallow baking dish large enough to hold the fish. Lay the fish, cut side up, in the dish and pour the remaining mixture over it. Bake in a preheated 350° oven for 50 to 60 minutes. The fish is done when it just flakes when tested with a fork. Serve immediately.

1 3-pound sea bream (porgy or sea bass)
2 lemons, thinly sliced

3 tablespoons olive oil
½ cup dry sherry
¼ cup minced white onion
2 cloves garlic, minced
2 tablespoons minced parsley
1 bay leaf, crumbled
¼ teaspoon salt
¼ teaspoon pepper

Turrón

Line a loaf pan with waxed paper cut to fit. Brush the waxed paper with vegetable oil. At the same time, prepare another piece of waxed paper brushed with oil and a piece of cardboard, both cut to fit just inside the pan.

a loaf pan
waxed paper
vegetable oil

Grind 1 cup of the almonds to a smooth paste in a blender, or crush with a mortar and pestle. Combine the remaining ½ cup whole almonds with the ground almonds.

1½ cups blanched almonds

Combine the sugar and water in a heavy-bottomed saucepan. Heat slowly until the sugar has completely dissolved. Increase the heat and boil 7 minutes. At this point, a few drops of sugar syrup should form hard balls when dropped into a bowl of cold water. Remove from the heat and add the almonds. Stir until the mixture forms a thick paste. It should come away from the sides of the pan as it is stirred. Add the egg yolks, stirring constantly. Press into the prepared pan and cover with the second piece of oiled waxed paper. Set the piece of cardboard on top of the waxed paper, securing it with a light weight on top. Set the loaf in a cool place.

1⅔ cups sugar
1⅛ cups cold water
4 egg yolks, beaten

Turn the loaf out of the pan. Remove the oiled papers. Cover the bottom of a plate with the sugar. Place the loaf topside down on the sugar. Turn the loaf right-side-up and set on a serving dish. Use a very hot skewer to burn a pattern of criss-cross lines in the top of the turrón.

¼ cup sugar

Avocado and Tomato Salad

27

Stuffed Artichokes
Mushroom Salad   Antipasto Salad
Stuffed Pasta Shells with Tomato Sauce
Shrimp with Garlic and Parsley
Zabaglione   Panettone

Stuffed Artichokes

6 large artichokes
½ lemon
3 quarts boiling, salted water

Rinse artichokes under cold running water. Remove and discard any discolored outer leaves. Trim off ½ inch from the top of each leaf with a kitchen scissors to remove the sharp tips. Trim the stem end of each artichoke with a sharp knife, so that it will stand. Rub each artichoke with the lemon. Squeeze the remainder of juice into the boiling water. Drop the artichokes into the water and cook for 15 minutes. Drain, top side down, until cool enough to handle. Pull out the centers and scrape out the chokes with a small spoon.

1 cup dry bread crumbs
1 cup grated Romano cheese
8 cloves garlic, minced
4 tablespoons chopped parsley
salt and pepper to taste

Combine the bread crumbs, cheese, garlic, parsley, salt and pepper in a small bowl. Put ½ teaspoon of the mixture in the spaces between leaves, using a small spoon. Fill the centers with the remaining mixture. Arrange the artichokes in a pan just large enough to hold them.

3 tablespoons butter
2 tablespoons olive oil

Melt the butter in a small saucepan and add the olive oil. Put a few drops between the leaves of each artichoke to moisten the filling. Add ½-inch boiling water to the pan. Cover and bake in a preheated 400° oven for 1 hour, or until tender.

Mushroom Salad

12 ounces fresh mushrooms

Rinse mushrooms quickly under cold running water, wiping them clean. Cut into thin slices and arrange in a salad bowl.

3 tablespoons olive oil
2 tablespoons lemon juice
1 tablespoon red wine vinegar
1 clove garlic, minced
½ teaspoon grated lemon rind
½ teaspoon sugar
pinch ground nutmeg
salt and pepper to taste
fresh parsley, chopped

Combine the olive oil, lemon juice, red wine vinegar, garlic, lemon rind, sugar, nutmeg, salt and pepper in a small glass jar. Cover and shake well to combine ingredients. Refrigerate for 1 hour. Let stand at room temperature for 15 minutes before serving. Shake the dressing again just before pouring over the mushrooms. Garnish the salad with the chopped parsley.

Antipasto Salad

1 pound fresh green beans
2½ quarts boiling, salted water

Drop the beans into the boiling water. Cook for 8 minutes until tender but still crisp. Rinse under cold running water for 1 minute. Lay the beans out on a towel to dry. Roll up and refrigerate.

Combine the olive oil, lemon juice, red wine vinegar, onion, parsley, sugar, salt and pepper in a small glass jar. Cover and shake well to combine the ingredients. Refrigerate for 1 hour. Let stand at room temperature for 15 minutes before serving.

3 tablespoons olive oil
1½ tablespoons lemon juice
1½ tablespoons wine vinegar
1½ tablespoons minced onion
1½ tablespoons minced parsley
½ teaspoon sugar
salt and pepper to taste

Arrange the tomatoes around the edge of a serving platter. Fill the center of the platter with the green beans. Shake the dressing and pour over the beans and tomatoes evenly. Wrap the olives with the anchovy fillets for garnish.

3 tomatoes, sliced
12 to 16 pitted black olives, drained
12 to 16 anchovy fillets, drained

Thin the mayonnaise with a little cream or milk to pouring consistency. Spoon over the salad.

½ cup mayonnaise
cream or milk

Stuffed Pasta Shells

Drop the shells into the boiling, salted water. Cook 15 to 20 minutes, testing occasionally. When the shells are tender but firm, drain in a colander under cold running water. Spread the shells in a single layer on a towel to dry.

1 12-ounce package jumbo pasta shells
6 quarts boiling, salted water

Cook the spinach according to package instructions, until most of the moisture has evaporated. Drain in a colander, pressing out any excess water.

2 10-ounce packages frozen spinach

For the filling:
Combine the ricotta cheese, spinach, Parmesan cheese, eggs, lemon juice, nutmeg, salt and pepper in a large bowl. Stir until well blended. Stuff each shell with the filling, distributing it evenly. Place the shells in a single layer in a buttered, shallow baking dish. Pour the tomato sauce on top. Bake in a preheated 350° oven 30 minutes, or until heated through.

1 15-ounce package ricotta cheese
the cooked spinach
½ cup Parmesan cheese
2 eggs
1 teaspoon lemon juice
pinch nutmeg
salt and pepper to taste

For the tomato sauce:
Heat the oil in a saucepan. Add the onion, garlic, celery, and carrot. Sauté slowly 10 minutes.

Peel, seed and chop the tomatoes. Add the tomatoes, tomato paste, wine, beef stock, water, sugar, nutmeg, salt and pepper. Bring to a boil, stirring. Lower the heat and simmer gently for 1 hour or until thickened, stirring occasionally.

Best when made a day ahead and refrigerated overnight.

2 tablespoons olive oil
1 onion, chopped
2 garlic cloves, minced
1 celery rib, chopped
1 carrot, grated
4 tomatoes
6-ounce can tomato paste
1 cup dry red wine
1 cup beef stock
1 cup water
1 tablespoon brown sugar
pinch nutmeg, salt and pepper

Zabaglione

Combine the egg yolks and sugar in the top of a double boiler. Beat the mixture with a wire whisk over barely simmering water. Gradually add the wine when the mixture is lemon-colored and slightly thickened. Beat until thick and foamy. Add the vanilla. Remove from heat and beat a few minutes. Pour into six individual serving glasses. Serve immediately.

6 egg yolks
6 tablespoons sugar
½ cup Marsala wine
½ teaspoon vanilla

Shrimp with Garlic and Parsley

Wash the shrimp under cold water. Peel and devein; lay on a towel to dry.

2½ to 3 pounds large shrimp

Heat the olive oil and butter in a large skillet. Place 1 layer of shrimp in the skillet. Season with salt and pepper. Sauté for 2 minutes. Turn and sauté for 1 minute. Transfer to a heated serving dish and keep warm. Sauté the remaining shrimp in the same manner.

3 tablespoons olive oil
3 tablespoons butter
salt and butter to taste

Add the garlic and parsley to the oil and butter remaining in the skillet. Heat and stir for a few seconds. Squeeze the lemon juice into the skillet. Pour sauce over the shrimp and serve.

4 cloves garlic, minced
½ cup minced parsley
juice of ½ lemon

Panettone

Combine the water, sugar and salt in a small saucepan. Bring to a simmer, stirring, to dissolve sugar. Remove from heat and add butter. Stir to melt butter and cool to lukewarm.

1 cup water
½ cup sugar
2 teaspoons salt
½ cup butter

Combine the lukewarm water mixture and yeast in a large mixing bowl. Stir to dissolve yeast. Add eggs, egg yolks, lemon peel and anise seed. Stir to combine thoroughly. Add flour and mix to form a smooth dough. Place on a floured board and knead, adding more flour if necessary until dough is smooth and satiny. Knead in the raisins, pine nuts and candied fruit.

2 packages active dry yeast
2 eggs, beaten
3 egg yolks, beaten
1 teaspoon grated lemon peel
1 teaspoon anise seed
5½ cups all-purpose flour
¾ cup raisins
¾ cup pine nuts
¾ cup mixed candied fruit

Place the dough in a lightly buttered bowl, turning to coat all sides. Cover with a towel and let rise in a warm place until doubled in bulk.

Deflate dough and knead again until smooth. Place in a greased 3-quart pudding pan or round pan. Cover and let rise until doubled in bulk. Cut a deep cross in the top of the loaf with a sharp knife or scissors.

Bake in a preheated 425° oven for about 8 minutes or until the surface begins to brown. Reduce temperature to 325° and bake about 1 hour longer. The bread is done when it is nicely browned and has a hollow sound when tapped.

Shrimp with Garlic and Parsley,
Stuffed Artichokes, Antipasto Salad

*Spinach Triangles
Lentil Soup
Beet and Onion Salad
Roast Stuffed Suckling Pig
Braised Celery   Glazed Carrots
Baklava*

Spinach Triangles

⅓ cup olive oil
1 large onion, chopped
8 scallions, chopped
1½ pounds fresh spinach, washed and chopped
3 tablespoons dried dillweed
1½ cups crumbled feta cheese
pepper to taste

For the filling:
Heat the olive oil in a large saucepan. Add the onion and scallions. Cook over moderate heat, stirring until soft. Lay the spinach over the onion, cover and cook for 5 minutes. Stir the mixture to combine ingredients. Remove from heat. Add the dillweed, feta cheese and pepper; stir gently. Set aside to cool.

½ pound phyllo pastry dough
olive oil

Cut the phyllo into 3 x 10-inch strips. Use the strips in double layers for each pastry. Place 1 tablespoon filling at one end of each strip. Fold one corner of the strip over the filling, forming a triangle. Continue to fold the pastry, maintaining the triangular shape (as you would fold a flag). Fill and fold each strip. Place the triangles on an oiled baking sheet. Brush with olive oil. Bake in a preheated 350° oven for 15 to 20 minutes until golden.

Lentil Soup

1 pound dried lentil beans
1 onion, chopped
2 celery ribs, chopped
3 cloves garlic, minced
½ cup olive oil
2 tablespoons tomato paste
2 whole cloves
½ bay leaf
salt and pepper to taste

Rinse the lentil beans in a colander under cold running water. Soak for 1 hour in lukewarm water. Drain in a colander and transfer to a kettle. Add 2 quarts water, onion, celery, garlic, olive oil, tomato paste, cloves, bay leaf, salt and pepper. Bring to a boil over moderate heat. Reduce heat, cover and cook for 30 minutes. Check the soup occasionally, adding more water if necessary. Soup should be fairly thick. Pour into a heated tureen and serve.

Beet and Onion Salad

2½ pounds medium-sized beets
1 tablespoon vinegar
1 tablespoon salt
1 large onion, sliced
salt and pepper to taste

Remove the leaves and stems from the beets. Wash under cold water. Place the beets in a kettle and cover with water. Add the vinegar and salt. Bring to a boil. Cover and cook for 45 minutes or until tender. Drain. When cooled slip off the skins by rubbing them between your fingers. Cut the beets crosswise into ¼-inch slices. Arrange the beets and onion in a salad bowl. Sprinkle with salt and pepper.

½ cup olive oil
2 tablespoons red wine vinegar
1 large clove garlic, split
½ teaspoon salt
¼ teaspoon pepper

The dressing:
Combine the olive oil, red wine vinegar, garlic, salt and pepper in a glass jar. Cover and shake to blend. Let stand at room temperature for 1 hour before serving. Dress the beet and onion slices generously.

Greece

Roast Stuffed Suckling Pig

Have the piglet cleaned at the meat market. Wash the piglet and pat dry. Rub the cavity and outside with salt and pepper. Set aside.

1 12-pound piglet
salt and pepper

For the stuffing:
Combine the raisins and sherry in a small saucepan. Simmer for 3 minutes until the raisins are plump.

⅓ cup seedless raisins
⅓ cup sherry

Heat the olive oil in a large heavy-bottomed skillet over moderate heat. Add the onion and sauté for 5 minutes. Add the ground pork, breaking it up as it cooks. After the meat has browned lightly, add the rice, raisins, pine nuts, parsley, sage, salt and pepper. Pour in the water and cook, stirring occasionally, for 15 minutes. The rice should be half cooked with the water absorbed. Remove from the heat. Cool before using.

3 tablespoons olive oil
3 tablespoons chopped onion
¾ pound ground pork
¾ cup uncooked rice
the plump raisins
½ cup pine nuts
½ cup chopped parsley
2 tablespoons sage
salt and pepper to taste
1 cup water

Fill the piglet loosely with the stuffing. Close the cavity with skewers and lace with kitchen string. Pull the front legs forward and tie them together. Do the same with the back legs. Place the piglet in the roasting pan, stomach down. Brush with olive oil. Make a few small, shallow cuts in the piglet's back with a sharp knife. Place the block of wood in the mouth to keep it open. Cover the ears with foil so they do not burn. Pour boiling water into the pan. Roast in a preheated 350° oven, basting occasionally with olive oil. Figure 30 minutes roasting time for every pound of meat. If the skin should begin to brown too quickly, cover loosely with aluminum foil. Uncover the piglet during the last 30 minutes of roasting to allow the skin to become crisp. When the piglet has finished cooking, remove to a warm platter. Cover loosely to keep warm.

the prepared piglet
skewers
kitchen string
olive oil
basting brush
1 small block of wood
foil
shallow roasting pan
2 cups boiling water

For the gravy:
Skim all but 2 tablespoons of the fat from the pan juice. Bring the juice to a simmer. Sprinkle the flour on the juice and stir until bubbly (2 minutes). Add the water, stirring constantly. Simmer until thickened. Season with salt and pepper. Serve in a warm sauceboat.

2 tablespoons flour
2½ cups water
salt and pepper to taste

Braised Celery

Remove the core and fibrous outer ribs from each bunch of celery. Trim off the tops, leaving the ribs 6 to 8 inches long. Quarter each rib. Rinse the celery under cold running water. Place in a saucepan, cover with water, and add the salt. Bring to a boil. Blanch the celery for 5 minutes. Drain in a colander.

2 bunches pascal celery
1 tablespoon salt

Heat the olive oil in a shallow casserole dish. Add the carrot and onion. Sauté over moderate heat for 8 to 10 minutes. Place the celery on top of the vegetables. Pour in the chicken stock. Add salt and pepper. Bring to a boil. Reduce heat, cover and simmer gently for 30 to 45 minutes. Celery should be tender. Remove celery with a slotted spoon to a heated serving dish and keep warm.

2 tablespoons olive oil
1 carrot, chopped
1 small onion, chopped
¾ cup chicken stock
salt and pepper to taste
2 tablespoons chopped, fresh
  flat-leaf parsley

33

Strain the chopped carrots and onion from the casserole; force the carrots and onion through a sieve back into the stock. Pour it over the cooked celery. Sprinkle with parsley and serve.

Glazed Carrots

1 pound small young carrots, peeled

If the carrots are small and garden fresh, they may be left whole. If not, slice them lengthwise into quarters, then crosswise in half.

½ cup cold water
2 tablespoons butter
2 tablespoons sugar
1 bouillon cube
pinch pepper

Place the carrots in a heavy saucepan. Add the water, butter, sugar and bouillon cube. Simmer gently, partially covered, until liquid is reduced to 2 tablespoons. Uncover and simmer until liquid becomes a glaze. Shake the pan, coating the carrots evenly with glaze.

Baklava

1½ cups walnuts, chopped
1½ cups walnuts, ground
¾ cups almonds, chopped
2 teaspoons ground cinnamon
¾ teaspoon ground cloves

1 pound unsalted butter, melted
1 pound phyllo pastry

For the filling:
Combine the chopped and ground walnuts, chopped almonds, cinnamon and cloves. Set aside.

Cut the layers of phyllo dough to fit a 9 x 12-inch baking pan. Set aside 4 layers for the top. Keep the phyllo dough covered at all times with a damp dish towel. It will dry quickly if exposed to the air. Brush the baking pan with the melted butter. Lay a sheet of phyllo in the pan and brush with butter. Sprinkle evenly with a handful of the nut mixture. Repeat this layering process until all the nuts are used. Lay the 4 remaining phyllo sheets on top, brushing each generously with melted butter. Using the tip of a sharp knife, cut a diamond-shaped pattern through the top 4 layers, leaving about 2 inches between each cut. Bake for 45 minutes in a preheated 325° oven until the top turns golden. Remove from the oven and cool slightly.

2 cups sugar
1¼ cups water
peel of 1 orange
4 whole cloves
1 cinnamon stick
6 ounces honey
juice of ½ lemon
½ teaspoon vanilla
¼ teaspoon almond extract

For the syrup:
Combine the sugar, water, orange peel, cloves and cinnamon stick in a saucepan. Simmer for 2 minutes. Add the honey and lemon juice. Boil for 5 minutes. Remove from the heat. Stir in the vanilla and almond extract. Allow to cool. Pour the syrup evenly over the baklavas. Cut through all the dough layers following the diamond-shaped pattern made earlier. Let stand overnight before serving.

Beet and Onion Salad, Braised Celery,
Glazed Carrots, Spinach Triangles, Baklava

Christmas Cheese Ball
Fish Soup
Paprika Chicken
Noodles and Cabbage
Chestnut Torte

Christmas Cheese Ball

2 8-ounce packages cream cheese, softened
⅔ cup crumbled blue cheese

Place the cream cheese in a large mixing bowl. Spread the cream cheese around the bowl with a heavy fork to allow it to soften. Add the blue cheese and blend well.

3 tablespoons sweet sherry
1 tablespoon Worcestershire sauce
1 clove garlic, finely minced
3 tablespoons minced chives
1 tablespoon caraway seeds
1½ cups finely minced parsley

Blend the sherry, and Worcestershire sauce into the cheese. Add the minced garlic, chives and caraway seeds. Blend all the ingredients together with a fork. Roll the mixture into a ball with your hands. Spread the minced parsley on a plate. Roll the cheese ball in the parsley, coating it completely. Wrap the ball in waxed paper and refrigerate for at least 4 hours or overnight.

1 7-ounce jar pimientos
pearl onions
stuffed green olives
toothpicks

Lay the pimientos on a cutting board. With a sharp knife, cut out decorations. Attach pimiento decorations onto the cheese ball with the toothpicks. Place pearl onions or olives on the ends of the toothpicks.

Fish Soup

2 pounds pike, sturgeon, halibut or flounder
1½ cups bottled clam juice
1 onion, thinly sliced
8 parsley stems
1 teaspoon lemon juice
¼ cup fresh mushroom stems
5 peppercorns
5½ cups cold water

Put the fish in a large heavy-bottomed kettle. Add the clam juice, sliced onion, parsley stems, lemon juice, mushroom stems and peppercorns. Cover with the cold water and slowly bring to a simmer. Simmer very gently, uncovered for 30 minutes. Strain the broth through a sieve and pour it into a large saucepan over low heat. When the fish is cool enough to handle, remove all the bones and break the fish into pieces. Cover the fish with foil and set aside.

3 tablespoons butter
3 tablespoons flour
6 cups of the simmering fish stock

Wash the kettle and place it over low heat. Melt the butter in the kettle. Add the flour, stirring over moderate heat for 3 minutes. Remove from the heat. Pour in the hot fish stock, stirring with a wire whisk to blend the stock thoroughly with the flour. Cook the soup over low heat until it thickens slightly. Simmer, stirring occasionally for 10 minutes.

¼ cup sour cream
¼ cup rice

Beat in the sour cream with the wire whisk. Rinse the rice in a sieve under cold running water and add to the soup. Partially cover the kettle. Simmer until the rice is tender, stirring occasionally.

the fish meat
lemon slices

Divide the fish meat among 6 heated soup bowls. Ladle the simmering soup over the fish. Garnish each bowl with a slice of lemon floating on top.

Hungary

Paprika Chicken

Rinse the chicken under cold running water. Pat dry thoroughly with a paper towel. Salt and pepper lightly and set aside.

Heat the butter in a Dutch oven. Add the onion and sauté for 8 minutes, stirring occasionally. Remove from the heat.

Add the paprika, chicken pieces, green pepper, tomato and water to the Dutch oven. Stir to combine ingredients and cover tightly. Return to the heat and simmer slowly for 1 to 1½ hours, turning the chicken once during cooking. Or bring to a simmer on top of stove and place in a preheated 325° oven for 1 to 1½ hours.

During the last 15 minutes of cooking time, add the sliced mushrooms. Cover and return to the oven.

When the chicken is tender, transfer it to a heated platter. Remove the vegetables with a slotted spoon and spoon over the chicken. Add the butter to the Dutch oven and set over low heat. Stir in the flour; continue stirring for 2 minutes. Remove from heat and pour in all the chicken broth at once, beating vigorously with a wire whisk until the sauce is smooth. Return to heat and stir occasionally while the sauce simmers, for 5 to 10 minutes. If the sauce becomes too thick, thin it with a little water. If it is too thin, continue to simmer until more liquid evaporates.

Blend the sour cream into the sauce, stirring until heated through. Do not allow the sauce to simmer or it will curdle. Spoon the sauce over the chicken. Garnish the platter with green pepper and tomato slices.

2½ to 3 pounds chicken, cut into serving pieces
salt and pepper to taste

6 tablespoons butter
1 large onion, sliced

2 tablespoons Hungarian paprika
the cut up chicken
½ green pepper, sliced
½ ripe tomato, sliced
⅓ cup cold water

¼ pound fresh mushrooms, cleaned and sliced

2 tablespoons butter
3 tablespoons flour
1½ cups boiling chicken broth

⅓ cup sour cream
½ green pepper, sliced
½ ripe tomato, sliced

Noodles and Cabbage

Melt the butter in a large heavy skillet. Add the onion and sauté for 8 to 10 minutes or until the onion is soft but not browned.

Remove any discolored leaves and quarter the cabbage, cutting out the core. Shred to measure 4 cups. Add to the skillet and sauté for 5 minutes until crisp and tender. Stir in the caraway seed; salt and pepper to taste.

Cook the noodles in salted water according to package directions. Drain well. Stir noodles into the cabbage. Add sour cream. Stir frequently for 5 minutes over low heat until heated through. Do not allow mixture to boil or the sour cream will curdle. Serve immediately.

¼ cup butter
½ cup chopped onion

4 cups shredded cabbage
1 teaspoon caraway seed
salt and pepper to taste

1 8-ounce package egg noodles
½ cup sour cream

Chestnut Torte

Place the chestnuts in a pan and cover with cold water. Bring to a boil for 1 minute. Remove from heat. Remove 3 chestnuts at a time from the pan. Peel off shells and inner skins.

Put the chestnuts in a pan and pour in enough milk to cover by 1 inch. Simmer slowly, uncovered, 45 to 60

1 pound chestnuts

milk as needed

minutes until the chestnuts are cooked through. Drain in a colander and press through a fine sieve. Set aside.

1 9-inch round cake pan
shortening
2 tablespoons flour
waxed paper

Grease the cake pan with the shortening. Add the flour coating the pan evenly. Cut a circle of waxed paper large enough to fit the bottom of the pan. Grease the waxed paper and dust it with flour.

6 egg whites
pinch salt
pinch cream of tartar
⅓ cup sugar

Beat the egg whites with the salt until foamy. Add the cream of tartar and beat until soft peaks form. Gradually add the sugar and continue beating until stiff peaks are formed. Set aside.

6 egg yolks
⅔ cup sugar
the beaten egg whites
the chestnut puree
1 tablespoon fine bread crumbs

Beat the egg yolks until light. Add the sugar and continue beating 2 to 3 minutes. Stir ¼ of the egg whites into egg yolk mixture with a rubber spatula. Place half the chestnut puree on top of the egg yolk mixture. Sprinkle on half the bread crumbs. Add half of the egg white mixture. Fold together. Repeat with the remaining ingredients.

Pour the batter into the cake pan, spreading to the rim. Bake in a preheated 350° oven 25 to 30 minutes. Cool on a wire rack 5 minutes. Invert the cake onto the wire rack and peel off the waxed paper.

1 16-ounce can peeled apricots
in heavy syrup
⅓ cup sugar

For the filling:
Drain the apricot syrup into a saucepan. Add the sugar. Bring to a simmer and stir to dissolve the sugar. Boil rapidly until thick and sticky.

the drained apricots
1 tablespoon lemon juice
½ teaspoon grated lemon rind

Remove the seeds from the apricots. Dice and stir into the syrup. Add the lemon juice and rind. Boil slowly for 5 minutes.

1 tablespoon kirsch or
orange-flavored liqueur

Remove the saucepan from the heat and add the kirsch or orange-flavored liqueur. Let the mixture cool before spreading. Split the cake evenly into 2 layers. Invert the bottom layer onto a serving dish. Place pieces of waxed paper under the cake to catch any drippings. Pour the apricot filling onto the bottom layer and spread evenly to the edge. Set the second cake layer on top of the first. Spread the remaining filling around the sides.

3 ounces semisweet chocolate
1½ tablespoons vegetable oil

For the chocolate topping:
Break the chocolate into pieces and put in the top of a double boiler set over simmering water. Pour in the oil. Cover for 5 to 10 minutes until the chocolate melts. Stir to blend and pour over the cake.

12 ounces almonds, sliced
maraschino cherries, halved
whole blanched almonds

Gently press the sliced almonds into the glaze around the sides of the cake until completely coated. Decorate the top with the maraschino cherries and blanched whole almonds.

Oxtail Soup
Prague Salad
Sautéed Mushrooms   Creamed Cabbage
Roast Pork   Potato Dumplings
Stuffed Baked Apples   Kolacky

Oxtail Soup

1½ pounds oxtail
2 quarts water

Cut the oxtail into 1-inch pieces. Bring water to a boil in a large kettle. Drop the meat into the water; return to a boil. Skim the surface with a large spoon as necessary. Lower heat and simmer, partially covered, for 2 hours or until tender.

3 tablespoons butter
2 parsnips, diced
3 carrots, diced
1 medium onion, diced
5 peppercorns

Heat the butter in a skillet. Add the parsnips, carrots and onion and sauté 10 minutes or until vegetables are soft, but not browned. Add the vegetables and peppercorns to the soup. Simmer 10 minutes. With a slotted spoon, remove the oxtail pieces from the soup. Remove the meat from the bones and return the meat to the soup. Remove and discard peppercorns.

salt
3 cups diced cauliflower
2 tablespoons minced parsley

Taste the soup for seasoning, adding salt if necessary. Add cauliflower and parsley; simmer 15 minutes. Serve immediately.

Prague Salad

½ cup cooked pork strips
½ cup cooked veal strips
1 cup sliced yellow onion
1 cup thinly sliced pickles
2 cups thinly sliced tart apples

For the salad:
Cut the pork and veal into strips 2 inches long by ½ inch wide by ⅛ inch thick. Combine the pork, veal, onion, pickles and apples in a mixing bowl.

1 cup mayonnaise
2 tablespoons cream
1 tablespoon lemon juice
salt and pepper
Romaine lettuce leaves

For the dressing:
Combine the mayonnaise, cream, lemon juice, salt and pepper in a small bowl. Blend thoroughly. Pour the dressing over the salad and toss to coat the ingredients. Refrigerate 4 hours. Arrange a bed of lettuce in a salad bowl. Place the salad on the lettuce leaves and serve.

Sautéed Mushrooms

¼ cup butter
2 cups sliced red onion
1½ pounds mushrooms, sliced
salt and pepper
1 teaspoon caraway seed

Heat the butter in a heavy skillet. Add onion and sauté for 5 minutes or until soft. Add mushrooms, salt and pepper to taste and caraway seed. Sauté for 10 minutes. Serve immediately.

Creamed Cabbage

1 large head of cabbage
¾ cup minced onion
5 tablespoons butter

Remove outer leaves from cabbage and discard. Cut cabbage into quarters, core and shred. In a large skillet, sauté cabbage and onion in butter for 5 minutes. Cover tightly and simmer until vegetables are just limp.

Czechoslovakia

Sprinkle vegetables with salt and pepper. Blend cream into flour and add to vegetables. Stir to blend thoroughly. Cover and simmer for 10 to 15 minutes or until tender.

salt and pepper to taste
1 cup heavy cream
1 tablespoon flour

Potato Dumplings

Drop the unpeeled potatoes into the boiling water. Cook until tender. Pour off hot water and cover the potatoes with cold water. Let stand until cool enough to handle. Peel and mash.

4 pounds potatoes
4 quarts boiling water

Add the water to a kettle and return to the heat; bring to a boil. In the meantime prepare the dumplings. Add flour, farina, eggs and salt to mashed potatoes. Mix into a stiff dough. To test the dough, form one small walnut-sized ball and drop it into the boiling water. If it falls apart, work more flour into the dough. Form the dough into 10 dumplings and drop immediately into the boiling water. Cook 15 minutes, stirring to prevent sticking.

4 quarts water
1⅓ cups flour
1 cup farina
2 eggs
2 teaspoons salt

Roast Pork

Rub the roast with the garlic. Combine the seasonings in a small dish; rub into the meat. Sprinkle the roast with the caraway seed.

4-pound loin of pork
1 clove garlic, halved
¼ teaspoon each rosemary, allspice, sage, thyme salt and pepper
1 teaspoon caraway seed

Place the meat in a glass dish. Cover loosely and let stand at room temperature for 1 hour before roasting.

Place the roast, fat side up, on a rack in a shallow roasting pan. Place in a preheated 450° oven. Immediately reduce heat to 325° and roast, basting occasionally, for 1 hour and 45 minutes. A meat thermometer inserted in the thickest part should register 175°. Transfer the pork to a heated platter and cover loosely while preparing the gravy.

Skim all but 2 tablespoons of fat from the roasting pan. Sprinkle on the flour and stir over moderately low heat for 2 to 3 minutes without browning. Add the water and milk. Stir with a wire whisk until the mixture is smooth and thickened. Add the brown sugar, salt, pepper and allspice. Transfer the gravy to a heated sauceboat and serve with the roast.

2 tablespoons flour
½ cup water
½ cup milk
½ teaspoon brown sugar
salt and pepper to taste
pinch allspice

Stuffed Baked Apples

Combine the raisins and rum in a saucepan. Bring to a simmer. Remove from heat and let stand for 30 minutes.

½ cup chopped raisins
¼ cup dark rum

Cut the tops off the apples and reserve. Core the apples but do not peel. Rub lemon juice over the cut surfaces of the apples to prevent discoloration.

6 large baking apples
lemon juice

Combine and blend the ground hazelnuts, cream, raisins and sugar in a mixing bowl. Stuff the apples with the mixture and cover with the reserved apple tops. Place apples close together in a deep baking dish.

1 cup ground hazelnuts
½ cup heavy cream
the raisins soaked in rum
½ cup sugar

Combine the honey and rum. Pour over the apples. Bake for 30 to 35 minutes in a preheated 400° oven, basting the apples often. Serve with whipped cream.

½ cup honey
½ cup dark rum
sweetened whipped cream

Kolacky

For the dough:
Scald the milk in a small saucepan. Remove from heat. Add sugar, shortening and salt. Stir to melt shortening. Cool to lukewarm.

1 cup milk
3 tablespoons sugar
¼ cup shortening
1 teaspoon salt

Combine the lukewarm milk mixture and yeast in a large mixing bowl. Stir to dissolve yeast. Add the eggs and stir well. Add flour and mix to form a smooth dough. Shape into a ball and knead until smooth and satiny. Place in a lightly buttered bowl, turning to coat all sides. Cover with a towel and let rise in a warm place until doubled in size.

1 package active dry yeast
2 eggs, beaten
4⅓ cups all-purpose flour

For the apricot filling:
Combine the apricots and water in a small saucepan. Simmer for 15 minutes or until the apricots are soft. Press the apricots and liquid through a sieve and return to the saucepan. Continue to simmer until thickened.

½ pound dried apricots
1½ cups water

Add sugar, stirring occasionally over moderate heat for 5 minutes. Remove from heat. Cool before using.

⅓ cup sugar

For the prune filling:
Combine the prunes and water in a saucepan. Cover and simmer for 5 minutes. Remove from heat. Transfer the prunes to a colander. When cool enough to handle, pit the prunes. Return the prunes to the liquid in the saucepan. Simmer, uncovered, for 15 minutes. Press the mixture through a sieve and return to the saucepan; add the sugar. Continue to simmer over moderate heat until thickened, about 5 minutes. Cool before using.

1 pound dried prunes
1½ cups water
1 tablespoon sugar

Roll the dough into 1-inch balls. Place each ball on a greased cookie sheet and flatten to make a 2-inch circle. Make an indentation in the center, leaving a ¼-inch rim. Fill with apricot or prune filling. Allow the pastries to rise until doubled in size. Bake in a preheated 350° oven for 25 to 30 minutes. Sprinkle with confectioners' sugar while still warm.

the apricot or prune filling
confectioners' sugar

Apricot and Prune-Filled Kolacky,
Stuffed Baked Apples

Christmas Eve
Menu for Six

Christmas Barshch
Herring and Apple Salad
Carp in Beer Sauce
Stewed Sauerkraut with Mushrooms
Cranberry Pudding   Poppy Seed Cake

Christmas Barshch

1½ cups fish heads, bones, tails or leftovers
3 carrots, sliced
2 celery ribs, sliced
2 onions, sliced
¼ head cabbage, shredded
1 clove garlic, halved
2 sprigs parsley

Combine the fish, carrots, celery, onion, cabbage, garlic and parsley in a heavy kettle. Cover with 2 quarts cold water. Bring to a simmer, keeping the heat low so the liquid never comes to a rolling boil. Simmer the stock gently, partially covered, for 1 hour. Strain the stock through a sieve, pressing the fish and vegetables with a wooden spoon to extract as much juice as possible. Discard the fish parts and vegetables.

8 medium beets
the fish stock
pinch allspice
1 tablespoon lemon juice
1 teaspoon sugar
salt and pepper to taste

Wash the beets under cold running water. Place the beets in a shallow baking pan. Bake for 30 minutes in a preheated 350° oven. Remove from the oven and let the beets set until cool enough to handle. Peel beets by rubbing the skins between your fingers. Grate coarsely. Add to the soup. Add allspice. Simmer for 5 minutes. Add the lemon juice and sugar. Taste for seasoning, adding salt and pepper if necessary.

Herring and Apple Salad

1 pound salt herring

Have herring cleaned, skinned and filleted at the market. Cut each herring diagonally into 2 pieces.

2 medium apples
1 tablespoon lemon juice
1 small mild onion, minced

Peel and grate the apples. Sprinkle grated apples with the lemon juice and toss to coat. Add minced onion.

¼ cup heavy cream
1 tablespoon sugar
½ cup sour cream
¼ teaspoon horseradish
salt to taste
lettuce or cabbage leaves
tomato or carrot slices
slices of leek

In a chilled bowl beat the cream and sugar until mixture holds a peak. Beat in the sour cream, horseradish and salt to taste. Pour into the apple-onion mixture and blend thoroughly.

Place a lettuce or cabbage leaf on each salad plate. Divide the apple-onion mixture among the plates. Place the pieces of herring on top and garnish with a tomato or carrot slice and a slice of leek.

Carp in Beer Sauce

1 4-pound carp

Have the fish cleaned and scaled at the market. Wash the fish in cold water and pat dry. Salt fish and let stand for 1 hour before cooking.

2½ tablespoons butter
1 large onion, chopped

Heat the butter in a heavy skillet over moderate heat. Add the onion and sauté for 2 minutes.

Add the sliced lemon, sugar, bay leaf, juniper berries and pepper to taste. Stir in the beer and simmer for 20 minutes. Strain the mixture through a sieve into a bowl. Discard the lemon slices, bay leaf and juniper berries. Pour the liquid into a pan large enough to poach the fish.

1 lemon, sliced
2 teaspoons sugar
½ bay leaf
4 juniper berries
pepper
2 cups dark beer or lager

Add the raisins and gingersnaps to the fish poaching pan. Cook the sauce over moderate heat until the crumbs have softened.

¼ cup golden raisins
¼ cup crushed gingersnaps

Place the carp in the pan. Bring the sauce to a simmer. Cover with a sheet of waxed paper and a lid. Poach the fish over moderately low heat for 15 to 20 minutes or until the fish just flakes when tested with a fork. Transfer the fish to a heated serving platter using 2 slotted spatulas to keep fish from breaking apart. Pour sauce over the fish and garnish with minced parsley and tomato quarters.

the carp
minced fresh parsley
2 tomatoes, quartered

Stewed Sauerkraut with Mushrooms

Soak the dried mushrooms in the water for 1 hour; slice. If using fresh mushrooms, slice and simmer in 3 tablespoons water for 5 minutes. Drain and reserve cooking liquid.

1 ounce dried mushrooms
  or ¼ pound fresh
½ cup water

If sauerkraut is uncooked, rinse and drain. Place in a kettle and cover with boiling water. Boil, partially covered, for 30 minutes. Drain the sauerkraut in a colander and press out any excess liquid.

1½ pounds sauerkraut

In a large skillet cook the mushrooms and onion in the shortening for 5 minutes over moderate heat. When the onions are soft, add the flour and reduce the heat, stirring constantly for 2 minutes. Remove from heat and pour in the mushroom liquid and a little water to make a thick, smooth paste. Stir in the sauerkraut. Add salt and pepper to taste. Cook the mixture, stirring, until heated through.

1 large onion, chopped
2 tablespoons shortening
2 tablespoons flour
the reserved mushroom liquid
the mushrooms
a few tablespoons water
salt and pepper to taste

Cranberry Pudding

Combine the cranberries and cold water in a saucepan. Bring to a simmer, and cook slowly just until the skins pop. Remove from the heat and run through a fine sieve or puree in a blender. Return to the saucepan. Add the sugar and stir to dissolve.

1 pound cranberries
1¼ cups cold water
½ cup sugar

Blend the cornstarch with the cold water in a small bowl. Stir into the cranberries and bring to a boil, stirring. Remove from heat and cool. Pour into a serving bowl or individual serving glasses. Spoon whipped cream on top and serve.

¼ cup cornstarch
¼ cup cold water
whipped cream

Poppy Seed Cake

Combine the yeast, sugar and milk in a small bowl. Stir to dissolve the sugar and let stand for 5 minutes. Stir in the flour, cover, and let stand in a warm place until double in size.

1 package active dry yeast
2 tablespoons sugar
1 cup lukewarm milk
1 cup all-purpose flour

In a large bowl, beat the eggs and the egg yolks until they are blended. Add the sugar gradually while beating. Continue beating for 2 to 3 minutes. The mixture should turn a pale yellow.

Add the flour, yeast mixture, vanilla and lemon rind. Knead the dough for 5 minutes. Add the butter a little at a time. Knead 5 minutes longer until smooth. Place the dough in a large buttered bowl, turning to coat on all sides with butter. Cover with a towel and place in a warm 100° oven with the door ajar until double in size.

For the filling:
Combine the milk and sugar in a saucepan. Bring the mixture to a boil over moderate heat. Stir to dissolve sugar completely. Stir in the poppy seed, raisins, orange and lemon rind. Remove from heat. Let the mixture cool completely before using.

Beat the egg whites lightly and fold into the poppy seed mixture. Stir in the butter.

When the dough has doubled in size, punch it down and roll into a 24 x 14-inch rectangle. Spread with the poppy seed filling, except 1 inch around the edge. Beginning with a long side, roll up the dough jelly-roll fashion. Arrange roll, seam side down, on a buttered baking sheet. Let it rise, loosely covered, in a warm place for 1 hour.

Brush the roll with water and bake in a preheated 350° oven for 45 minutes. Cool on a rack while preparing the glaze.

Beat the confectioners' sugar, lemon juice, boiling water and vanilla in a small bowl until the mixture is light and fluffy. Spread on the cooled cake. Let the cake stand until the glaze has set.

Apricot and Prune Compote

Rinse the fruit and place in a bowl. Cover with the water and let soak for 24 hours.

Transfer the fruit to a serving bowl. Pour the liquid into a saucepan. Add the sugar. Cook, stirring, over low heat until the sugar is dissolved. Remove from the heat. Add the lemon juice and rind. Pour over the fruit and refrigerate.

---

1 egg
3 egg yolks
½ cup plus 1 tablespoon sugar
3½ cups all-purpose flour
the yeast mixture
1 teaspoon vanilla
1 teaspoon grated lemon rind
¼ pound butter, melted

1 cup milk
1 cup sugar
½ pound ground poppy seed
⅓ cup raisins
1½ teaspoons grated orange rind
1½ teaspoons grated lemon rind

2 egg whites, lightly beaten
2 tablespoons softened butter

2 cups confectioners' sugar
2 tablespoons lemon juice
1½ tablespoons boiling water
1 teaspoon vanilla

¼ pound dried apricots
¼ pound prunes
2 cups water

1 cup sugar
1 tablespoon lemon juice
grated rind from 1 lemon

Christmas Barshch,
Herring and Apple Salad

Christmas Day Menu for Six

Caviar-Stuffed Eggs
Eggplant Zakuski with Black Bread
Cucumber and Radish Salad
Roast Duck with Madeira Sauce
Veal Stuffing   Roast Potatoes
Buttered Cauliflower and Green Peas
Raisin and Almond Mazurka

Caviar-Stuffed Eggs

6 eggs
4 tablespoons red or black caviar

Boil the eggs for 8 minutes. Rinse under cold water. Peel the eggs; cut in half lengthwise. Remove the yolks, press through sieve and reserve. Divide the caviar among the egg white halves.

mayonnaise
2 tomatoes, quartered
6 green onions
fresh parsley or dill
the sieved egg yolks

Spoon some mayonnaise into a small serving bowl. Place the bowl in the middle of a large round platter. Surround the bowl with tomato wedges. Arrange the caviar-stuffed eggs around the tomatoes. Peel and slice the green onions. Garnish with the green onion, parsley or dill and sieved egg yolks.

Eggplant Zakuski with Black Bread

2 medium eggplants
olive oil

Wash the eggplants and score with a fork. Brush with the oil. Bake in a preheated 350° oven 30 minutes, until tender. Cut the eggplants in half lengthwise and remove all the pulp, discarding peels. Chop very fine. Drain.

¼ cup olive oil
2 tablespoons wine vinegar
2 tablespoons lemon juice
1 clove garlic, minced
sugar, salt and pepper to taste

For the dressing:
Combine the olive oil, wine vinegar, lemon juice, garlic, sugar, salt and pepper in a jar. Cover and shake to blend the ingredients. Refrigerate for 1 hour. Let stand at room temperature for 15 minutes before serving.

1 medium onion, minced
1 green pepper, minced
2 tomatoes, seeded and minced
the dressing
small pieces of buttered black bread

Combine the onion, pepper and tomatoes in a bowl. Pour in the dressing. Add the prepared eggplant. Blend the mixture thoroughly. If the mixture is too moist for spreading, simmer it slowly in a saucepan to evaporate moisture. Chill thoroughly. Place in a serving bowl, and serve with the buttered black bread.

Cucumber and Radish Salad

1 fresh cucumber
2 bunches radishes
salt

Wash the cucumber. Score the cucumber with a fork. Cut into thin slices. Salt lightly. Set aside. Trim the radishes. Wash and cut into thin slices. Arrange the cucumber and radish slices in a shallow salad bowl. Coat evenly with the sour cream dressing.

6 tablespoons sour cream
1 tablespoon wine vinegar
1 tablespoon lemon juice
½ teaspoon sugar
pinch salt

For the dressing:
Combine the sour cream, wine vinegar, lemon juice, sugar and salt in a jar. Cover and shake to blend the ingredients. Refrigerate for 1 hour. Let stand at room temperature for 15 minutes before serving.

Roast Duck with Madeira Sauce

Wash the duck under cold running water. Pat dry with a towel. Salt the inside and outside of the duck.

1 5-pound duck
salt

The veal stuffing:
Remove the crust from the bread and reserve for another use. Cut the bread into ½-inch cubes. Place the bread cubes in a large baking pan. Set in a preheated 300° oven for 20 minutes, turning the cubes occasionally. Transfer the dried cubes to a bowl and soak with milk. Press out any excess milk and set aside.

½ loaf stale white bread, such as Vienna or Italian
1 cup milk

Heat the butter until foaming in a large heavy skillet. Add the onion and sauté for 5 minutes. Beat the eggs with the water in a small bowl. Pour into the skillet. Scramble the eggs with the onion. Set aside.

1½ tablespoons butter
1 large onion, chopped
2 eggs
2 tablespoons cold water

Chop the veal coarsely. Put the veal, bread, and scrambled eggs with onion in a food processor to blend. Or put the ingredients through a meat grinder and combine in a large bowl. Add the scrambled eggs and onion, salt, pepper and nutmeg. Stir to blend.

1 pound cooked veal
the milk-soaked bread
the scrambled eggs and onion
1 egg
salt, pepper and nutmeg to taste

Stuff the body and neck cavities of the bird loosely with the veal stuffing. Close the cavity with skewers and lace with kitchen string. Close the neck cavity with a skewer. Truss the bird securely with the string so it will keep its shape while roasting. Pierce through the skin around the thighs, back and lower breast with a fork so the fat will drain during roasting. Place the duck, breast side up, on a rack in a shallow roasting pan. Set the pan in the middle level of a preheated 425° oven for 15 minutes to brown the skin lightly. Reduce the heat to 350° and turn the bird on one side. Remove fat occasionally from the pan with a bulb baster. The duck will not need to be basted. After 30 minutes turn the bird on the other side. Figure 15 minutes roasting time for every pound of meat. To test whether the bird is done, pierce the thigh with a small knife. If the juice is rosy-colored, roast another 5 to 10 minutes. When done, discard the trussing strings and skewers. Scoop stuffing into a heated serving bowl. Set the duck on a heated platter, cover loosely and keep warm.

the duck, cleaned and salted
the veal stuffing
skewers
kitchen string
shallow roasting pan
wire rack

For the Madeira sauce:
Pour off all but 2 tablespoons fat from the roasting pan. Set the pan over moderate heat. Add the flour. Cook, stirring, for 3 minutes. Pour in the stock and simmer, stirring, until thickened. Add the lemon juice and Madeira, cover and cook for 2 minutes. Spoon some sauce over the duck. Serve the remaining sauce in a heated sauceboat.

1½ tablespoons flour
1¼ cups duck or chicken stock
juice of ½ lemon
1 cup Madeira wine

Roast Potatoes

Peel the potatoes and cut in half lengthwise. Place on the rack of the roasting pan along with the duck during the last 45 minutes of roasting time.

3 red potatoes
3 sweet potatoes

Cauliflower and Green Peas

4 quarts water
2 tablespoons salt
1 head cauliflower, cut into flowerets
2 tablespoons butter

Bring water to a rapid boil in a large kettle. Add salt. Drop the flowerets into the water, and bring to a boil again. Boil slowly, uncovered, for 9 to 12 minutes. Cauliflower should be tender, but retain a suggestion of crunchiness. Remove the flowerets with a slotted spoon and place in a colander. Let the moisture evaporate for a moment. Arrange the flowerets around the circumference of a heated vegetable dish. Dot with the butter.

2 quarts water
1 tablespoon salt
2 cups peas, fresh or frozen

Bring salted water to a rapid boil in a large kettle. Add the peas and cook slowly, uncovered, for 4 to 8 minutes, until just tender. Drain the peas in a colander.

1 teaspoon sugar
salt and pepper to taste
2 tablespoons butter, cut into pieces

Place the peas in a saucepan immediately after draining. Sprinkle in the sugar, salt and pepper. Roll the peas gently around over moderate heat for a few minutes to evaporate the moisture. Pour into the center of the heated vegetable dish.

Raisin and Almond Mazurka

8 x 10-inch cake pan
shortening
2 tablespoons flour

Grease the bottom and sides of the cake pan with the shortening. Dust with the flour, coating the bottom and sides evenly. Set aside.

1 orange
1 lemon

Remove the outermost, orange-colored skin from the orange with a vegetable peeler. Do the same with the lemon. (The white part on the inside is bitter.) Drop the peelings into the saucepan and cover with cold water. Bring to a rapid boil and simmer for 2 minutes. Drain in a colander under cold running water for 1 minute. Pat the peels dry and cut into ⅛-inch strips.

¾ cup sugar
2 eggs
1¾ cups all-purpose flour
½ cup butter, melted
1 cup seedless raisins, chopped
½ cup almonds, blanched and chopped
the orange and lemon peel

Combine the sugar and eggs in a large bowl. With an electric mixer, beat the mixture 2 to 3 minutes until it is pale. Sprinkle in ½ cup of the flour. Continue to beat while pouring in half of the melted butter. Sprinkle in another ½ cup of the flour and pour in the remaining butter, beating all the while, until the mixture is blended and smooth. Sprinkle in the chopped raisins. Sprinkle ¼ cup of flour over the raisins. With a rubber spatula, fold the mixture together. Sprinkle in the almonds, ¼ cup of the flour and fold together again. Sprinkle in the orange and lemon peel. Sprinkle in the remaining flour and fold together to blend thoroughly.

Press the dough mixture evenly into the cake pan. Bake in the middle level of a preheated 350° oven for 30 minutes. Cool on a wire rack for 5 minutes before serving.

Caviar-Stuffed Eggs with Garnishes,
Eggplant Zakuski with Buttered Black Bread

*Holiday
Menu for Six*

*Winter Melon Soup
Cold Sweet and Sour Vegetables
Prawns with Sweet Peppers
Spiced Lamb   Fried Rice
Eight=Precious Pudding*

Winter Melon Soup

**9 small dried Chinese
mushrooms
½ cup warm water**

Place the mushrooms in a small bowl; cover with the warm water. Soak for 30 minutes. Drain. Trim the stems of the mushrooms. Set aside.

1½ pounds winter melon

Peel the melon. Discard the inner seeds and stringy fibers. Cut the pulp into ¼-inch slices; cut the slices into 1½-inch pieces.

1 ⅛-inch thick slice cooked ham

Cut the ham into 1½-inch pieces and set aside.

**4½ cups chicken broth
the trimmed mushrooms
the melon pieces
the ham pieces**

Combine the chicken broth, mushrooms and melon in a heavy saucepan. Bring to a rapid boil. Reduce heat to low, cover and simmer for 15 minutes. Remove from heat and stir in the ham. Ladle the soup into a tureen and serve.

Cold Sweet and Sour Vegetables

**1½ teaspoons salt
¼ cup soya sauce
2 tablespoons wine vinegar
2½ tablespoons brown sugar
1½ tablespoons sesame oil**

For the soya sauce mixture:
Combine the salt, soya sauce, wine vinegar, brown sugar and sesame oil in a small glass jar. Cover and shake until the sugar is dissolved. Use as needed for the vegetables.

**1 large cucumber
2 tablespoons soya sauce
mixture**

Peel the cucumber. Dice into ¼-inch pieces. Place in a small serving bowl and add the soya sauce mixture. Stir to coat the cucumber. Chill well before serving.

**6 ribs celery
3½ tablespoons soya sauce
mixture**

Wash the celery under cold water. Cut the celery into 1-inch slices. Place in a saucepan and cover with water. Bring to a rapid boil. Immediately drain in a colander and rinse under cold water for 1 minute. Drain. Place the celery slices in a small serving bowl and add the soya sauce mixture. Stir to coat the slices. Chill well before serving.

**2 bunches small radishes
4½ tablespoons soya sauce
mixture**

Trim, wash and drain the radishes. Smash each radish slightly with the flat handle of a heavy knife, but leave the radish whole. Place the radishes in a small serving bowl and add the soya sauce mixture. Stir to coat the radishes. Chill well before serving.

Prawns with Sweet Peppers

**3 sweet red peppers
¼ pound fresh mushrooms
¼ pound fresh broccoli**

Wash and core the peppers. Cut the peppers into rings. Set aside. Wash the mushrooms quickly under cold water and wipe clean. Trim off the stems. Wash the broccoli under cold water. Cut off the tough bottom stalks. Trim

China

the broccoli into 1½-inch pieces. Blanch the broccoli in 2 quarts boiling salted water for 5 minutes. Drain in a colander and rinse under cold running water. Drain on paper towels.

Heat the oil in a wok over moderately high heat. Add the sweet peppers and mushrooms and stir for 1 minute. Add the water, cover and simmer for 5 minutes. Remove with a slotted spoon and keep warm.

2 tablespoons oil
the peppers
the mushrooms
2 tablespoons water

Combine the prawns and broccoli in the wok. Sprinkle on the chopped onion and salt. Stir-fry for 2 to 3 minutes. Add the soya sauce, brown sugar, sherry and cucumber. Cook for 1 minute.

1 pound prawns, or shrimp, shelled and deveined
the broccoli
2 spring onions, chopped
½ teaspoon salt
2 tablespoons soya sauce
2 teaspoons brown sugar
2 tablespoons sherry
2-inch piece of cucumber, peeled and diced
2 teaspoons cornstarch
½ cup water

Mix the cornstarch with the water to a smooth paste. Lower the heat and add to the wok, stirring, until slightly thickened. Return the peppers and mushrooms to the pan and mix well. Serve immediately.

Spiced Lamb

Wipe the meat and rub the salt into the skin. Place in a saucepan. Cover with water. Bring to a rapid boil. Reduce heat to a low simmer. Skim any froth that rises to the surface. Simmer the lamb, covered, for 20 minutes. Drain and set aside.

1 4-pound lamb leg or shoulder
1¼ teaspoons salt

Mix the soya sauce and sherry together in a small bowl. Crush the garlic and shred the ginger into the bowl. Blend together and rub into the lamb. Let stand for 10 minutes.

1½ tablespoons soya sauce
1½ tablespoons sherry
3 cloves garlic
1½ ounces green ginger or 1 teaspoon ground ginger

Heat the oil in a Dutch oven. Add the lamb and brown on all sides for 15 minutes. Pour on the beef bouillon. Bring to a rapid boil. Reduce heat to a simmer, cover and cook for 2½ hours.

5 tablespoons peanut oil
6 cups beef bouillon

Mix the cornstarch and water to a smooth paste in a small bowl. Lift the lamb onto a heated serving platter. Cover loosely and keep warm. Add the cornstarch mixture to the liquid in the pan. Bring to a boil, stirring constantly, until thickened. Pour the sauce over the lamb. Garnish with watercress.

1½ teaspoons cornstarch
1½ tablespoons cold water
watercress leaves

Fried Rice

Pour the rice into a bowl. Cover with cold water. Stir the rice and water around with your hand. Drain. Repeat the washing process and drain again.

1½ cups long grain white rice

Place the rice in a saucepan with a tight-fitting lid. Measure in the water. Bring to a rapid boil, uncovered, over high heat. Boil for 2 to 3 minutes until holes appear in the surface of the rice. Cover the pan tightly and reduce heat to low. Cook the rice for 20 minutes. Turn off the heat but do not remove the lid. Let stand for 10 minutes. Remove the lid and fluff the rice with a fork.

the washed rice
3 cups cold water

salt and pepper to taste
2 tablespoons oil or lard
the cooked rice
2 eggs, lightly beaten

Season the rice with salt and pepper. Heat the oil or lard in a skillet or wok. Add the rice. Fry gently over medium heat for 10 minutes or until all the fat has been absorbed. Lower the heat. Pour the eggs onto the rice in a thin stream, stirring constantly. Continue to stir until the egg is mixed with the rice and just set. Serve immediately.

Eight-Precious Pudding

1½ cups glutinous rice
(sweet rice)
1½ cups water

Cover the rice with cold water. Soak for 1 hour. Drain. Add the rice to 1½ cups water; bring to a simmer. Simmer for 15 minutes. Drain.

2 tablespoons lard
3 tablespoons sugar

Add lard and sugar. Stir to mix.

20 red dates
⅓ cup peanuts
⅓ cup walnut halves
¼ cup white seedless raisins
½ cup raisins
½ cup red and green candied cherries
¼ cup candied orange or lemon peel, cut into small pieces

Oil a 6-inch mold or heat-proof bowl. Decoratively arrange the fruits and nuts on the bottom and sides of the bowl. (They will cling to the sides.) Carefully place half of the rice in the bowl, covering the fruits and nuts.

½ cup canned sweet red bean paste

Spoon the red bean paste on the rice. Spoon on the remaining rice, gently packing it. Place the bowl in a steamer or on a rack in a wok. Steam the pudding for 1¼ hours.

¾ cup water
3 tablespoons sugar
1 tablespoon cornstarch, mixed with 2 tablespoons cold water
½ teaspoon vanilla

For the syrup:
Combine water and sugar in a small saucepan. Bring to a boil. Reduce heat to a simmer. Add cornstarch mixture; stir over low heat until thickened and clear. Stir in vanilla. Unmold pudding onto a serving plate. Spoon the syrup over the pudding. Serve hot.

Clear Soup with Tofu and Shrimp
Crab Meat with Vinegar Dressing
Glazed Chicken Wings
Sukiyaki
Peas and Rice
Fresh Fruit in Pineapple Halves

Clear Soup with Tofu and Shrimp

2 cups cold water
6 ounces tofu (soybean curd), cut into 6 cubes
1 2-inch square kombu (dried kelp), washed

Bring the water to a simmer in a small saucepan. Add the tofu and kombu. Return to a simmer and immediately remove from the heat. Set aside until ready to serve.
Note: Tofu and Kombu may be obtained at Oriental specialty stores or larger supermarkets.

2 cups salted water
6 spinach leaves

Bring the salted water to a boil in another saucepan. Add the spinach. Return to a boil. Remove the spinach with a slotted spoon. Rinse under cold water. Squeeze the leaves to remove excess water and dry on a towel. Reserve the pan of cooking water.

the reserved spinach water
6 medium-sized shrimp, shelled and deveined

Return the reserved spinach water to a boil over high heat. Add the shrimp and boil for 30 seconds. Drain in a sieve and set aside.

1½ quarts water
1 2-inch square kombu (dried kelp)
⅔ cup preflaked katsuobushi (dried bonito)

For the stock:
Pour the water into a saucepan. Bring to a boil. Drop the kombu into the water. Return to a boil. Remove the kombu from the pan immediately with a slotted spoon and set aside. Stir the katsuobushi into the boiling water and remove from the heat. Let the stock rest for 2 minutes until the katsuobushi sinks to the bottom of the pan. With a large spoon, skim any froth that rises to the surface. Place a double thickness of cheesecloth in a sieve and set over a large bowl. Pour in the stock and drain slowly. Remove the katsuobushi and set aside.

1½ teaspoons salt
½ teaspoon Japanese soy sauce
1 teaspoon sake

Return the stock to the saucepan. Bring to a simmer over moderate heat. Stir in the salt, soy sauce, and sake.
Note: Reserve 2½ tablespoons of the stock for the following recipe.

the spinach leaves
the tofu cubes
the shrimp
6 thin strips lemon peel
6 soup bowls
the soup stock

Arrange a spinach leaf, a cube of tofu, 1 shrimp and a strip of lemon peel in the bottom of each bowl. Carefully fill each bowl ¾ full with the simmering stock. Serve immediately.

Crab Meat with Vinegar Dressing

1 large cucumber
½ cup cold water
1 teaspoon salt

Peel the cucumber lengthwise in a striped pattern, cutting away and leaving alternate ¼-inch strips of peel. Halve lengthwise. Scoop out the seeds with a small spoon. Cut the halves crosswise into paper-thin slices. Combine the

Japan

water and salt in a small bowl. Add the slices; soak for 30 minutes at room temperature. Drain, squeezing the slices to extract excess water.

Flake the crab meat and discard any cartilage or bone. Shred the meat with a large, sharp knife.

Equally divide the cucumber and crab meat into 6 small serving bowls. Wrap the ginger in a piece of cheesecloth and squeeze juice into each bowl. Serve with the dipping sauce.

For the dipping sauce:
Combine the rice vinegar, stock, sugar, soy sauce and salt in the small saucepan. Bring the sauce to a boil over high heat, stirring constantly. Immediately remove from heat and set aside. Cool to room temperature. Serve the dipping sauce in 6 tiny cups or dishes.

12 ounces fresh or canned crab meat
the cucumber slices
the crab meat
3 tablespoons coarsely grated fresh gingerroot
2½ tablespoons rice vinegar
2½ tablespoons fish stock, from preceding recipe or bottled clam juice
4 teaspoons sugar
2 teaspoons Japanese soy sauce
⅛ teaspoon salt

Glazed Chicken Wings with Teriyaki Sauce

Lightly salt the chicken wings on both sides. Arrange the wings in a shallow baking pan. Place under a preheated broiler for 4 minutes. Turn over and broil 4 minutes.

For the sauce:
Combine the soy sauce, mirin and sugar in a small saucepan. Stir until heated through and sugar is dissolved. Cook the sauce for 2 minutes until thickened.

Remove the wings from the broiler. Dip the wings into the sauce and drain. Return the wings to the broiler and broil for 4 minutes. Remove and dip into the sauce once more. Broil 2 to 3 minutes.

18 meaty chicken wings
¾ teaspoon salt
⅓ cup Japanese soy sauce
⅓ cup mirin (syrupy rice wine)
2 tablespoons sugar
the broiled chicken wings

Sukiyaki

Freeze the beef for 30 minutes to stiffen it slightly. Cut against the grain into ⅛-inch slices with a sharp, heavy knife. Cut the slices in half lengthwise.

Bring the water to a boil. Drop in the shirataki and return to a boil. Drain and cut into thirds. Scrape the base of the bamboo shoot; slice in half lengthwise and cut the slices crosswise. Rinse under cold water and drain. Leave 3 inches of stem on the scallions. Cut into 1½-inch pieces. Peel the onion and cut into ½-inch slices. Wash the mushrooms and cut into ¼-inch slices.

Arrange the meat, shirataki, bamboo shoot, scallion, onion, mushrooms, tofu and watercress attractively in separate rows on a large platter.

Use an electric skillet preheated to 425°, or heat a heavy skillet on a table-top cooking unit at the dining table.

1½ pounds beef sirloin
1 8-ounce can shirataki (long thread-like noodles), drained
1 cup water
1 canned bamboo shoot
6 scallions
1 yellow onion
¼ pound fresh mushrooms
the sliced beef
the shirataki
the sliced bamboo shoot
the scallion pieces
the sliced onion
the sliced mushrooms
2 cakes tofu, cut into 1-inch cubes
2 ounces watercress

Hold the beef suet with chopsticks and rub it over the bottom of the hot skillet. Add 6 to 8 slices of meat. Pour in ¼ cup soy sauce. Sprinkle the meat with the sugar. Cook for 1 minute, stirring. Turn the beef and push to one side of the skillet. Add ⅓ of the shirataki, bamboo shoot, scallions, onion, mushrooms, tofu and watercress. Sprinkle with ¼ cup rice wine. Lower the heat and maintain a steady simmer for 4 to 5 minutes. Transfer the meat and vegetables to individual serving plates with chopsticks and serve. Continue cooking in the same manner. If the skillet becomes too hot, lower heat and cool with a few drops of cold water.

1 large piece beef suet
¼ to ¾ cup Japanese soy sauce
3 tablespoons sugar
¾ cup rice wine

Peas and Rice

Drop the peas into the boiling water. Cook for 1 minute. Drain in a colander and rinse under cold water. Drain again and set aside.

1 cup shelled fresh peas
2 quarts boiling salted water

Place the rice in a large bowl. Cover with cold water. Stir the rice and water around the bowl with your hand. Drain in a fine sieve. Repeat the process twice to remove any starchy powder. Drain thoroughly.

1½ cups short grain rice

Place the rice in a medium-sized saucepan with a tight fitting lid. Add the water and let stand for 10 minutes. Add the mirin and stir. Place the covered saucepan over high heat. Cook for 4 to 5 minutes. Reduce to medium heat and cook for 8 to 10 minutes.

the washed rice
1¾ cups water
1½ tablespoons mirin (syrupy rice wine)

Add the peas to the rice, cover and cook over high heat for 20 to 30 seconds. This will help dry the rice. Remove from the heat. Let the cooked rice steam itself, covered, for 10 to 15 minutes.

the blanched peas

Gently toss the rice and peas. Scoop out individual portions. Sprinkle the sesame seed and salt mixture over each portion. Serve immediately.

1½ tablespoons mixture black sesame seeds and coarse salt

Fresh Fruit in Pineapple Halves

Hull and wash the strawberries. Halve the cantaloupe. Scoop the flesh into balls with a melon-ball cutter. Halve the pineapple lengthwise keeping the leaves in place. Cut out the core, remove flesh and cut into 1-inch pieces. Fill the pineapple halves with the fruit and serve.

1 pint fresh strawberries
1 cantaloupe
1 pineapple

Clear Soup with Tofu and Shrimp

*Christmas Day
Menu for Six*

*Cranberry-Orange Relish
Poached Pear Halves
Ham Baked in Pastry Crust
Raisin Sauce
Curried Corn Timbale
Cheesecake with Raspberry Sauce*

Pear Halves Filled with Cranberry-Orange Relish

1 16-ounce package of fresh cranberries
½ cup cold water

For the relish:
Combine the cranberries and water in a saucepan. Bring to a simmer. Cook slowly just until the cranberry skins pop. Remove from heat and stir for a moment. Set aside.

1 medium, bright-skinned orange

Peel the outermost, orange-colored part of the orange skin with a vegetable peeler. Reserving the fruit, place the peelings in a saucepan and cover with water. Bring water to a simmer for 2 minutes. Drain in a colander under cold running water. Return the peel to the saucepan and repeat the process, simmering for 2 minutes. Remove from heat and drain in a colander under cold running water. Cut the peel into strips 1/16 inch wide. Add to the cranberries.

1 medium orange
the peeled orange
⅓ cup firmly packed brown sugar
pinch cinnamon

Completely peel the oranges, removing as much of the membrane as possible. Separate the oranges into sections and chop into small pieces. Add to the cranberries. Add the brown sugar and cinnamon, stirring until well blended. Taste the cranberries. If too tart, add more sugar. Refrigerate until chilled.

½ cup sugar
1½ cups water
¼ cup lemon juice

For the poached pears:
Combine the sugar and water in a saucepan. Bring to a simmer, stirring until the sugar is dissolved. Add the lemon juice. Simmer for 5 minutes. Cover and set aside.

juice of ½ lemon
a bowl of cold water
6 firm ripe pears

Add the lemon juice to the bowl of cold water. Peel, halve and core the pears; drop into the bowl of cold water with lemon juice.

Return the syrup to a simmer. Add 4 pear halves to the syrup. Simmer for 8 minutes until the pears are tender. Remove the pears with a slotted spoon and put in a bowl. Poach the remaining pears in the same manner. Pour the syrup over the pears and chill until ready to use. Before serving, drain the pear halves on a wire rack. Fill the centers with the cranberry-orange relish. Arrange the pear halves around the ham.

Ham Baked in Pastry Crust

12-pound boneless, smoked ham

Remove the rind from the ham. Cut off all but ⅛ inch of the fat from the ham with a sharp knife.

Set the ham in a deep roasting pan. Combine the wine, raisins and sugar in a small saucepan. Bring to a simmer. Remove from the heat and let stand 10 minutes. Pour the mixture over the ham. Roast, uncovered, in a preheated 350° oven for 2½ hours, basting frequently.

1 cup red Burgundy wine
½ cup raisins
1 tablespoon sugar

For the pastry:
Combine the flour, baking powder, salt, mustard and sage in a large bowl. Stir with a fork to blend thoroughly.

Drop the butter into the flour mixture a few pieces at a time and cover with the flour. Cut chilled shortening into the flour with a pastry blender until the mixture resembles coarse meal. Gradually add the cold milk to make a soft, but not sticky, dough. Place the dough on a lightly floured board. Knead for 1 minute, shaping into a smooth ball. Wrap in a sheet of waxed paper and refrigerate.

6 cups sifted all-purpose flour
4 teaspoons baking powder
1¾ teaspoons salt
¾ teaspoon powdered mustard
¼ teaspoon powdered sage
½ cup cold butter, cut into pieces
½ cup shortening, chilled
1½ cups cold milk

When the ham has finished roasting, carve into serving slices. Assemble the slices into original shape of the ham.

Mix the honey with the wine basting sauce. Using a pastry brush, coat the ham with the mixture.

3 tablespoons honey
3 tablespoons wine basting sauce
cold milk

Roll out the refrigerated dough in a sheet ¼ inch thick. Fold over the ham, covering it completely. Make a hole in the top of the dough to allow steam to escape during baking. Place the ham on a large, lightly buttered baking sheet. Make cut-out Christmas designs with the leftover dough. Place on the dough covering the ham. Bake in a preheated 450° oven for 15 minutes. Lower the heat to 350° and bake the ham 45 minutes. Brush the crust twice with cold milk during the baking time. The crust will turn a delicate brown. Let the ham stand at room temperature for 15 minutes before serving.

Raisin Sauce

Spoon off fat from the wine basting liquid. Strain through a sieve into a saucepan. Discard the basting raisins. Add the ¾ cup fresh raisins and sugar to the pan. Simmer for 2 minutes. Add the brown sauce. Serve in a warmed sauceboat with the ham.

¾ cup wine basting liquid from the cooked ham
¾ cup seedless raisins
1½ tablespoons brown sugar
1 cup brown sauce

For the brown sauce:
Melt the butter in a heavy saucepan. Add the chopped vegetables. Sauté, stirring occasionally, until they just begin to turn golden.

2 tablespoons butter
¼ cup chopped carrot
¼ cup chopped onion
¼ cup chopped celery

Stir in the flour. Cook the vegetables, stirring constantly, until they are a rich brown color. Remove the pan from the heat. Stir in the beef stock, using a wire whisk to blend smoothly. Add the parsley, bay leaf, garlic and thyme to the sauce. Continue to cook, stirring the mixture frequently, until it thickens.

2 tablespoons flour
1 cup beef stock, heated
1 sprig parsley
⅓ bay leaf
½ clove garlic, crushed
pinch thyme

Add the beef stock and tomato paste. Simmer slowly for 1 hour. The sauce should reduce to 1 cup. Skim off any fat that has accumulated on the surface. The sauce is ready to use or may be refrigerated overnight.

1 cup beef stock, heated
1 teaspoon tomato paste

Curried Corn Timbale

Beat the eggs until well blended in a large bowl. Add the corn and the creamed corn. Stir in the Swiss cheese, Cheddar cheese, cream, bread crumbs, minced onion, parsley, curry powder, salt and pepper.

Butter the bottom and sides of the 8-cup mold. Line the bottom with waxed paper cut to size and shape. Pour the mixture into the mold. Set in a baking dish filled with boiling water ⅔ the way up the side of the mold. Place the dish on the lower-middle level of a preheated 350° oven and bake 30 minutes. Reduce the heat to 325° and bake 45 to 60 minutes. Be sure the water surrounding the mold never reaches a simmer. The timbale is done when it has risen to the top of the mold and cracked open on top. Keep the timbale in the turned-off oven, with the door open, for 10 minutes before unmolding. Place a plate upside down over the top of the mold and turn the timbale onto the plate.

6 eggs
1½ cups fresh or frozen corn
1 12-ounce can creamed corn
⅓ cup grated Swiss cheese
⅓ cup grated Cheddar cheese
⅔ cup heavy cream
⅔ cup fresh bread crumbs
3 tablespoons minced onion
¼ cup chopped fresh parsley
½ teaspoon curry powder
1 teaspoon salt
¼ teaspoon pepper

an 8-cup timbale or charlotte mold or soufflé dish
softened butter
waxed paper

Cheesecake with Raspberry Sauce

Blend the crumbs and sugar in a bowl. Pour in the butter. Stir with a fork to moisten the mixture. Grease a 9-inch springform pan with softened butter. Using a soup spoon, press the crumbs firmly onto the bottom and sides of the pan.

1½ cups graham cracker crumbs
1 tablespoon brown sugar
¼ cup butter, melted
1 tablespoon butter, softened

For the filling:
Place the cream cheese in a large mixing bowl to soften. Or you may soften the cream cheese more quickly if you spread it around the bowl with a fork. Blend in the vanilla, flour, sugar and salt. Beat with an electric mixer until fluffy. Add the egg yolks and beat thoroughly. Beat in the lemon juice and heavy cream.

1 pound cream cheese
1 teaspoon vanilla
¼ cup all-purpose flour
2 tablespoons sugar
¼ teaspoon salt
4 egg yolks, lightly beaten
1 tablespoon lemon juice
1 cup heavy cream

Beat the egg whites in another bowl until soft peaks form. Gradually beat in the sugar until the meringue is stiff and glossy. Fold the meringue into the cream cheese mixture. Pour the mixture into the pan. Bake in a preheated 325° oven for 1½ hours until set in the center. Turn off the oven, leave the door ajar and let the cake cool in the oven. Chill the cake until firm before removing from the pan.

4 egg whites
2 tablespoons sugar

For the raspberry sauce:
Heat the jelly in a medium-sized saucepan. Add the raspberries and simmer for a moment. Stir in the lemon juice. Remove from heat and force through a fine sieve. Chill and serve with the cheesecake.

1 cup currant jelly
1 quart raspberries
2 tablespoons lemon juice

Ham Baked in Pastry Crust, Poached Pears
Filled with Cranberry-Orange Relish, Raisin Sauce